Critical Essays on Cervantes

Critical Essays on
World Literature

Robert Lecker, General Editor
McGill University

Critical Essays on Cervantes

Ruth El Saffar

G. K. Hall & Co. • Boston, Massachusetts

Publisher's Note:
Square brackets in the text indicate material that appeared in Spanish in
the original publication and has been translated for this volume.

Library of Congress Cataloging-in-Publication Data
Main entry under title:

Critical essays on Cervantes.

(Critical essays on world literature)
Bibliography: p. 211
Includes index.
1. Cervantes Saavedra, Miguel de, 1547-1616 — Criticism and
interpretation — Addresses, essays, lectures. I. El Saffar, Ruth S.,
1941-   . II. Series.
PQ6351.C75 1986   863'.3   85-24809
ISBN 0-8161-8825-4

CONTENTS

INTRODUCTION

> Why is it that across the ages no two people have been able to agree on the meaning of *Don Quixote?*[1]

> The hall-mark of a masterpiece is that though primarily a work of art it makes us unquiet about its meaning and sense.[2]

After months of wrestling with the many-headed monster that is the body of criticism Cervantes's genius has spawned, I sit before my stacks of articles — many more of which have been dismissed than included in this volume — with a feeling of dismay: how can any one selection of articles possibly represent the outpouring of interpretation that nearly four hundred years with Cervantes's texts have inspired? How can any bibliographical list, limited to thirty books and articles, do justice to the critical imagination of our collective effort to interpret Cervantes's opus? Perplexed, just as Cervantes represented himself to be in his wonderful prologue to Part 1 of *Don Quixote*, I sit with head propped on hand, elbow on my writing desk, wondering how ever to justify to my readers the choices made herein.

On the one hand, the editor of a collection such as this faces the question of how to give fair coverage to the entirety of the author's literary production. *Don Quixote*, though it has captured a disproportionate amount of interest among Cervantes's readers and critics, is neither the only, nor, perhaps, from Cervantes's point of view, the most accomplished of his works. A volume dedicated to presenting a critical survey of Cervantes must give some, if not equal, time to the other works: to *La Galatea*, an early pastoral novel both responsive to the traditions of that genre, as Jennifer Lowe has shown in her article, and profoundly aware of its shortcomings, as Mary Gaylord Randel invites us to recognize; to the *Novelas ejemplares*, a collection of short stories which are nothing less than a writer's workshop, giving insight into the issues of literary theory with which Cervantes was grappling, as William C. Atkinson tells us; to the mock-heroic long poem *Viaje del Parnaso*, whose humorous yet painful expression of Cervantes's disillusionment as a writer Elias Rivers explains; to the collection of three- and one-act plays, *Ocho comedias y*

1

ocho entremeses, which contain unsuspected literary and socio-economic complexities as outlined in articles here by Jean Canavaggio and Nicholas Spadaccini respectively; and finally to the much-disputed Byzantine romance the *Persiles*, whose riches modern critics such as Alban Forcione and Diana Wilson are just beginning to excavate.

On the other hand, as a glance at the Table of Contents reveals, *Don Quixote*, which represents far less than half of Cervantes's total literary output, clearly remains the critic's choice. Were my task simply to capture the flavor of *Don Quixote* criticism alone I would still have to come humbly before the reader in an introduction such as this, and ask, as Cide Hamete asked in *Don Quixote*, to be praised not so much for what I have included as for what I have left out.[3] The editor's task, however, is not only to select articles on all of Cervantes's works, but to offer, through that selection, some idea both of the history of Cervantes criticism and of the varying contemporary approaches to an understanding of Cervantes. For all that I have sought to accomplish this, in my own nightmarish journey to Parnassus I see the likes of Américo Castro, Menéndez Pelayo, Unamuno, Ortega y Gasset, Victor Schlovsky, Joaquín Casalduero, E. C. Riley — all of those whose basic readings on Cervantes I have used extensively in my own work and yet had ultimately to reject for this volume — hurling their books at me in anger. And in the background I see the hosts of great writers who have left commentaries on Cervantes — Flaubert, Coleridge, Dostoevsky, Proust, Mann, Fuentes — cheering them on.

My selection, I find myself explaining, has been dictated by a number of exigencies, not all of which are strictly scholarly. And here again I take refuge in Cervantes's own example, hoping thereby to appease my imagined hosts of discarded and disgruntled critics. In Chapters 3 and 4 of *Don Quixote* Part II a frequently-cited discussion takes place in which the young student fresh from Salamanca — Sansón Carrasco — reveals to Don Quixote and Sancho that a book about their adventures has already been published. Don Quixote is not only amazed ("He could not persuade himself that such a history existed, for the blood of the enemies he had slain was scarcely dry on his own sword-blade"), but disheartened upon learning that his author is a Moor who has not had the delicacy to omit from his narrative Don Quixote's episodes of defeat and humiliation. No less shocked and upset is Sancho, when, a few pages later, he learns that the Moor intends to write a Second Part, motivated more by profit than by desire for praise. "Does the author expect to make money by it?" Sancho asks. And here the reader might well echo, "Is this editor basing her selection on extrinsic, material concerns?"

Alas, the days are long gone when a translator can be picked up at the marketplace and paid in raisins and wheat for an on-the-spot translation such as the one contracted by the "Second Author" in *Don Quixote* after he found the remaining chapters of *Don Quixote* in Arabic manuscript.

Neither time nor money allowed me the luxury of providing a forum in this volume for all the untranslated commentaries I would have liked to include: the many Spanish, French, Russian, and German critics whose work has been so seminal to Cervantes studies. Other wonderful essays — one by Leo Spitzer,[4] another by Marthe Robert[5] — had already been translated into English but were finally excised for their length. What remains are articles that fit the criteria of being both reasonably short, and, with a few notable exceptions, already in English. Within the tight confines of this volume are the survivors: those articles or chapter excerpts which capture some aspect of the work of Cervantes in question while not presenting too many complications of length or translatability. I offer these, with no pretense to comprehensiveness, as what the post-structuralists, echoing Derrida, would call "traces." The articles here must be understood as pointing towards, without ever succeeding in capturing, the experience of four centuries of reading and contemplating the works of Cervantes.

The general problem of the degree to which words can in any case express a reality beyond themselves is one discussed in this volume by Mary Gaylord Randel with respect to *La Galatea*, and by Michel Foucault regarding *Don Quixote*. The question of referentiality can also be turned towards Cervantes criticism itself. It does not take long, when working with the body of commentary on a given author, before one comes to sense that the studies refer as much to other studies as to the author in question and his or her works. We are dealing here, not only in particular essays, but in the volume as a whole, with the basic issues of self-referentiality and of intertextuality. Critics write within a tradition, responding, often unconsciously, to the mind-set of their time and place, and to the precepts and preconceptions of other critics. Only recently have serious efforts been made among some Cervantes scholars to distinguish between the philosophical and literary dominants of our time and the concerns that fueled Cervantes's own writing. The topic of authorial intentionality and its relation to the task of interpretation, debated in the larger arena of literary criticism in general, has not gone without its resonances in Cervantine circles.

Out of respect for the importance of the question of intentionality and interpretive dominants, I have opened the section of essays devoted to *Don Quixote* with Luis Murillo's article, which traces the history of the term "irony" as applied to Cervantes's masterpiece. Murillo's historical perspective regarding the development of the notion of irony in Cervantes criticism is included here to give voice to what might be called the anti-perspectivist school, and to lead those readers interested in pursuing that avenue of study to longer works which challenge the Romantic underpinnings of twentieth-century Cervantes criticism by such writers as P. E. Russell,[6] Anthony Close,[7] and Arthur Efron.[8]

In addition to placing first in the *Don Quixote* section of this volume an article which gives historical perspective to certain key terms in recent Cervantes criticism, I have selected as the opening essay of the entire collection Helmut Hatzfeld's 1947 overview of the prevailing trends in twentieth-century studies on Cervantes. My intention in selecting both the Murillo and the Hatzfeld texts has been to provide some sense of chronology to the topic of Cervantes's reception, while giving over the bulk of the articles collected here to samplings of the many different ways contemporary critics approach the question of Cervantes's works. Hatzfeld's categories of critical response, while terminologically somewhat outdated, are ones that can still be fruitfully applied to the most recent varieties of approaches to Cervantes. His article, therefore, provides a bridge between the diachronic and the synchronic impulses at work in the creation of this collection, allowing us to see how current critical trends continue the patterns of response to Cervantes's work established over time. The more basic challenge to interpretive biases implied in the Murillo study allows us to recognize that all the approaches presented here are conditioned by factors having to do with our own place in time and culture. Taken together the two articles both extend our perspective on Cervantes criticism back in time and give a provisional, conditioned quality to the many viewpoints on Cervantes's work which follow.

Javier Herrero's article on Part I of *Don Quixote* provides a fine example of what might be called thematic criticism. Focusing on the question of the conflicts between neo-Platonic and Erasmian notions of romantic love and marriage, Herrero brings light to the vexed question of the role of Don Quixote with respect to the interpolated tales of Part I of *Don Quixote*. The issue of Erasmus, Christian marriage, and love is central not only to an understanding of *Don Quixote* but to Cervantes's entire *opus*. It has attracted commentary from many excellent recent critics, most notable among whom are Marcel Bataillon,[9] whose two-volume study of the presence of Erasmus in Cervantes's work has become a classic; Cesáreo Bandera,[10] who has shown how Cervantes breaks down the supposed charms of romantic love in *Don Quixote* Part I; and, most recently, Alban Forcione, in his *Cervantes and the Humanist Vision*.[11]

Another approach entirely is provided in the studies by Charles Aubrun and Dámaso Alonso. Although ideological issues come very much to the fore in both articles—Aubrun being concerned with the economic constraints that affected Don Quixote's social class, and Alonso with the mix of idealism and realism built into the the major characters of the novel—these two critics emphasize primarily characters and character analysis in their commentaries. I chose the two articles as examples of readings which turn on an effort to understand character motivation—that of Don Quixote in the case of the Aubrun article, that of Sancho in the Alonso study.

Although anticipated in seminal studies early in this century by Rudolph Schevill,[12] and picked up later by Atkinson, whose study on the

Novelas ejemplares appears in this volume, and Entwistle, cited in the Annotated Bibliography[13] it was really with the publication of E. C. Riley's *Cervantes's Theory of the Novel*[14] that critics began to look closely at the role of neo-Aristotelian and neo-Platonic literary theory in the development of Cervantes's craftsmanship as a writer. Several articles in this collection show a special interest in Cervantes's awareness of poetics, most especially those by Bruce Wardropper, who addresses the question of history and poetry as it is revealed in *Don Quixote*, George Haley, who works on the role of the fictional narrator and the problem of the story within the story, and Alban Forcione, who shows how the *Persiles* reflects Cervantes's interest in Renaissance literary trends.

The socio-economic situation out of which Cervantes wrote, and its effects on his world view is tangentially related to the Erasmian currents so many critics have noted in Cervantes's work. Américo Castro in particular saw the connection between ideology and the racially-oriented caste system in sixteenth-century Spain and moved from his early, almost exclusive concern for the ideological aspects of Cervantes's work to a much more profoundly historical analysis in his later writings on the author.[15] Castro has been as decisive an influence for socio-historical analyses of Cervantes as has been Riley for the question of Renaissance literary theory. The above-mentioned Aubrun article reflects some of the concerns of the literary critic oriented toward history and economics. Also in that line of analysis is the article by Nicholas Spadaccini, who analyzes the kinds of messages Cervantes was sending through his eight plays and eight interludes—most of them never actually produced for the stage—to an audience clearly understood to be reading, not viewing, his dramatic works. Elias Rivers, studying Cervantes's late satirical-autobiographical long poem *Viaje al Parnaso*, also gives insight into the political and economic realities of Cervantes's life as a writer.

Much recent work on Cervantes and his characters reflects our twentieth-century involvement with psychology and the role of the sub-conscious in the interplay of characters and events. A recent major work by Louis Combet[16] uses Cervantes's texts to trace back to the author himself a particular, and constant, structuring of the psyche. Another book just out by Carroll Johnson[17] trains a Freudian eye not so much on Cervantes as on Don Quixote, revealing the unresolved Oedipal conflicts that motivate and explain so much odd behavior on the part of the gentleman of La Mancha. Marthe Robert, in two excellent books,[18] shows how the strategies of the fictional narrator, and certain patterns in Don Quixote's behavior mirror and reveal the author. My own latest book on Cervantes[19] also borrows from twentieth-century notions of the unconscious to show how Cervantes worked through a series of basic problems in the course of his life as a writer. Unfortunately none of these interesting psychological studies were short enough, or excerptible in sizes reasonable enough to be collected here.

I have given considerable space, however, to another pet theme in twentieth-century criticism — the topic of the text as in some way self-reflective. The issue is approached from the point of view of language in Mary Gaylord Randel's intriguing article on *La Galatea*, in which she shows how that early pastoral novel is constantly commenting on its own inability to transform into words the experience from which it purports to draw. The short Foucault piece on *Don Quixote* from *The Order of Things* addresses the problem of the relationship between word and referent from a historical vantage point, locating Cervantes's major novel on the very fulcrum between a view which saw the word as label for a world-text, and a view which came to see the word as referring only to other words in a system that created worlds out of words. Borges continues the theme of the relation between "reality" and story by speculating on the way Cervantes builds himself into the text, calling into question which of the two is more real, which the creator of which. Finally, in the Canavaggio article, and to a lesser degree in the Haley article, we have a consideration of the phenomenon of the play within the play, the story within the story, and how that phenomenon deepens and problematizes the relationship between audience and performance, reader and text. Though each of these articles has its own special stamp and flavor, they have in common a tendency to pull words and texts away from the world which may have conditioned them and to turn them in on themselves, following a tradition in literary criticism in this century that has its origins in formalism and New Criticism and that has developed into what is now called post-modernism.

A collection of essays on Cervantes designed to reflect the gamut of approaches now being applied to his works would not be complete without some attention to the burgeoning area of feminist criticism. Although throughout this century occasional studies on women in Cervantes's works have been published, serious consideration on the role of the female characters has only just begun. Diana Wilson's work on the *Persiles*, especially written for this volume, gives an excellent introduction to the problematics of the feminine in Cervantes, while opening up Cervantes's little-understood and less-read *Persiles* to some unsuspected depths. Not unlike Castro or Spadaccini, Wilson has succeeded in showing the profoundly iconoclastic, subversive nature of Cervantes's work, a feat all the more notable because it is accomplished in a text so often considered Cervantes's bow to conservatism, or, at best, his hypocritical accommodation to the conventions of his times.

So now it is time to face head on my critics, those hosts of commentators of Cervantes's works whom I have perhaps offended by omitting from this all-too-slender volume. I have tried in this collection, given the constraints of space and money, to present a wide variety of critical approaches, picking up on the major contemporary trends in

Cervantes criticism while giving some hint of the history of the readings of Cervantes out of which they have emerged. And I have given time and place both to critics for whom "extra-literary" concerns are paramount and to those who prefer to turn the text in on itself. Still, as I cast my eye over the list of articles that have finally found their place here, I find unmistakable signs of my own preferences. Following Cervantes's observation in his Prologue to *Don Quixote* I, I have to admit, as he did, that "I have been unable to transgress the order of nature, by which like gives birth to like." My own biases are evident in the preponderance of articles that highlight language's problematic relation to the things and feelings it purports to express (Mary Gaylord Randel, Michel Foucault); the mirroring effects of texts within texts (Jean Canavaggio, George Haley, Jorge Luis Borges); the metaphysical and psychological implications of authors within texts (Borges); and the subversive, iconoclastic nature of Cervantes's work with respect to dominant cultural values (Rivers, Spadaccini, Wilson).

More than half of the articles printed here, and the very preference I have revealed for synchrony over diachrony, support in one way or another my conviction that Cervantes's texts belong to, and are completed by, the readers who interpret him in every age. While this understanding by no means minimizes the importance of careful philological, historical, and literary studies of Cervantes's intentions, concerns, and interests, it insists on the inevitable filtering process all such studies go through upon being undertaken by us. The filters of age, sex, culture, and historical moment are not an encumbrance to be lamented, but are rather added enrichments to the ongoing discourse of Cervantes with his readership. I am delighted that women are now in a position actively to engage the question of the feminine in Cervantes's work—to register in another key Cervantes's challenge to the dominant world view of his time. And had it not been for the racial conflicts brought to the fore in Nazi Germany we might never have had studies such as Américo Castro's, which have brought to light similar struggles in the Spain of Cervantes's time. Freud and Jung set the stage for a twentieth-century engagement in the nature of the unconscious which has also borne fruit in studies on Cervantes. The point is that critics need tools—categories by which to order the material observed and highlighted in their readings. Those tools might be literary constructs such as "the Baroque" or "mannerism." They might also be terms borrowed from the sixteenth century, such a "the marvelous," or "verisimilitude." Whatever the terms, however, they are only important as an interpreter finds them so, and applies them. Both the selection and the application of terms reflects inevitably on the interpreter. Because I find literary criticism only compelling if it implies an exchange between reader and author, I have valued especially those studies which reveal the reflective, and interrelated nature of the critical enterprise. And because I find what is best in Cervantes in his ability to see beyond the narrownesses of his age, to break past the confines of the traditions in which so many others were caught, I also value those readings sensitive to Cervantes's iconoclasm.

In the final analysis, I hope that my biases are such that they open rather than close doors on critical discourse. I have tried to include studies not favorable to my own approaches, in support of my ultimate belief that any genuine effort at establishing new areas of understanding is a gift to all students of Cervantes, and that each reading should be honored as an example of the way one consciousness interacts with another. I hope the reader, accordingly, will find enough here of interest to feel strengthened in pursuing his or her own version of Cervantes, to feel safe in engaging in his or her own dialogue with that ever-engaging author.

For the long and selflessly given hours spent excavating articles from the library, photocopying, cutting, pasting, translating, and doing general troubleshooting, I want to thank my student and colleague Nikki Beidleman. Without her constant help and support I could never have so quickly expedited the assembling of this volume. I want also to thank another student, Janet Ingrassia, for her expert typing and managerial work connected with the production of this book. Her quick and accurate work saved me from many hours of anguish, and her record keeping made the task of gathering reprinting permissions possible in the midst of my own too busy schedule. Financial support, in the form of an unexpected research grant from the University of Illinois, proved also to be a great help in making this collection possible. I am grateful to all the wonderful resources that were made available to me just as I was embarking on this editorial task, and to all the people, named and unnamed, through whom it came.

RUTH EL SAFFAR

University of Illinois at Chicago

Notes

1. Bruce Wardropper, "*Don Quixote*, Story or History?," *Modern Philology* 63 (1965): 1–11.

2. Helmut Hatzfeld, "Thirty Years of Cervantes Criticism," *Hispania* 30 (1947): 321–28.

3. See *Don Quixote* Part II, Chapter 44.

4. Leo Spitzer, "Linguistic Perspectivism in the *Don Quixote*," *Linguistics and Literary History* (Princeton: Princeton University Press, 1948).

5. Marthe Robert, *Origins of the Novel* (Bloomington, Indiana: Indiana University Press, 1980).

6. P. E. Russell, "*Don Quixote* as a Funny Book," *MLN* 64 (1969): 312–26.

7. Anthony Close, *The Romantic Approach to "Don Quixote"* (Cambridge: Cambridge University Press, 1978).

8. Arthur Efron, *Don Quixote and the Dulcineated World* (Austin: University of Texas Press, 1971).

9. See especially *Erasmo y España*, translated by A. Alatorre. Two volumes. (Mexico City: Fondo de Cultura Económica, 1950), and also his "Cervantès et le 'marriage chrétien,' " *Bulletin Hispanique* 49 (1947): 129–44.

10. Cesáreo Bandera, *Mímesis conflictiva* (Madrid: Gredos, 1975).

11. Alban Forcione, *Cervantes and the Humanist Vision* (Princeton: Princeton University Press, 1982).

12. See, for example, Rudolph Schevill's "Studies in Cervantes: 1. *Persiles y Sigismunda*: The Question of Heliodorus," *Modern Philology* 4 (1907): 677–704.

13. William Entwistle, "Cervantes, the Exemplary Novelist." *Hispanic Review* 9 (1941): 103–9.

14. E. C. Riley, *Cervantes's Theory of the Novel* (Oxford: Clarendon Press, 1962).

15. Castro's most famous early work on Cervantes is his 1925 *El pensamiento de Cervantes*, revised and reprinted in a second edition in 1972 (Barcelona: Noguer). After World War II, however, Castro repudiated the strongly idealistic nature of his earlier work, publishing a series of studies on history and caste in Spain. His collection of essays, *Hacia Cervantes* (Madrid: Taurus, 1967), and his study of Cervantes's probable New Christian background in *Cervantes y los castecismos españoles* (Madrid: Alfaguera, 1966), mark his turn away from ideology to history, and offer us a view of Cervantes conditioned by and reacting against the majoritarian trends of his time.

16. Louis Combet, *Cervantès ou les incertitudes du désir* (Lyons: Presses Universitaires de Lyons, 1981).

17. Carroll Johnson, *Madness and Lust: A Psychoanalytical Approach to "Don Quixote"* (Berkeley: University of California Press, 1983).

18. Marthe Robert, *The Old and the New: From Don Quixote to Franz Kafka*. Translated by Carol Cosman (Berkeley: University of California Press, 1977), and *Origins of the Novel* (Bloomington, Indiana: Indiana University Press, 1980).

19. Ruth El Saffar, *Beyond Fiction: The Recovery of the Feminine in the Novels of Cervantes* (Berkeley: University of California Press, 1984).

General

Thirty Years of Cervantes Criticism

Helmut A. Hatzfeld*

It is a gratifying fact that Cervantes, four hundred years after his birth, has not diminished but increased in general interest and admiration. To prove this point no method seems to me more appropriate than to review the criticism of Cervantes since the tercentenary of his death in 1916. Writers from all nations and of all possible convictions have declared Cervantes to be the mouthpiece of their creed and Don Quijote the symbol of their ideals.

There is of course a scholarly and an impressionistic criticism. Whereas the latter sees Cervantes apart from the limits of epoch, nationality, and belief, the former never loses sight of the fact that the critic is confronted with a Spaniard, a Catholic and a man belonging to the Golden Age. The problem is complicated by the circumstance that the values historically realized in Classical Spain and in the work of Cervantes coincide with the ideals which man at his best has everywhere and at all times pursued, the same ideals which Father David Rubio has characterized as the philosophy of *El Quijote*: ["a philosophy of faith in the ideal, in the value of effort, in the triumph of justice and in the merits of sacrifice"].[1] In the same year 1924, when those words were first written, the late Professor Cesare de Lollis of the University of Rome, while not denying these ideals of Cervantes, regretted that they were not counterbalanced by some of the pagan ideas of the Italian Renaissance. He called his book accordingly *Cervantes Reazionario.*[2]

The "Reactionary." De Lollis saw in Cervantes a reactionary because he supposed Cervantes to be a particular advocate of the ascetic spirit of the Counter-Reformation. With this preconceived idea in mind he ran into great difficulties in the interpretation of the humorous, ironical, lively *Don Quijote*. Karl Vossler was moved to remark at the time that Cervantes' great novel unfortunately was an event which is in conflict with De Lollis's thesis. But even De Lollis's interpretation of *Los trabajos de Persiles y Sigismunda* proved a failure. For these two lovers, separated for a long time and reunited after innumerable hardships, conclude their labors by a

*Reprinted with permission from *Hispania* 30 (1947):321–28.

11

merry marriage, and do not enter religion after having come closer to God during their trials, as in more classical fashion did Luzmán and Arbolea, the principals of Jerónimo de Contreras's truly ascetic novel *Selva de aventuras* (1565).

The "Nonconformist." In his book *El pensamiento de Cervantes*, 1925, Américo Castro went to another extreme. He considers Cervantes a late representative of the Renaissance, who seems to dislike the discipline which Church and State in Spain had adopted in order to check dangers from within as well as those threatening from the Protestant North and from the neo-pagan Italian East. Castro therefore supposes a Cervantes in whom an intellectual relativism is manifested by the motif of the [sleight of hand]; in whom a moral relativism disguises sin by the euphemism "error"; in whom an aristocratic idealism is symbolized by Don Quijote [the wise], full of contempt for the gregarious, vulgar spirit of Sancho, [the fool], representing the masses of the people. Castro's Cervantes is a smiling non-conformist who says with Montaigne: ["What do I know?"] His irony, hiding a destructive criticism under sanctimonious and patriotic sentences, is Cervantes's defense against possible troubles with the Inquisition. If this picture of a hypocritical non-conformist were true, it would deprive Cervantes of his decisive rôle as typical representative of Spain during the epoch of the Catholic Reformation.[3]

It can easily be understood that the positions of De Lollis and Castro, though extreme, were based on much erudition. This made it very difficult for scholarly and responsible Cervantes criticism to show what the poet hero of Lepanto actually was like if he was neither an ascetic nor a neo-pagan in spirit. The negative proof, that Cervantes was not an unorthodox Spaniard, seemed relatively easy. It could be based on vocabulary, character, psychology, historical circumstances. Aubrey Bell, Díaz Plaja, Leo Spitzer, and Margaret Bates have made some contributions in this line. But in support of Castro's thesis it must be conceded that there remains a suggestion of non-conformity and secularism in a Cervantes who, however orthodox, puts the active [knights], as it seems, on the same level with the contemplative [saints], praises [freedom of conscience] in Germany, and draws the picture of a model Christian gentleman in Don Diego de Miranda, *el Caballero del Verde Gabán*, which seems not free from irony, because this perfect gentleman enumerates his virtues himself, so that Sancho kneels down at once to worship him as a saint.

The "Relativist." The opponents of Castro must also agree that Cervantes's [sleight of hand] is something quite different from Calderón's idea of [*Life Is a Dream*]. Cervantes does not seem to illustrate a world of Baroque symbolism which has its unity only in [the mind of God] and appears to men as though it were broken through a prism. If you never can be sure whether windmills are giants or inns are castles, you never will be able to seize the meaning behind the symbol, and you renounce the decision whether an object is a basin or a helmet and accept the compromise of a ["basin-helmet"]. Therefore the French Hispanophile Jean Cassou[4] tried to interpret Cervantes's [mirror-tricks] as a poetic though tragic vision of the modern world erected on the débris of the Middle Ages. The geocentric and accordingly anthropocentric picture of Ptolemy has been destroyed, and man from his new Copernican peripheral view is driven into relativism and perspectivism. None the less, who will decide, with exact methods, whether Cervantes is a medieval realist, a neo-platonic idealist, a Baroque symbolist, or a modern relativist, according to the behavior of Don Quijote?

A political relativism in Cervantes has been stressed by Thomas Mann. This famous German writer happened on his way from Europe to the United States to read the *Don Quijote*.[5] He is sympathetic to a Cervantes whom he considers very cautious and therefore necessarily a little hypocritical when his loyalty towards Spain and his personal feelings are at odds. Thus Cervantes praises and blames at the same time the expulsion of the [Spanish Moors]. He finds kind words for Ricote, the [Spanish Moor], who, banished by the decree of Philip II, returns to Spain devoured by homesickness. Thomas Mann, then in a situation similar to Ricote's, says that when reading this passage "sorrow, love, compassion, and veneration without limits for Cervantes invaded him" and he sees in Cervantes a noble mind whose human feelings could not be stifled by any *raison d'état*. Thus the actual modern relativist Thomas Mann was overwhelmed and conquered by Cervantes's boundless charity.

The "Anti-Superman." Though the scholarly critic always will mistrust an emotional appraisal, he certainly must be alert to the possibility that from parallel situations in history there may come particularly pertinent insights. Thus during the Nietzchean Renaissance in Germany preceding the rise of National Socialism, Joseph Bickermann found that the ["never-enough-praised Don Quijote"] was not an ideal but a reprehensible extreme,[6] representing the superman who imposes his own arbitrary standards on society and therefore precipitates his own defeat in due course of a dialectical process of justice. On this continent a similar conception has been suggested by Ambrosius Czakó, who considers the hero Don Quijote a failure because the idealist who tries to elevate the actuality of life to his illusions and refuses to adjust his standards to life is bound to destruction.[7] Though there is some specious justification for Bickermann and Czakó in Don Quijote's repentance before his death, they come close to simply reviving the old criticism of Heinrich Heine, who considered Don Quijote's idealism as absolute folly ridiculed by Cervantes and Sancho's materialism as the pattern of reason.

The "Psychologist." In view of the obsession of our time with psychology it should not surprise anyone that it has been possible for J. Goyanés[8] to see in Don Quijote and Sancho two contrasting patterns of behavior in the attempt to master life, the schizothymic and the cyclothymic, which depend on circumstances beyond the human will. Another psychological approach, helpful for a new evaluation of the *Don Quijote*, has been made by José Vicente Castro Silva.[9] For him the two parts of the *Don Quijote* illustrate the problem of social readjustment. The reintegration of Don Quijote into his environment cannot be achieved by ["voices, shouts, confusion, apprehension, sudden dread, misfortunes, blows, beatings, kicks and spilling of blood"], as is attempted in the First Part of the novel, but can only come about through friendly understanding in nobler and more cultivated surroundings, as is the case in the Second Part with the Duques. These noble hosts permit the madman to develop into a sympathetic critic in the role of a courtly fool.

The "Communist." Your curiosity as to what a Soviet Russian critic may think about the Don Quijote may be satisfied by the work of Pavel I. Novitsky,[10] who declares that Cervantes' two protagonists together represent the alleged tragic dualism of a bourgeois-class civilization hesitating between an aimless dream of spiritualism and a well-planned policy of money-making. For the bourgeois has not the courage of a choice between spirituality or radical materialism. Another critic, Alberto Gerchunoff,[11] makes out of De Lollis's *Cervantes reaccionario* a *Cervantes revolucionario*, and declares: ["Don Quijote is an eternal rebel. His metal visor challenges the establishment with the fierce audacity of a revolutionary of later centuries. . . . If in front of rustic people he evokes the primitive organization of society, it is to magnify, in the poetry of a clear night . . . the communism of remote times"].

Returning to the more serious criticism of the scholars, we find ourselves confronted with two positions which certainly represent an aftermath of the conflict between the two opposite views of a conservative and a revolutionary Cervantes. But this time there are not at issue *a priori* ideologies, but two ways of analyzing the text, in view of the historical *péripéties* during the sixteenth century. There was of course at the beginning of the [Golden Age] a particular Spanish Renaissance, the Renaissance of Luis Vives and Fox Morcillo, of Cardinal Jiménez de Cisneros and Antonio de Nebrija, of Garcilaso de la Vega and the brothers Valdés. This Renaissance, Erasmian in kind, tried to attain a harmonious combination of Christian standards and humanistic concepts. Now Cervantes, born in the first half of the sixteenth century, is full of the ideas of Christian humanism, but he writes at a moment when this Erasmian harmony has given way to the overwhelming pressure of a radical theocentric and even theocratic Christianity. This pressure met with some resistance, and the Spaniards now appear divided into an older group of mystically-minded writers like San Ignacio de Loyola, Santa Teresa, San Juan de la Cruz, and ["the two Luises"] on the one side, and a younger group of disillusioned worldlings like Mateo Alemán, Vincente Espinel, Góngora, and Quevedo on the other. Nothing seems more natural therefore than the question whether Cervantes is a late Erasmian humanist, and whether his Quijote and Sancho are the two severed aspects of the former unity which Cervantes attempts to reunite like the famous Platonic halves of the Symposium; or whether Cervantes himself is a typical seventeenth-century writer who sides with this lofty spiritualism, which he wants to put in the place of the chivalrous and pastoral illusions, condemning at the same time in Sancho the new materialism of the rich adventurers returned from the colonies. In other words, is Cervantes a Renaissance or a Baroque writer? Nothing is more difficult than an answer to this decisive question, which seems a formal problem, but is the very core of the historical meaning of Cervantes.

The "Erasmian." Ludwig Pfandl, in his famous History of Spanish Literature,[12] declares Cervantes to be by all means the typical Renaissance writer. His Cervantes is aware of all the dangers of the Baroque in Spain, with its threat of splitting a politically disillusioned nation and its failure to provide a middle road between the mystic and the pícaro. This prophetic Cervantes is eager to underscore the values of a moral balance in the mind of Don Quijote whenever the ["sane madman"] has his great moments of lucidity, and the dangers of an idealism out of place when the mono-maniac turns out to be an incorrigible illuministic knight. Likewise in the sound Manchego Sancho he demonstrates the common sense of the old popular wisdom of Spain, mirrored in his [sayings] and [proverbs], but also a catastrophic greediness and cowardliness, when his peasant ambition overwhelms him and he sets out to gain an island to dominate and to exploit. Pfandl thus also says rather clearly that Cervantes is not a representative of his own epoch but a critic of its culture. He rather is the laudator temporis acti, who curses his contemporaries like a prophet:

> [Now laziness triumphs over diligence,
> indigence over work,
> vice over virtue,
> arrogance over valor
> and theory over practice . . .] (II,1).

The "Timeless Spaniard." Aubrey Bell also considers Cervantes a late Renaissance genius, but on quite other grounds. Bell sees in the late-sixteenth and early-seventeenth-century styles a genuinely Spanish Renaissance, harmoniously developing and embodying the ideals of the Council of Trent.[13] Therefore he sees only a well-balanced, unpolitical, harmless, smiling Cervantes who created a poetic synthesis of the eternal Castilian mind out of the idealistic thesis and the realistic antithesis: "If Sancho," he says, "may be described as the medieval Aristotelian recorder of reality, external common sense accepting objects as they are impressed on his mind, Don Quijote is the Renaissance Platonic mind, the inner vision creatively, imaginatively impressing itself on things. Between them they embody what may be termed the spiritual realism of Castile."[14] Aubrey Bell's concepts of Renaissance and Baroque are subordinated to a belief in an unchangeable Hispanidad stronger than history itself. They recently have been sharply criticized by Stephen Gilman in his study "An Introduction to the Ideology of the Baroque in Spain."[15] Bell actually so minimizes the historical implications around Cervantes that he almost denies the existence of the problems we have just been considering.

The "Man of the Middle Ages." A more original philosophical approach to Cervantes was made by Professor Mario Casella of Milan, whose two volumes on Cervantes and *Don Quijote*[16] were honored in 1938 by the Premio Isidre Bonsoms of the Institut d'Estudis Catalans in Barcelona. Casella thinks that Cervantes epitomizes in the form of pure poetry, as he calls the novel in contradistinction to technical philosophy, the essentials of the Augustinian-Thomistic tradition in metaphysics, esthetics, and ethics. Don Quijote starts from an illusionary love of self, because his chivalrous and pastoral illusions so hide the truth from him that he can not see himself as he ought to. But though illusion bound his enthusiastic nature, his fight for justice, his refining experiences, his high ideal of love reflected in Dulcinea, his Beatrice, prove that he wants to sublimate blind justice into mercy, sensuous desire into the love of charity, a sinful world into a more palpable establishment of the kingdom of God. As Nature is enhanced by Grace, so he wants this world of the *caballeros* to become a true analogy to the world of the *santos*, the *Civitas Dei*, and to the Divine. Casella sees in Cervantes practically the last representative of the Middle Ages, a man who defends unshakeable truths against the mirage of a modern world, which seems successful only because, as Don Quijote complains, the personal valor of a daring knight is bound to succumb to the blind technical force of ambushed artillery. Casella, excluding all other interpretations of *El Quijote*, asserts that he alone interprets the entire novel with all the details, whereas other commentators have confined themselves to selected details. Casella however ranges Cervantes too much among the conscious philosophers and obscures the problem that Cervantes's Middle Ages are the new Middle Ages called Baroque, whose opposition to the Renaissance is precisely the contribution of Spain to modern Europe. For it was Spain, under the leadership of men like Cervantes, that gave Europe the cultural stamp for its whole seventeenth century.

The "Baroque Man." The problem of a Baroque Cervantes writing a work of baroque art has been tackled, most fortunately, by Marcel Bataillon,[17] for the subject-matter, and by Joaquín Casalduero,[18] for the form. Marcel Bataillon has demonstrated that Cervantes is as much a typical representative of post-Tridentine Spain and consequently, we should add, a Baroque man, as Lope de Vega, but he presents other problems. Which ones? A humane mind — and therefore loved by everybody, [a lay genius] in a theological age, Cervantes is aware of not having the high spiritual tendencies required by Santa Teresa's verdict: ["Everything is nothing"]. So he becomes the melancholy, smiling, resigned writer who admires the sublime and follows the average and tries to justify his choice. This is the reason why he gives only one half of his divided soul to Don Quijote, the other half to Sancho Panza. Cervantes is however no new Erasmus, because he does *not* believe in the Renaissance dream of a full harmony between the divine and the too human on earth, possible only in a Golden Age, in which ["the clergy ask Heaven in peace and calmness for well-being on earth; but it is the soldiers and knights who carry out what they ask for"] (I, 13).

This truly Baroque picture of the meaning of the *Don Quijote* is supplemented by Joaquín Casalduero's account of its composition. According to this scholar, the first modern novel with a considerable perspective, where all the details serve a greater unity according to Wölfflin's principles of art, appears a maze but represents ["a disorderly order"]. Therefore Casalduero sees the various sallies of the knight as circular movements with tangential adventures, harmonized in number and tone, with tales and criticism correspondingly inserted in the balanced whole. The chivalrous, the amorous, and the literary themes, however, are intertwined. With its central core in the very middle of each Part, the tale is overlapped with a four-fold passional action, an organization of four "cascades" beyond the sallies, the adventures, the returns. With the problems, the landscape alters: steep, wild, nightmareish; or pathetic; or burlesque. There are atmospheres and climates of dust, and light and shades, and noises; the words are arranged accordingly. There is psychic reaction to these climates, mainly in Sancho, but also in the other central characters: from the Housekeeper to Dulcinea, the Priest and the Barber to the Duchess and Sansón Carrasco. There are love and womanhood in a hundred shadings. There is the crying contrast of flesh and spirit, even more in Maritornes and Doña Clara than in the squire and the knight. There is a masterwork of Baroque, rich with the humanistic past, endless in perspective toward the future.

Considering Casalduero's statements, we are inclined to say that in Cervantes studies the results of the esthetic method seem to be more satisfactory than those based on the historical or philosophical approach. But they are less stimulating. The hall-mark of a masterpiece is that though primarily a work of art, it makes us unquiet about its meaning and sense. And with all the findings of De Lollis and Castro, Pfandl and Bell, Casella and Bataillon, there remains still the truth formulated by Padre Bruno Ibeas: ["In the *Quijote* each one sees what he wants to, according to the nature of his spirit"].[19]

The last and definite word about the meaning of the *Don Quijote* probably will never be said. If such a thing were possible, the handicraft of scholarship would be superior to the lofty intuition of the poetical mind and this is, as Cervantes would have put it himself: ["of all impossibles, the most impossible"] (I, 22; II, 3; II, 53). Therefore the student of literature will always bow in admiration before Cervantes, the genius, and be grateful to Spain, which gave him, as her greatest literary treasure, to the entire world.

Notes

1. David Rubio, ¿Hay una filosofía en el Quijote? (New York, 1924), 165.

2. Cesare de Lollis, Cervantes Reazionario (Rome, 1924).

3. Américo Castro, El pensamiento de Cervantes (Madrid, 1925).

4. Cervantes (Mexico, 1939).

5. "A bordo con Don Quijote," in Cervantes, Goethe, Freud (Buenos Aires: Losanda, 1943.

6. Don Quijote und Faust (Berlin: Colignon, 1929).

7. Ambrosio Czakó, Don Quijote, A Commentary (Winnipeg: The Christian Press, 1943).

8. J. Goyanés, Tipología de El Quijote (Madrid, 1932).

9. Epílogo de Don Quijote (Bogotá, 1939), 29.

10. Cervantes and Don Quijote (New York, 1936).

11. Alberto Gerchunoff, La jofaina maravillosa: Agenda cervantina (Buenos Aires: Losada, 1938), 39–40.

12. Geschichte der spanischen Nationalliteratur der Blütezeit (Freiburg, 1929), 289–96.

13. Aubrey F. G. Bell, "Spanish Renaissance," Revue Hispanique, 80 (1930), 524.

14. Aubrey F. G. Bell, "The Character of Cervantes," Revue Hispanique, 80 (1930), 704.

15. Symposium, 1 (1946), 82.

16. Mario Casella, Cervantes: Il Chisciotte (Firenze: Monnier, 1938, 2 vols.).

17. Erasme et l'Espagne (Paris: Droz, 1937).

18. "La composición del Quijote," Revista de Filología Hispánica, II (1940), 323–369.

19. España y América, 11 (1916), 193.

La Galatea (1585)

The *Cuestión de Amor* and the Structure of Cervantes' *Galatea*

Jennifer Lowe*

The term 'Spanish pastoral novel' presupposes a certain similarity of elements in the individual works. A pastoral setting is, clearly, a fundamental requirement although its particular function will vary from book to book and, indeed, within the individual novel. It may be presented as the world of nature in harmony with the lovers; it may be an element in a Court/Country antithesis or it may be little more than a conventional backcloth to the events in the book.[1] Closely linked with the pastoral setting are the shepherds and shepherdesses, by profession and adoption, resident and visiting. Through the narratives of courtiers and ladies who have donned pastoral garb the atmosphere of the Court is introduced to us and we temporarily forget the realm of nature. No real variety is to be found in the themes and topics which are conveyed to us through the numerous stories, episodes and songs. Love, *desamor*, disdain, jealousy, friendship, Fortune, the ravages of Time all appear with almost monotonous regularity. Many of the novels are closely allied to the ideology of the Neoplatonic love treatises and may include *verbatim* an extract from one of these treatises or, at least, will echo much of their attitude and terminology.

It seems, therefore, that individuality in the pastoral novel will be restricted either to the way in which the novel is written and presented or to any particular emphasis given by the author. However, there is again a similarity in the methods used by these authors in the presentation of their novelistic material. We find a combination of narrative describing past events, events taking place in the present and lyrical passages which may help to heighten the emotional atmosphere. On reading a pastoral novel we are immediately aware of the numerous interruptions in the stories, the interweaving of the various episodes and the complex relationships between the characters. This technique is derived from the novelistic tradition which is nowadays termed Byzantine.[2] In the majority of Byzantine novels the narration swings between past and present events in an attempt to link the two and hold the interest of the reader. The pastoral

*Reprinted with permission from *Bulletin of Hispanic Studies* 53 (1966):98–108.

novel uses this device to greater purpose for such an interweaving of stories and juxtaposition of situations can serve to highlight particular topics and contrast the attitudes and fortunes of different characters. Moreover, by using such a technique the author is better able to present the *cuestiones de amor* which were an important part of most Spanish pastoral novels.[3]

The origin and development of the *cuestión de amor* are complex. In the Provençal poetry of the twelfth and thirteenth centuries are found the *tensor* which was a personal debate on varied subjects between two or more poets and the *partimen* or *joc-partit* in which a question, usually connected with love, was posed and contested. This literary fashion spread to Northern France, Italy and Spain. In Castile there was no exact equivalent of the *joc-partit*, but we find in the *Cancionero de Baena* poems known as *preguntas* or *requestas* in which a question, often connected with love, is formulated and answered in a separate poem or poems called *respuestas*. It is, however, the later development of the use of questions in Italy which had the most profound effect on Spanish literature.

In Book IV of Boccaccio's *Filocolo* (written 1338–40) we find a series of thirteen *questioni* or *dubbi*. (In theory a *dubbio* always poses a choice between two or more situations whilst the *questione* poses a straight question. In practice, however, this distinction in terminology is not always maintained). The wandering hero, Filocolo, and his shipwrecked companions find a group of noblemen and ladies in a beautiful garden. The latter have decided to pass the time by posing *questioni* and *dubbi*, many of which were probably prompted by Andreas Capellanus' *De amore*, a work in its turn influenced by the Provençal poets. Fiammetta is chosen as Queen or President of the proceedings and it is thus her task to pronounce judgement on each of the *questioni*. Each topic is introduced by one of the company, Fiammetta gives her opinion, this is immediately contested by the first speaker who presents the opposite view and finally, Fiammetta sums up and gives more detailed reasons for her judgement. The actual manner of presentation varies. Sometimes a direct question is asked as in *Questione* VII: Should a man fall in love? and *Questione* IX: Should a man fall in love with a young girl, a married woman or a widow? More important from the literary point of view, however, are those occasions on which a story is told to illustrate the question before it is actually formulated. In *Questione* I the account of the giving and receiving of garlands between a girl and her two admirers prompts the question: Does the girl love more the one from whom she receives or the one to whom she gives? In *Questione* IV a *novella* introduces a question about the respective values of three different types of magnanimity. This section of the *Filocolo* is self-contained and presents in miniature the basic elements for the framework of the later *Decamerone*.

In the *Filocolo* the *questioni* were used to create an artistic structure in one section of the book and to provide interest and amusement.

Questioni later appeared in a different setting, becoming an important feature of many of the love treatises where the various aspects of a topic were debated by the interlocutors. Yet they were not confined to the written word as they became the subjects of debates in the Academies which proliferated in sixteenth-century Italy, thus providing academic exercise and social diversion.[4]

In an age when Italian literature so frequently influenced that of Spain it is not surprising to find there the development of a similar phenomenon: the *cuestión de amor*. The anonymous *Question de amor* (published c.1510) has, as its title implies, a single *cuestión* as its basis. Two gentlemen, one mourning the death of his beloved and the other suffering from unrequited love, ["argue over which of the two suffers greater pain"]. This *cuestión* provides the core of the work in which a great deal of other material is introduced.[5] A similar conflict is, of course, presented in Garcilaso's First Eclogue where Salicio complains that his Galatea no longer loves him and Nemoroso laments the death of his beloved Elisa. Other Spanish works, including novels in the Byzantine tradition such as the *Historia de los amores de Clareo y Florisea* and the *Selva de aventuras*, contained sections in which *cuestiones* were suggested and resolved.

When we come to the realm of pastoral fiction we continue to find examples of the openly-stated *cuestión* as, for example, Sireno's question which prompts Felicia's long discourse in Montemayor's *Diana* (Book IV). The poetic debate between two or more shepherds is also represented. More interesting, however, is the way in which the *cuestiones* are made part of the whole structure of the work, so that the various stories and episodes narrated often prove to be illustrations of the several aspects of a *cuestión*. There are, of course, some obvious *cuestiones* such as that provided by the opening scene of the *Diana* where the two shepherds lament the marriage of the Diana they love. But, which has the greater cause for complaint and suffering: Sireno who was once loved by Diana or Silvano who was continually disdained by her? This situation is echoed in the initial presentation of Elicio and Erastro in the *Galatea*. However, most of the *cuestiones* are implicit and merely suggested to us by the various episodes and stories. The reader is able to compare the attitudes and fortunes of the various characters, using the clues provided by the author in the form of juxtaposition of characters or incidents and verbal comments and may, if he wishes, formulate the *cuestiones* himself. This is not the only way in which the reader could participate in the working out of the book. It is a well-known fact that the names and stories of many of the personages are but the disguise for real people. Thus, the reader would be able to exercise his ingenuity in trying to discover the links between fictional characters and contemporary figures. Moreover, great pleasure — albeit intellectual — would doubtless be derived from identifying the passages or reminiscences from the love treatises. Important too was the emotional appeal of these books which provided another possibility for reader-participation.[6]

Although he usually employed these conventional elements and techniques in the composition of his work, the skill of the author could be shown by the way in which he combined them. In addition, all could be used to illustrate an overall theme or to underline the author's particular purpose, thus giving his book individuality. Montemayor's *Diana* and Gil Polo's *Diana enamorada*, generally recognized as the best examples of the Spanish pastoral novel, make very different use of the conventional material.

The *Diana* has structural symmetry resulting from the distribution of the material between the seven books: I–III present the problems; IV introduces Felicia's intervention and V–VII offer some of the solutions.[7] Further cohesion is provided by the pilgrimage of many of the lovers to Felicia's palace. Through the interweaving of the stories various individual *cuestiones* are formed, many of which contribute to the overall *cuestión* of the book: Who are the more fickle in love, men or women? The book serves also to illustrate Montemayor's theory that ["they are best who suffer most"], a claim which is disputed by Gil Polo in the *Diana enamorada*. Although he retains many of the characters of the *Diana* and presents similar situations, his attitude to love and his purpose in writing are radically different from Montemayor's.[8] Gil Polo wishes to warn his readers against the ["harmful sickness"] of love and this dominant aim gives a unifying element to his book. Story and structure, though possessing individual merits, are subordinate to this end.

When we come to Cervantes' *Galatea* we are not immediately conscious either of a thematic unity or of a particular purpose on the part of Cervantes or of any skilful symmetry in the ordering of the material. Criticism, moreover, has not been at all favourable to Cervantes' pastoral novel. Many critics dismiss it in a very cursory manner as Cervantes' initial failure or his attempt to pander to contemporary fashion. Of those who do discuss it in more detail some allow their general dissatisfaction with the pastoral genre to influence their attitude to what they consider a particularly poor example of it; while others try and find in it hints of Cervantes' later work. Cervantes follows the established pastoral tradition; he includes *cuestiones* and the conventional dialectical passages; there are stock situations and characters and the customary quota of songs. We shall, in fact, be disappointed if we hope to find in the *Galatea* an original concept of the pastoral novel or a revolutionary method of presentation. It undoubtedly has many defects, but I hope to show that much of it has been constructed and written with great thought and skill on the part of Cervantes. However, before looking in detail at the structure we must first consider the content.

The main themes and topics of the *Galatea* have been listed by López Estrada, proving that Cervantes shows no originality in his choice of material.[9] His intention in the *Galatea* seems to be not so much to distinguish between the different types of love or to take up a moralizing standpoint as to show the many and varied obstacles with which love is confronted and the way in which these obstacles may be overcome. Is there, then, any thematic unity in the book?

Cervantes has made an attempt to give continuity to his book by the way in which he has presented the main conventional topics. He portrays them through a variety of characters and in differing situations which thus reveal numerous facets. This can be seen more clearly by considering the three chief topics. The theme of jealousy is presented first from a negative point of view when Elicio claims that Erastro's love for Galatea arouses no envy in himself (I,9).[10] Our opinion of this apparently altruistic attitude is diminished when we later learn that Elicio has no real cause to be jealous since he alone is not completely ignored by the proud Galatea (II,141). A more profound treatment of the Elicio / Erastro situation is found in the story of Timbrio and Silerio who, though both in love with Nísida, are each moved, because of their friendship, to generous action to obtain the other's success in love, rather than to selfish jealousy. The violent, destructive force of this passion is exemplified in the story told by Lisandro whilst the potential dangers and resulting effect are revealed by the Rosaura / Grisaldo episode which also serves as a practical example of Damón's invective at the end of Book III. Friendship has already been mentioned and it, too, is a constant theme throughout the book. Cervantes shows us the passive relationship of Elicio and Erastro, the active, magnanimous friendship of Silerio and Timbrio and the way in which the name of friend is abused in Lisandro's tragic story.

Most pastoral novels present the conventional figure of the *desamorado* or *desamorada* and the *Galatea* is no exception. Galatea herself is proud of her immunity from love and takes pleasure in taunting Elicio and Erastro. Teolinda is, initially, a similar character but soon becomes *enamorada* whilst Gelasia presents a more extreme case of *desamor*. This, however, is not a feminine prerogative for we are shown that the now ardent Elicio was once a *desamorado* and that Lauso progresses from *desamor* to *amor* ["before becoming *desamorado* once again"].[11] The rebellious Lenio's condemnations of love play a large part in the book but eventually even he succumbs and falls in love with the harsh Gelasia.

This necessarily brief summary shows that Cervantes has succeeded in creating a certain amount of continuity in the *Galatea*. Through the repetition of these and other topics he has linked together characters and situations which might otherwise have remained unconnected. Yet this does not mean that the book thereby achieves thematic unity. There is no one dominant theme or aim to which these various topics can be subordinated. Are there, then, any qualities in the structure of the book which might compensate for the weak content? A glance at the views of the critics would suggest that this is not necessarily so. The extreme point of view is represented by comments such as that of H. A. Rennert: "There seems to be no attempt at plot or connected narrative and it is with the greatest difficulty that the reader keeps track of the various characters."[12] López Estrada has a much more sympathetic approach to the book but can find little to say in favour of its construction: ["the threads of the plot are entangled in the author's hand . . . and one must struggle to untie them. Thus one finds violent interruptions in the discourse, or aglomerations of characters which cause confusion"].[13] Cesare de Lollis takes the view that these interruptions in the narrative serve merely as a means of holding the attention of the reader: ["because suspense, which was an epic trait most loved by Cervantes . . . increased interest in the story"][14] J. A. Tamayo, on the other hand, praises the construction of the book pointing out that ["the essence of the work's plot is no longer limited to the presentation of the classic chain of enamored shepherds. . . . The presentation . . . is now much more complicated and the author gives his work a wiser and more perfect architecture"].[15] He draws up a skeleton plan of the book but can find no particular purpose in the order of events. Indeed, he then feels that the ["criss-cross of topics and themes . . . generates a certain amount of confusion"].[16] Avalle-Arce believes that ["the number of those tales and the evident thematic relations woven among them" helps Cervantes to establish a "series of perspectives" describing "the tragic love . . . of Lisandro, the idyllic love of Teolinda, and the failed love of Rosaura"].[17] He also gives a more elaborate explanation of the way in which the interweaving of the stories creates a ["poetic solar system"].[18] Avalle-Arce's approach is part of his general view of the presentation of reality in the book. The other critics fault the structure chiefly on the grounds of confusion and over-frequent interruptions of the narrative. I hope to show that there is a purpose behind many of these interruptions and that the structure is, for the most part, well integrated.

The opening situation in the book presents us with a *cuestión de amor*. Which of the two shepherds is the more unfortunate and, consequently, the more unhappy? Is it Elicio who has a little, but not sufficient, success with Galatea, or Erastro who is continually disdained by her? A similarity with the plight of Sireno and Silvano in the opening scene of the *Diana* is at once apparent. The distinction between the two shepherds in the *Galatea* is, however, more subtle and as soon as he has introduced the *cuestión* Cervantes implies that, despite a superficial difference, the attitude of Galatea towards them and the effect of that attitude is basically the same. He suggests this through the words of Erastro who refers to Galatea as ["she who is so rejecting of my demands as she is harsh regarding my constant complaints"] (I. 7). Because of this: ["if you with your skill and extreme grace and reason cannot soften her, little will I be able with my simplicity to make her care for me"] (I. 8). They are equated again later in the story in the words of Elicio: ["sometimes Erastro's hope *weakens* and in me it *grows cold*, so that he takes it as *certain*, and I as *beyond question* that we will be dead before our hopes are realized"] (I, 109. The italics are mine). Thus, having first sketched in a *cuestión de amor* between the two friends, Cervantes then suggests there is no real difference between their situations — an answer which is important in connexion with the following episode with the arrival of the distraught Lisandro telling of the tragic and violent death of his beloved Leonida. A *cuestión* at once suggests itself: Which is the more unfortunate, Elicio and Erastro or Lisandro? Which brings the greater suffering, disdain or death? The tragic story told by Lisandro and his obvious lack of consolation in this life are beginning to persuade us that he is definitely the more unfortunate when the arrival of Galatea (I, 41–42) and her disdainful attitude to her two lovers make us reconsider our opinion. The emphasis of the *cuestion* has been altered and its terms must now be qualified, which is worse: to know that you are loved and then to lose the beloved by death or to know that the beloved is alive and see her, and yet know that she may never love you? *Amor* and death or *desamor* and life?

Soon after these relationships have been established Teolinda appears (I, 46). Although it is possible to form a *cuestión* between her and Galatea — which is the preferable state: *amor* or *desamor*? — this is not the main reason for her introduction at this particular juncture. She serves chiefly to show the possible consequences of Galatea's behaviour if her pride encourages her to persist in her *desamor*. When she begins to tell the story of her past life similarities between herself and Galatea are at once established. She had been proud of her immunity from love and mocked at lovers (I, 52–53) as Galatea still does (I, 43). She had spent her time gathering flowers (I, 52), an occupation pleasing to Galatea (I, 46). Teolinda's pride preceded the traditional fall even if it was not the actual cause of it and she fell passionately in love with Artidoro, only to be separated from him by unforeseen circumstances. Earlier, Erastro when vexed by the attitude of Galatea had expressed the wish that, one day, she might have her love similarly scorned: ["may heaven destroy the good will I have if I do not wish to see you in love with one who values your complaints as you value mine"] (I, 44). These words are re-echoed now as Teolinda recalls the words of the passionate Lidia to herself when out of love: ["I pray to God . . . that you will soon find yourself in a state compared to which mine will seem happy, and that love will treat you in such a way that you tell your pain to someone who will listen and value it to the same degree as you have done with my pain"] (I, 54). The first part of this wish has already been fulfilled and, as she tells her story to Galatea, Teolinda fears that the second part of Lidia's wish is also coming true and that, as she once mocked Lidia, so Galatea will mock her. The implications of the situation are obvious: Cervantes wishes us to assume that, like Teolinda, Galatea will eventually succumb to the power of love.

The arrival of the *desamorado* Lenio (I, 68) provides a male counterpart to Teolinda and Galatea. His attitude to love and lovers is even more extreme than that once held by Teolinda. The introduction of Lenio in the middle of the account of Teolinda's "conversion" is indicative of the fact that he will probably suffer the same fate and this surmise is again emphasized by a prophecy similar to the two mentioned above, for Erastro, incensed by Lenio's hostility to love, exclaims: ["I hope that some day you will pay for what you have said, and that whatever you may say in your defense will be of no use"] (I, 73). Later, when he too is in love, Lenio admits rather sadly that ["love brought him to such a state to avenge itself all at once for all the offenses he had committed against it"] (II, 172). The wish of Erastro has been fulfilled more completely than he could ever have imagined. Teolinda is flanked, therefore, by two *desamorados*; one hears her story, the other does not. A certain tension is thus created as the reader wonders whether Galatea or Lenio will be the first to succumb to love.

In Book II Teolinda continues her story, telling how her separation from Artidoro came about. The tentative *cuestión* formed between her and Galatea can now be adapted and expanded: Which is better, *desamor* and freedom from unhappiness or *amor* and the suffering connected with it? This topic is to be constant throughout the book. A different sort of *cuestión* in a more stylized form, reminiscent of the earlier poetic debates, is now presented in the song of Tirsi and Damon (I, 96–100). It poses the question: Which is worse, to be afflicted by separation from the beloved or by her disdain? Here the answer is clear from the arguments which are adduced to support the two claims: absence is easily remedied, disdain is not. Its thematic connexion with the situations so far introduced into the novel is noticeable.

The story told by Silerio is complete in itself in many respects but does have some contact with the rest of the novel.[19] The first part of the narration seeks to determine which of the two companions shows the greater conception of the meaning of friendship whilst the second part continues this *cuestión*, coupling it with another problem: Which should have the greater claim in a person, love or friendship? Obviously it is possible to link Silerio with other characters in the book in an attempt to assess which of them is the unhappiest, but a more interesting and subtle connexion can be formed between him and Mireno (I, 172), who sings tragically of the way in which he has been deceived in love by Silveria who is about to marry Daranio. His appearance at this juncture is deliberate. His position is similar to that of Silerio in that they have both lost the girl they loved. But there the similarity ends. Mireno has not willingly relinquished Silveria; nor can he reconcile himself to Daranio's marriage to her by rejoicing at the good fortune of a friend. Silerio, on the other hand, had deliberately forfeited his own chance of happiness and had shown how his sadness at the loss of his beloved Nísida was attenuated by the fact that she would marry his friend Timbrio: ["if luck yielded me any pleasure in this pain, it was in considering the welfare of my friend Timbrio"] (I, 169). This, then, is the basis of yet another *cuestión*: Which is worse, to lose the beloved to another person because you wish it or against your will? Mireno, moreover, seeks to contrast his lot with that of Elicio, for he claims that the latter has the hope of being loved some day whilst he himself can have only the certainty of being forgotten (I, 185). Which of them, then, is the more to be pitied? Here, Mireno, while pleading his own case, has in fact formulated yet another *cuestión*.

Another stylized *cuestión* is presented in a four-part song by Orompo, Marsilio, Crisio and Orfenio who lament their sufferings caused respectively by death, disdain, absence and jealousy (I, 199–222). This poetical debate helps to bring into sharper focus some of the points and details which may perhaps have escaped our notice when we were considering the stories of the various characters. Moreover, these characters did not seek to present their stories merely as evidence that they deserved more pity than the next person or as the explicit illustration of one aspect of a *cuestión*. The chief value and interest lay in the stories themselves and the reader could probably find additional pleasure in discovering the comparisons and contrasts established by Cervantes. In this four-part song the last *pena* to be dealt with is jealousy which had not, as yet, received much attention in the book. Now it is discussed by Damón (I, 226–29) and soon given a practical demonstration in the story of Rosaura and Grisaldo.

Lauso is next introduced and his case-history recounted, the emphasis being placed on the fact that he has fallen in love after being a confirmed *desamorado* for so many years (II, 30). Then follows the long debate between Lenio and Tirsi, the *desamorado* and the *enamorado*. That the "conversion" ["the free Lauso"] has just been shown to us is a suggestion that Lenio, too, may soon change his attitude. We may perhaps have forgotten how Lenio was previously paralleled with Teolinda; the introduction of Lauso reminds us of this fact.

The debate is followed by the arrival of Timbrio, Nísida and Blanca, preluding their reunion with Silerio. The story of Teolinda is recalled by the incident involving her, Leonarda, Gelasia and Galercio (II, 83–89). It is important in that it shows us the nature of the harsh Gelasia with whom Lenio will soon fall in love. In the ensuing pages we learn, among other things, of Timbrio's wanderings before he eventually reached Silerio, of Galatea's projected marriage to an unknown shepherd, of the aftermath of Rosaura's foolhardy behaviour, of Lenio's passionate and unrequited love for Gelasia, of the development of the Teolinda / Artidoro situation with the additional complications of the perfidious behaviour of Teolinda's sister Leonarda, of old Arsindo's love for Maurisa and of Galatea's changing attitude towards Elicio. Towards the end of the novel Belisa, another *desamorada*, loved by Marsilio, is introduced (II, 252–54). That she is going to be presented as another Galatea is obvious from the equation between the attitudes of Elicio and Erastro and Marsilio to their respective ladies (II, 239).

The *Primera parte* ends with the hint of various stories and situations which would clearly have been continued and, if possible, resolved in the *Segunda parte*. From the brief outline of the novel I have given it can be seen that the second half of the novel as we know it is not as well constructed as the first section. There, a rigid plan was often evident and stories and incidents were arranged so as to give the best possible effect and to underline similarities and differences between the characters. Much of this was achieved by juxtaposition of the characters or by verbal similarities between their comments. We are not confronted with a meaningless tangle of stories, with numerous interruptions merely for the sake of suspense. The Byzantine technique and the *cuestión de amor* have both been used by Cervantes in the construction of his *Galatea*. He does not, for the most part, openly state a *cuestión* and then tell stories to illustrate the various points. Rather, he succeeds in giving us the impression that the *cuestiones* emerge naturally from the narration of the stories and incidents. The reader himself can thus attempt to formulate some of these *cuestiones* and to guess the ultimate fate of some of the characters. The skilful and rigid plan of the first section disintegrates toward the end of the book: now Cervantes has so many stories and parts of stories operating simultaneously that he is obliged continually to swing from one to the other in order, not so much to emphasize contrasts, as to keep the reader up to date with all of them. An artistic device has become a practical necessity.

Thus, although it would be wrong to claim that the *Galatea* is an outstanding book which clearly bears the stamp of Cervantes, it would be equally wrong to dismiss it as a complete failure. It was obviously not intended solely as the setting for the rather mediocre poems,[20] nor is it true that our only interest is in the way that the characters speak.[21] There is, undeniably, similarity between one character and another[22] but this is often deliberate similarity which serves Cervantes in the presentation of the *cuestiones*. The lack of an overall theme may, quite rightly, disturb us at times but does not prevent much of the book from having a structural unity. Twentieth-century readers may not find the same amount of enjoyment as those of Cervantes' day in following the clues, tracking down the quotations and recognizing the disguised courtiers. However, we can at least appreciate much of the author's skill and applaud his aim as expressed in his Prologue, ["which was to please"].

Notes

1. The role of the pastoral background is discussed by B. W. Wardropper, "The *Diana*: Revaluation and interpretation', *S Ph*, XLVIII (1951), 127–43.

2. F. López Estrada deals with the links between the Byzantine and the pastoral novel in the introduction to his edition of *Historia etiópica de los amores de Teágenes y Cariclea* (Madrid 1954).

3. They are not, of course, confined to the pastoral novel and are used to great effect in Cervantes' own *novela Las dos doncellas*.

4. For a detailed study of this aspect of the *questioni* see T. F. Crane, *Italian Social Customs of the Sixteenth Century* (New Haven 1920).

5. The *Question de amor* is included in *Orígenes de la novela* (*NBAE*, VII).

6. E. C. Riley, *Cervantes's Theory of the Novel* (Oxford 1962), 33.

7. B. W. Wardropper, *op. cit.*, 133.

8. Discussed in detail by A. Solé-Leris, 'The Theory of Love in the two *Dianas*: a contrast', *BHS*, XXXVI (1959), 65–79.

9. F. López Estrada, *La 'Galatea' de Cervantes. Estudio critico* (La Laguna de Tenerife 1948).

10. All refrences are to *La Galatea* ed. R. Schevill and A. Bonilla (Madrid 1914), 2 vols.

11. López Estrada, *op. cit.*, 21, incorrectly states that Lauso merely passes from *amor* to *desamor*. In fact, in the *desamor / amor / desamor* cycle Cervantes has presented a much more complex situation.

12. H. A. Rennert, *The Spanish Pastoral Romances* (Philadelphia 1912), 117.

13. López Estrada, *op. cit.*, 65.

14. Cesare de Lollis, *Cervantes reazionario* (Florence 1947), 24.

15. J. A. Tamayo, 'Los pastores de Cervantes', *RFE*, XXXII (1948), 389.

16. *Ibid*, 394.

17. J. B. Avalle-Arce, *La novela pastoril española* (Madrid 1959), 200.

18. *Ibid*, 200.

19. This story is, of course, based on one in Boccaccio's *Decamerone*, Tenth Day, *novella* VIII. Many of the ideas on love and friendship recall those in Cervantes' own *Curioso impertinente*.

20. This was the story of L. Astrana Marín, *Vida ejemplar y heroica de Miguel de Cervantes Saavedra* (Madrid 1948–5), III, 236.

21. L. Rosales, *Cervantes y la libertad: I – La libertad soñada* (Madrid 1960), I, 273.

22. *Ibid*, 272.

The Language of Limits and the Limits of Language: The Crisis of Poetry in *La Galatea*

Mary Gaylord Randel*

[His whole pleasure and pastime was to sing to the tune of his *rabel* the events — whether fortunate or adverse — of his love, in accordance with his natural inclination . . .]

One might say of the [pastoral books] what the narrator says of ["the enamored Lauso"] in Book V of *La Galatea* (II, 123).[1] They find their whole and sole pleasure in songs of love. If the shepherd symbolizes love by the very nature of his calling, the world of literary pastoral is one in which not love but *talk about love* dominates, in which shepherds are not obliged

*Reprinted with permission from *MLN* 97 (1982):254–71.

actually to tend sheep but rather to engage in constant reflection on that "occupation." The pastoral world, in short, is a world of representation and of self-representation, as Cervantes makes clear in the ["false Arcadia"] episode of *Don Quixote*.[2]

From its beginnings, the literature of shepherds has presented what Elias Rivers calls the "pastoral paradox of natural art."[3] While it promotes an ideal of Golden Age innocence, it insists on its own position as art. Pastorals have tended to be highly conscious of their own traditions; their world is a world of inherited words.[4] Classical versions of pastoral, furthermore, were written entirely in verse, many of them consisting largely of poetic competitions. By virtue of their fidelity to tradition, the contestants of these matches vie implicitly not only with their immediate rivals, but with the tradition which their songs carry on. The "natural" language of shepherds does not simply accept imitation of poetic models. It makes that imitation a central principle of its art. Pastoral, then, advertising itself as poetry, can readily become *poetry about poetry*. Quite predictably, we often find pastoral works addressing the nature, the claims and the status of the poetic enterprise.

La Galatea provides a particularly rich illustration of this tendency. In his prologue, Cervantes, invoking ["the inclination toward poetry that I have always had"] (I, 6), complains about the disfavor which poetry (and especially the eclogue) suffers in his day. He makes his first major literary effort an implicit defense of poetry:

> [It cannot be denied that studies of the [poetic] faculty — so rightly admired in the past — carry with them more than mediocre advantages, among which are the enrichment of the poet upon considering his own language, and the mastery of the elocutionary skills of poetry, for the carrying out of higher and more important undertakings.] (I,6)

Cervantes' enthusiasm associates him with a host of sixteenth-century defenders of the vernacular and its poetic aspirations.[5] *La Galatea*'s obvious concern with poetry does not, however, end here. Tirsi and Damón, ["two honored and famous shepherds"] (I, 104), who represent the celebrated poets, Francisco de Figueroa, "el Divino," and Pedro Laínez, join the shepherds on the banks of the Tagus in Book II. These poets guide the company toward the wedding of Book III, the debate of Book IV and finally to the commemorative rites at the tomb of another poet, Meliso (Diego Hurtado de Mendoza), in Book VI. Along the road to the tomb, Tirsi and Damón participate — both as poets and as judges — in numerous poetic contests. At graveside in the Valley of the Cypresses, the shepherds witness the marvellous nocturnal appearance of Calíope, the muse of poetry, who offers a lavish verse tribute to one hundred of Cervantes' poet contemporaries. By their sheer bulk, Caliope's imposing hyperboles oblige us to focus on the place of verse in what we can come to call the pastoral novel.[6]

Two prevalent notions interfere with our disposition to read *La Galatea* as primarily a defense of poetry. Cervantes himself promoted both of these conceptions, which have become persistent axioms of Cervantes criticism. One is the idea of the "failure" of *La Galatea*, suggested in the prologue (["in this (the will to please) the work does not fulfill its intent"] (I, 9); and in the famous judgment voiced in the "inquisition scene" of *Don Quixote* ["it proposes something and concludes nothing"] [*DQ* I, 6]). The other is the portrait of Cervantes as "failed poet." Again in the "inquisition scene," the priest describes *La Galatea*'s author as ["more versed in misfortune than in verse"]. The prologue of the *Eight Plays and Eight Interludes* reports the book dealer's blunt verdict: ["from the prose one can expect much, but from the poetry, nothing"].[7] Despite equally frequent tributes to poetry scattered throughout his works, we have most often elected to accept at face value—that is, as signs valid apart from contexts—Cervantes's self-deprecating remarks about his poetic talents. These negative self-appraisals have tended to bolster "disappointed" modern reactions to *La Galatea* and to provide readers with an excuse for skipping over its verses in search of Cervantes, the apprentice novelist.

La Galatea, while it purports to defend poetry, is not exclusively a verse pastoral or eclogue, but a pastoral romance, the Renaissance hybrid of prose and verse modeled on Sannazaro's *Arcadia*. Recently Joaquín Casalduero cautioned against viewing this hybrid form as a simple pretext to ["collect a few poems"].[8] He challenges readers to uncover the "intimate need" that causes verse to give way to prose and prose to verse, in alternating rhythm. The question is highly suggestive. It pinpoints, in fact, another pastoral paradox, the formal paradox of the pastoral romance, which uses prose to privilege verse, at the same time that it acknowledges the insufficiency of the verse. Pastoral romance is thus always meta-poetry. That is, by virtue of the decision to supplement verse with prose, it always makes an implicit commentary on the original vehicle. In what follows we propose to show how *La Galatea* explicitly makes the power of poetry its central concern, and how the text exploits the alternation of prose and verse to dramatize a struggle with the very limits of language.

Cervantes, says Casalduero, attacks the pastoral composition at its center. From the temple of Love in Montemayor's *La Diana*, we move in *La Galatea* to the sacrament of marriage, for Casalduero a sign of Cervantes' Christian social and moral consciousness, new to the genre. Two weddings, mirror images of each other, share the center of *La Galatea*: the public wedding of Daranio and Silveria toward the end of Book III and the secret vows of Rosaura and Grisaldo at the beginning of Book IV. These events raise many questions which are left unresolved. The "justice" of both matches remains in doubt. The weddings, toward which the shepherds journey and from which they move on in a symbolic, unwitting, pilgrimage toward Death, serve as foreshadowing of Galatea's own destiny.[9] If the weddings occupy the off-centered center, the work does not give a prominent place to the consideration of marriage in itself. The dramatic encounter of Rosaura and Grisaldo briefly claims the narrative foreground with its intensity, but the wedding of Daranio and Silveria seems strangely remote. It functions as silent backdrop to a series of poetic events, particularly the Eclogue.

In effect a "pastoral within a pastoral," the Eclogue situates the traditional poetic competition within a pastoral romance. Its stilted form, its commitment to abstract expression and its static quality stand in marked contrast to the tangle of love-lives that surrounds it. Even before it begins, Cervantes seems to invite us to reject it as a form of discourse inadequate to the task of evoking the intricacies of sentimental life. He introduces his four shepherd-poets, famed for their "disputas y competencias," with elusive irony:

> [many times they had come together so that each one could highlight the cause of his torment, each trying to show as best he could that his pain was greater than that of any other, taking as the highest glory to be richer in pain. And they were all so clever, or rather, they all suffered such pain, that however they expressed it, they showed it to be as great as could be imagined.] (I, 198)

Orompo, Marsilio, Crisio, Orfenio, representing respectively the pain of Death, Disdain, Absence and Jealousy, renew an old question: Which of them is the most wretched and most deserving of pity?[10] Cervantes turns the standard oxymoron of "sweet pain" into the paradoxical emblem of poetic competition. Whoever can prove himself most miserable — by eloquence or by the "truth" of his grief — will be most glorious.

Yet there is more at stake here than Montemayor's axiom that ["he is best who suffers most"].[11] This passage and the Eclogue which follows oblige us to suspend that consideration. How, they ask us, are we to go about answering the question? Does one judge the merits and miseries of a soul on the basis of rhetorical skill or on the basis of actual suffering? Orompo describes himself as

> [A shepherd who dares
> With words grounded
> in the pure truth of his torment
> to show that the feeling
> of his intensified pain
> is stronger than yours
> No matter how you value
> raise and glorify it.]
> (I, 209–10)

The Eclogue, we now perceive, is *a poetic competition about poetic competition*. Cervantes here makes the central issue of pastoral art not sentiment but the way that sentiment can be expressed. Orompo's words call into question the power of language to communicate truth about the self.

Orompo echoes Salicio's famous refrain from Garcilaso's first Eclogue (itself an echo of an earlier poem). He addresses, however, not his *tears* but his *words*: ["come out from the depths of an afflicted breast / *bloodied words* mixed with death; / and if sighs keep you bound / open and break down the confining ribs"] (I, 205). And even if his words break out of his heart's prison, will they succeed as self-representation and communication?

> [Because even if you escape, words, trembling,
> which of you will be able to say what I feel,
> if my fierce torment is incapable
> of coming out as it is from truth to an image of it?
> But even though I have no *how* or *when*
> to represent my pain and loss
> that which is lacking and that my words cannot say
> will come through my eyes in continual crying.]
>
> (I, 206)

Orfinio, victim of jealousy, rejects eloquence as a valid standard for judging sentiment: ["since it is not in elegance / and manner of speaking that one finds grounding / and true sustenance for the tale; / in pure truth it has its foundation"] (I, 215–16). This passage is most often read as confirmation of Cervantes' campaign against affectation. Language must make the ["pure truth"], as Orfinio says, its sustaining base. Yet his words voice an anxiety: "truth" may give words a foundation; but only words, trembling in their incapacity, can provide evidence of that truth.

The indictment of refined speech — whether through distrust of its excess expressive capacity or through the agonizing realization of its insufficiency — is nothing less than an indictment of pastoral as a whole. In this most poetic of genres, shepherd-lovers rehearse and exalt their intimate feelings in verse. They operate on the tacit premise that subtlety of feeling can best be communicated by the subtle refinement of language called "poetry."[12] Cervantes plays with that assumption by permitting several characters to champion less polished speech as proof of sincerity. But the private anxiety of the individual sufferer-competitor that he will be found unworthy of sympathy is secondary to the questions which the competition poses about the relationship of language to its object, to the "truth." Is the idea of language as mimesis a viable one in the area of feeling? In short, can the self ever aspire to "go directly from the real thing to its image?"

The traded verses of the Eclogue seem largely oblivious to this problem. Each shepherd argues the pressing nature of his own particular claim. Only Orompo perceives the devastating logic of their competition, an interminable duel of hyperboles, a ["They will never end"]: ["and since no one senses / what the other feels, each exaggerates his own pain, / and thinks that he surpasses the other thereby"] (I, 222). The performance of the four ends in a kind of truce: the shepherds offer final summation of their cases without conceding. An outsider, Damón, must decide the question. The Eclogue must end, because each shepherd ultimately *listens only to himself*. As attempted communication of intimacy, the Eclogue has failed.

Nonetheless Damón, without hesitation, ["leaving everyone satisfied of the truth that he had so fully demonstrated to them"] (I, 232), names Orfinio's torment, Jealousy, winner of the contest. Damón's discourse introduces a pair of favorite Cervantine themes: jealousy and the figure of the *curioso impertinente* (from the interpolated tale of that name in *Don Quixote* and the story of Timbrio and Silerio in *La Galatea* itself). These themes have such a recognizable profile in Cervantes' work generally that readers have not felt the need to articulate their particular function within *La Galatea*. In a work which poses to itself the problem of the power and limits of its own discourse, the figure of the jealous, curious one clearly paints the limit of distress. As curious, burning for absolute certainty, and as jealous, beyond all of language's power of persuasion and consolation, condemned to invent *ex nihilo* his own seductive fictions, he inhabits a *purgatory of language*, which cannot reach that which it claims for its foundation and its object.

> [There is no antidote that will protect him, advice that will help him, nor explanation that makes any sense; all of this belongs with the jealous lover and more: that any shadow terrifies him, and foolishness upsets him, and any suspicion, true or false, undoes him. . . . And having no other medicine for his jealousy but excuses, and not wanting to express them, the jealous lover's illness continues without remedy, taking precedence over all other problems.]
>
> (I, 203)

The true lover, Damón adds, shares the jealous lover's purgatory, if not his frenzy. Neither can have certainty beyond fear in love: ["The good lover fears and will fear . . . and this fear must be so secret that it does not reach the tongue to be spoken, nor even the eyes to be expressed"] (I, 231). The discreet lover's language must serve him as a mask.

From the Eclogue and subsequent commentary, we draw two remarkable conclusions. First, language cannot tell the truth; it fails absolutely as a mimetic mirror in the domain of feeling. Second, language *should not* tell the truth; its mask necessarily, rightfully, conceals. Finally, the paradoxical result: despite language's lamentable inadequacy, the greatest misery comes of finding one's self beyond its civilizing power. The Eclogue's concern with discourse and what it struggles to tell suggests a key to the unity of the episodes which proliferate around it. Fragments of discourse leave as much mystery as information in their wake. The relentless pace of narrative interruption — introducing other figures with more stories to tell — creates a chain of partial understandings and misunderstandings. Daranio and Silveria, unique among the wordy shepherds in their speechlessness, are only more mysterious in degree than the other characters in *La Galatea*. Their absolute silence is only slightly more perplexing than the faltering aid which discourse lends to the exploration of intimacy. Again and again, the text's lurching movements, sudden breaks and incompletions — its interruptive aesthetic — remind us that we cannot know with certainty, that ["one does not feel what another is suffering"].

La Galatea's shepherds and shepherdesses break into song when they overflow with emotion, when they contemplate a beloved person or a private grief. ["Let not my torment keep silence," "let my soul come out with my voice / *for greater feeling*"] (II, 108). As the language of the soul, verse aims to intensify, even to exaggerate feeling. Timbrio offers his verses here as the handmaidens of hyperbole. Verse is presumed better equipped than prose to maintain a high emotional temperature and to reproduce emotion in the listener. Charged with saying the most that language can say, verse nonetheless presents itself as a problematical vehicle of communication.

Of course, it is always the challenge of poetry to say what it means by not saying what it means. "Poetry," writes Jonathan Culler, "lies at the center of the literary experience because it is the form that most clearly asserts the specificity of literature, its difference from ordinary discourse by an empirical individual about the world. The specific features of poetry have the function of differentiating it from speech and altering the circuit of communication within which it is inscribed."[13] Within the mimetic world created by the book, the shepherd's decision to "speak in song" necessarily changes the nature and aims of his communication. Verse in *La Galatea* always attaches to a specific "I," identified by name at the head of the composition. If speaking in verse means choosing to speak *from* the deepest seat of emotion, however, it also means deciding not to speak directly, exclusively, *to* anyone. Even though the song may be addressed rhetorically to a certain figure, it reaches for a wider audience. While claiming to be in some sense more intimate, poems become at the same time more impersonal. In the pastoral romance, verse tends to function as a kind of *indirect direct discourse*: it always presents the paradox of alluding to and simultaneously avoiding its fictional context.

A shepherd (like Elicio at the opening of Book I) may sing to no one but his own ["thoughts of love"] (I, 18), hinting at his circumstances, but aware of no audience. Such songs are, of course, in what Cesáreo Bandera calls a ["world of watchers"][14] fated to be overheard by listeners who eventually reveal their presence and pursue the significance of what they have chanced to hear. Or a shepherd or shepherdess may be asked to sing in order to demonstrate the sweetness of his or her voice. The poem is always presumed to address a circumstance or a person which may or may not be recognized by its listeners. If the addressee happens to be present, the verses may press a specific complaint by innuendo, without ever revealing an identity. If the addressee is absent, the verses may say more than they would dare to say in his or her actual presence. Verses may even be delivered from a presumed speaker to a presumed addressee, while the poem's impersonal discourse hides the actual identity of either from the character-listeners. The most complex instance involves the two friends, Timbrio and Silerio. Silerio tells of his own sentiments to Nísida *as though they were* — and in fact they *are* — Timbrio's (I, 150–51). Later he sings of his love *for* Nísida *to* Timbrio *as though it were for* Blanca (I, 159–60). In these situations, the language of verse is *double-talk*. It does and simultaneously does not want to be understood. It claims, through the privilege it enjoys over prose, a special significance for its message, but it cloaks that significance in a *mask of language*.

This bizarre kind of communication which hopes to succeed and simultaneously works to blunt its own purpose has a familiar name in the courtly ethos: discretion. As an ethic, discretion dictates reserve. The lover must remain silent lest he endanger his beloved's reputation. But even in private, in the protected intimacy of her presence, he must not — like the *curioso impertinente* — say all. He must repress his inmost fears and offer his lady the image of his trust. He must mask her to others and himself to her. As an aesthetic principle, then, discretion imposes the *language of the mask*, another name for the inner distancing action for language, its irrevocable separateness from the thoughts whose image it presents. The shepherd paints an image of self — a ["simulation of himself"] in Alarcón's phrase — which is and is not his own.

By convention and by desire, *La Galatea*'s shepherds speak a verse language both abstract and heavily metaphorical. Abstractions naturally work to obscure intratextual references. The dependence on metaphor, however, creates a different kind of difficulty. The theorists of Cervantes' day wrestled with the connexion between metaphor and clarity of style. Fernando de Herrera, while recommending clarity, acknowledges that ["the words for things"], which call things by their own names, do not always have the force of ["distanced words"] or metaphors. Metaphors are desirable, provided they are used judiciously. Keep the comparison just, says Herrera, and the expression will retain both clarity and energy.[15] Cervantes, however, makes the notion of transparent metaphor problematical. When Orompo laments in the Eclogue that he cannot find the means to express his pain and loss, the subsequent exchange of verses makes it clear that metaphor is at the heart of the problem. Each of the four poets in turn takes up a well-worn metaphor (the *locus amoenus*, the fruits of love and the *albergue* or haven of repose) and tries to make that metaphor *stand for* his own grief. He attempts, in other words, to make it *more proper* to *appropriate* it, but in the end none succeeds in taking

permanent possession of any of these images. The proliferation of metaphors traces only the search for that oxymoronic impossibility, the *proper
metaphor*.

The obstacles which metaphoric speech erects to communication
become acutely obvious in Book IV, when Lenio and Tirsi debate the
nature of Love. Their traded poems belong to the medieval tradition of
["questions"], where the answer imitates the form of the question. After
hearing Lenio's poem, Tirsi offers one ["which seems to have been made in
competition with yours"] (II, 68). Each lays claim to a traditional body of
metaphors (fire, ice, rope, net, yoke, army, blind man, etc.) to bolster his
own view of Love. With subtle irony, Cervantes permits Lenio to boast
that ["I lift my voice / to the true song / which is formed in attack against
love, / with such sincerity, / and in such a style and manner, / that its evil is
revealed to all the world / and the certain harm which love disguises / is
openly exposed"] (II, 55). The next moment Lenio's adversary Tirsi
congratulates himself for the ["truths which . . . I have declared"] (II, 68).
Cervantes makes Tirsi in some degree conscious of the dependence of his
"truth" on metaphor. When Tirsi attacks his adversary's version of the
figure of Cupid, he alleges, ["Since they paint him as a child, blind,
naked, with wings and arrows, it means nothing other than that the lover
is a child"] (II, 67). The dependence on metaphor makes poetry always a
desire to mean, a desire to invest things with meaning. Since poetic
language cannot say directly what it means without saying less than it
means, it must expose itself to the perils of metaphor. In the contest
between Lenio and Tirsi, the *shepherds'* desire for meaning stands
squarely on Tirsi's side. That is to say, Tirsi's listeners want Love's
language to signify purity, faith, innocence, beauty and trust — not suffering and despair. Despite the fact that *La Galatea*'s narratives alternately
support and contradict that vision, by showing that Love is both glory and
inferno, even critics fall into the trap of equating desire with truth.[16]

Lenio's and Tirsi's philosophical and poetic exchange occupies a
position similar to that of Book III's Eclogue. As an explicit, traditional
cuestión de amor, it is really a question within a question. The status of
the prose debate and supporting verses is metaphorical: they stand for,
before or in front of, the narrative fabric, and thus inevitably apart from
it. The extreme views they oppose are never reconciled, either with each
other or with the narrative. Despite the tacit promise that there is some
"truth" about Love to which language can provide access, the debate and
the text as a whole cultivate contradictions as obstacles to reduction. With
both verse eclogue and debate held at arm's length from narrative, Books
III and IV suggest a model for describing the structure of the work as a
whole. In *La Galatea* narrative itself stands conspicuously apart from its
subject. Galatea's book does not tell *her* story: she functions as the silent
center. ["Rejection"] is merely the name of her opacity. The *Primera parte*
makes her image its premise, its hyperbolic limit, which the text points to

but does not approach. The text, in this sense, is never at one with itself. Galatea's and Elicio's destinies are available to us—even to them—only as foreshadowing. In the genre which supposedly allows its characters to concern themselves with being rather than contingency, wholeness shines precisely by its absence. The text's internal distances—between philosopher and philosopher, poet and poet, between debate and narrative and event—confirm the inevitable exteriority of all discourse to the vision of truth or of self that it pursues.

The games people play in *La Galatea* revolve around the ambiguous signifying power of language. Following the Eclogue and Damón's discourse on jealousy, the old man Arsindo puts a question to the poet-visitors. Two shepherds, Francenio and Lauso, have written verse glosses of a couplet which had been composed during a game of "propósitos." A sort of poetic game of "telephone," "los propósitos" involves a chain of whispered communications. The first speaker whispers a verse into the ear of his neighbor, who completes the couplet and passes the whole on around the circle. On the occasion in question the first speaker and his neighbor happened to be lovers. To his ["Hope is fleeing"], she returned ["Catch it with desire"] (I, 233). The ["wit"] of the reply won general approval. The poets applauded it by composing glosses of their own, and between these glosses the visiting poets are now asked to decide. Damón and Tirsi decline to make the choice, on the grounds that ["the laurel ought to be given to the shepherdess who initiated such a curious and laudable competition"] (I, 235). The sequence as a whole alludes to an intimate communication, the couplet which that secret exchange produces, and the verses which the imitative chain of admiration-rivalry produces. The initial energy of the couplet derives from a mysterious sentimental transaction that lies before and beyond language. In the amplifications of their discourse the glossers, desiring to exploit the rich implications of the original, concentrated verses, instead dilute its energy. Their verses in fact prove most interesting to the other shepherds as veiled allusions to their own sentimental adventures. In terms of the original moment, however, more verses have produced not more truth but less.

In a symmetrical position in Book VI we find another game: *enigmas* or riddles. The eminently literary game of verse riddles is really nothing other than a metaphor matching. Each speaker presents a catalog of metaphors; the listener who can name the unspoken referent of the series wins the chance to continue the game with a catalog of his own. The play reaches its climax with Elicio's riddle:

> [It is very dark and very clear;
> it has a thousand contradictions;
> it blinds us to its truths
> and then reveals them to us.
> It is born sometimes of cleverness
> other times, if exalted, of fantasies,

and it tends to create complaints
even though it deals with vagueries.
Now it is foolish, now curious,
now easy, now complicated,
but whatever it may be,
tell me now, can you guess what this is?]
(II, 245)

"Qué es cosa y cosa," the popular form of the riddle's question, asks roughly, "can you guess what this is?"[17] Timbrio supplies the answer: ["Just as I thought that your riddle, Elicio, was dark, so with that very darkness it seems to reveal itself, and since the last line says that we should guess what this is, I will answer by saying that your question is the 'qué es cosa y cosa' "] (II, 246). The "answer" turns out to be none other than the question itself: ["it blinds us to its truths / and then reveals them to us"]. The "truth" of the reply only reiterates its own question: what does this mean?

These formal entertainments mirror two games which *La Galatea*'s characters play in real earnest: hide-and-seek and what Geoffrey Stagg calls the "matter of masks."[18] The riddle contest is interrupted by a "real" game of hide-and-seek that involves Gelasia, Galercio, Lenio and ultimately Maurisa, Arsindo, Theolinda, Artidoro and Leonarda. In fact, *La Galatea*'s narrative structure follows the shepherds and shepherdesses through a woodsy labyrinth, pursuing and fleeing, finding and losing one another, by design and by chance. In Cervantes' hands, the hackneyed pastoral topic of unsynchronized love recovers its energy, emerging not only as a sentimental problem but as an aesthetic question as well. The lack of synchrony becomes a basic principle, a "natural law" of the book's universe. The central experience of *La Galatea*, in physical, sentimental and linguistic terms, is that of being perpetually *out of phase*, of pulling backward or forward to a condition whose full enjoyment seems ever to elude the grasp.

["Covered faces"] merges hide-and-seek and the mask in another unacknowledged game in which identity is withheld for strategic reasons, as when Nísida, Blanca and Timbrio approach Silerio's hermitage (II, 98ff.). Geoffrey Stagg reminds us that the desire for positive identification of characters propelled the sixteenth-century reader beyond the confines of the book. That reader mirrors the characters themselves, who strain throughout *La Galatea* to uncover and fix identities. With the riddles, the metaphor-matching duels, and the opacity of the lovers' lyrical double-talk, the name of the game is really the *game of the name*. "Name" stands here for the power of language to establish presence and identity. In *La Galatea*, the name always turns out to be another game, the answer always poses a new question. The riddles offer the shepherds a kind of ritual satisfaction. They *play at* achieving the desired moment of naming, a satisfaction which is denied to many of them in the world of the book

outside of the game. The play verses of the riddles suggest that the
shepherds' earnest verses obey similar aims. Their metaphorical enterprise
is self-consuming.[19] Metaphors strain for names, for the full presence
which will render them needless.

In another important respect, *La Galatea*'s verses are self-consuming.
Poetry operates in the limit region of sentiment, where it always risks
extinguishing itself. Elicio's songs in praise of Galatea regularly give way
to paroxysms and fainting spells. When Galatea learns of her father's plans
to marry her to a "Lusitanian shepherd," her songs of grief dissolve:
["where my tongue fails, let my eyes show it to you"] (II, 134). The intense
sentiments which it is verse's mission to cultivate threaten to obliterate the
vehicle of their expression. One of *La Galatea*'s most dramatic moments,
the reunion of Timbrio and Silerio in Book V, comes as a breaking off of
poetry. Timbrio, his face concealed, sings a sonnet which he had composed ["at the fever pitch of my love"], and which (like his passion) is
familiar to Silerio. He does not, however, succeed in finishing, ["because
for Silerio, hearing his voice and recognizing him took place at one and the
same instant. Without thinking of anything else, he got up from where he
was seated and went to embrace Timbrio with such a show of joy and
confusion, that *without saying a word*, he was transported, remaining for
a moment in a state of unconsciousness"] (II, 103). As the verses succeed,
they become perfectly superfluous. To the extent that the story of Timbrio
and Silerio presents an unusually successful communication of intense
emotion, it serves also to illustrate the dangers of success. So eloquently
does Timbrio communicate his affection for Nísida that Silerio actually
experiences that emotion, thereby becoming his best friend's rival. ["The
one does not feel what another is suffering"]: the exteriority of language to
both speaker and listener in fact affords a necessary protection. Lovers
who invoke their inmost feelings do not consciously aim at kindling
identical sentiments in others. When the lover of the popular song says, "If
you knew Suzy like I know Suzy," he does not really want to share that
experience, only to validate his exclamation ("Oh, oh, oh what a gal!").

Poetry's hyperbolizing mission — the communication of extremes of
beauty and sentiment — is placed in jeopardy by both success and failure.
It should not surprise us, then, to hear the Muse of Poetry herself, the
Caliope of the *Canto*, owning up to serious difficulties as she faces the
challenges of sustaining her verse hyperboles through the celebration of a
full hundred *ingenios*. The music of ["the most beautiful voice that can be
imagined"] (II, 190) holds her listeners enraptured. Not only her extraordinary voice (she is the very fountain of eloquence) but her subject, the
veneration of that eloquence and its practitioners, makes her song into a
kind of poetry to the second power. What first appears to be a cheerful but
tedious catalog of superlatives turns out, on closer inspection, to be the
Muse's meditation on the limits of the art she patronizes. Caliope spends
many of the more than one hundred octaves lamenting *her own* inade-

quacy. For human eloquence, the task she faces would be hopeless ["it is foolishness for a human tongue to try it"] (II, 217), but in the heady regions of hyperbole even the Muse finds herself at a loss for words: ["For my own rude tongue cannot, / however many routes it probes and tries, / find one that is as I would want it / for praising what I see and feel in you"] (II, 218). At the outer limit of eloquence, she discovers silence: ["With the most appropriate words, / with whatever cleverness heaven may bestow on me, / I admire and praise you here in silence, / and I reach a place I cannot reach by speaking"] (II, 219). None other than the custodian of the poetic word here confesses her ultimate impotence. As she finishes singing, the Muse is immediately engulfed in the miraculous flames from which she appeared. The flames (["little by little consuming themselves"]) soon disappear altogether; Caliope's enterprise has quite literally consumed itself. The shepherds must accreditate (*acreditar*) the truth of her praise. Telesio, sage and elder shepherd, must second and supplement the Muse's poetic tribute with a prose discourse on the merits of Spanish poetry.

In the hybrid form of pastoral romance, the limit of poetry always takes the form of a *return to prose*. His *song* concluded or interrupted, the shepherd can usually be persuaded to tell his *story* as validation of his verses. Timbrio invites his friends to judge the success of his long narration. ["Consider if, because of the life I have had and am now having, I can be called the most afflicted and fortune-crossed man now living"] (II, 121–22). A story's capacity to amaze *authorizes* its narrator's poetic ejaculations; poems in turn validate narrative hyperboles. Don Quixote makes Poetry first lady of the sciences: ["she is to use all the others, and they will find their validation in her"] (DQ II, 16). Poetry will use all the other sciences; they will take their authority from her. Verse and prose in *La Galatea* coexist in this sort of relation of mutual dependence, each requiring the reinforcement of the other. Nor does this amount to a comfortable symbiosis of prose and verse, the one flowing harmoniously into the other. The dynamic of narrative, propelled by the desire of both character-narrators and curious character-readers to make it complete (["so as not to leave my story, once started, imperfect"], in Teolinda's words [I, 80]), seeks scenes of recognition and presence, scenes which should belong to verse in its capacity as custodian of exalted sentiment. Yet at the moment of its greatest power, poetry discovers its limit. Either it breaks off, obliterated by its own success, into the speechless silence of delight or pain, or it leaves its significance cloaked in a veil of language, sending the curious hearer back once again to disentangle the threads of narrative.[20]

["Poetry"], says Don Quixote, defender of poetry as well as of damsels, ["is like a young and tender maiden of extreme beauty . . . but this maiden does not want to be mishandled, nor dragged through the streets, nor exposed either at the edges of the marketplace or in the corners of palaces"] (*DQ* II, 16). Her intimacy and fragility must be safeguarded; she must not be paraded daily through the public plazas of discourse. Like the damsel, poetry will arouse desires she cannot satisfy. Hers is the language of the limit, and poetry is the limit of language. In trying her strength, we test the capacity of eloquence to fulfill its most delicate charge, the communication of human experience and feeling.

Not only in the Eclogue and the *Canto*, but throughout the six books, the shepherds constantly invoke language's inadequacy for expressing sentiment: ["What words will suffice?"] (I, 101), ["the joy I feel cannot be said"] (II, 27), ["I cannot exaggerate with words my pain"] (II, 116), ["let them say what they felt if they dare"] (II, 117), to quote only a few instances. The "inexpressibility topos," a standard disclaimer often used to voice the false modesty of the super-articulate, in *La Galatea* calls attention to the limit regions in which hyperbole operates.[21] The works' insistent concern with the power of language gives coherence to a whole range of familiar pastoral topics: persuasion, consolation, unwitting failures of communication, deceit and disdain. Even the interpolated tales (of Lisandro, Teolinda, Timbrio and Silerio, and others), which have been seen to represent the world of history or of action within the book,[22] are also stories about communication. In these tales, lovers often speak to one another first in the masked language of verse. Their stories subsequently demonstrate the potential for misreading of verbal and visual signs even within the intimacy of mutual desires. The motif of doubles (look-alikes and think-alikes, rivals, and friends) dramatizes the gap which separates appearance and expression from feeling. Silerio's hermitage offers him temporary refuge from the chaos of human communication: ["disillusioned with the things of this false world in which we live, I have decided to turn my thoughts toward a more noble goal, and to spend what little of life is left to me in the service of *Him who esteems our desires and deeds in the degree to which they are worthy*"] (I, 187). Only God knows the truth of desire. The crisis of poetry in *La Galatea* only describes at the limit the crisis of all language.

As *La Galatea*'s central preoccupation, the ultimate impotence of words inscribes itself clearly in the work's "ending." Galatea learns shortly before the book ends that her father plans to marry her to a "Lusitanian shepherd," obliging her to leave the banks of the Tagus. Under this threat, she at last acquiesces to Elicio's offer of assistance. Suddenly much like the Erastro who once proposed to teach Lenio a lesson in love with his fists (I, 86), Elicio plans three strategies. First he will try persuasion with Galatea's father, then threats to discourage his rival. Failing all else, he will resort to force (II, 263). As his fellow shepherds fall in behind him, vowing to ["keep their word"], we suspect with them that words will ultimately fail to keep order in the fictional world. The book's final moment, that of *keeping the word*, is also the moment of *breaking the word*. Words can only carry thought and feeling to the limit, where desire reaches beyond discourse.

Cervantes' references to poetry and the pastoral should, by their very range, suggest to us the author's capacity for ironic distance from himself. His wry smile suggests that he is not at one with himself about a poetic enterprise as immensely appealing as it is fraught with peril. In the context of *La Galatea*'s testing of the limits of language and poetry, Cervantes' protestations about the distance between his texts and his desires assume a new value. The *themes* of *La Galatea*'s shortcomings and its author's meager poetic talents acquire their full resonance from the text's concern with the failure of language itself and the super-language of verse to produce a "pure truth" of thought and desire. Cervantes' defense of poetry, then, also indicts; his version of pastoral is also a subversion. The text's ambivalence about poetry helps us to see why its verses are so rarely read. In a sense, we have already accepted what the text discovers. We already distrust pastoral's claim that refined language can best render intense feeling or describe an essential self. We regard the mask of language with suspicion, but we find its veil more powerful than the unveiling. By attending to narrative, we perhaps acknowledge that a literary vehicle which exploits the dynamic of desire and curiosity exerts a greater pull than "still-life" in verse. Like all poetry, *La Galatea* makes promises which it cannot keep ["It proposes something, and concludes nothing"]. Cervantes ultimately subverts the pastoral not by asking it to be something other than pastoral, but by asking pastoral to deliver on its own promises.

Notes

1. All references to *La Galatea* cite the edition of Juan Bautista Avalle-Arce, Clásicos Castellanos (Madrid: Espasa-Calpe, 1968), by volume and page number.

2. *Don Quixote de la Mancha*, Part II, Chapter 58. Because of the large number of editions in use, I have chosen to refer to passages from *Don Quixote* in the text of the article, by part and chapter number, preceded by the initials *DQ*, to distinguish from passages of *La Galatea*. All emphasis in quoted passages has been added.

3. Elias L. Rivers, "The Pastoral Paradox of Natural Art," *MLN* 77 (1962), 130–44.

4. This aspect of Renaissance pastorals is treated at length by Pilar Fernández-Cañadas Greenwood, "Pastoral Poetics: The Uses of Convention in Renaissance Pastoral Romance," Diss. Cornell 1980.

5. See Avalle-Arce's note (I, 6) for a list of these defenders.

6. Carroll Johnson undertakes such an inquiry in the case of *La Diana*. See his "Montemayor's *Diana*: A Novel Pastoral," *BHS* 48 (1971), 20–35.

7. Miguel de Cervantes, *Comedias y entremeses*, ed. Schevill and Bouilla, I (Madrid, 1915), 9. A recent antidote to the critical neglect of Cervantes' verse is José Manuel Blecua's "La poesía lírica de Cervantes," in his *Sobre poesía de la edad de oro* (Madrid, 1970), pp. 161–95.

8. Joaquín Casalduero, "*La Galatea*," in *Suma cervantina*, eds. Juan Bautista Avalle-Arce and E. C. Riley (London: Tamesis, 1972), p. 35.

9. Ruth El Saffar rules out such a pilgrimage in *La Galatea*, on the grounds that it does not involve the main characters. See her "*La Galatea*: The Integrity of the Unintegrated Text," *Dispositio* 9 (1978), 337–51. I argue for the pilgrimage as symbolic undercurrent of *La Galatea* in "Góngora Reads Cervantes: *La Galatea* and *Soledad primera*," Spanish Section, Prose and Poetry of the Golden Age, MLA Convention, New York, 30 Dec. 1978.

10. For the *cuestión* as structural key to the work, see Jennifer Lowe, "The *Cuestión de amor* and the Structure of Cervantes' *La Galatea*," *BHS* 43 (1966), 98–108.

11. Jorge de Montemayor, *Los siete libros de la Diana*, ed. Francisco López Estrada, Clásicos Castellanos (Madrid: Espasa-Calpe, 1966), p. 167.

12. I use the term "poetry" somewhat loosely throughout. The strict formal distinction between prose and poetry would require the term "verse." "Verse" does not, however, render the honorific sense that "poetry" has in English and that "la poesía" (meaning something more like "high literature") had for the sixteenth-century Spaniard.

13. Jonathan Culler, *Structuralist Poetics* (Ithaca: Cornell University Press, 1975), p. 162.

14. Cesáreo Bandera Gómez, *Mímesis conflictiva. Ficción literaria y violencia en Cervantes y Calderón* (Madrid: Gredos, 1975), p. 124.

15. *Garcilaso de la Vega y sus comentaristas*, ed. Antonio Gallego Morell (Granada, 1966), p. 294.

16. Avalle-Arce calls Tirsi's speech "el documento válido con que comulga Cervantes." *La novela pastoril española* (Madrid: Revista de Occidente, 1959), p. 207. Using the Marcela-Grisóstomo sequence in *Don Quixote*, Javier Herrero sustains the opposing view. "Aracdia's Inferno: Cervantes' Attack on Pastoral," *BHS* 55 (1978), 289–99.

17. See Avalle-Arce's note (II, 245).

18. Geoffrey Stagg, "A Matter of Masks," in *Hispanic Studies in Honour of Joseph Manson*, eds. D. M. Atkinson and A. H. Clark (Oxford, 1972), pp. 255–67.

19. I borrow the term from Stanley Fish, *Self-Consuming Artifacts* (Berkeley: University of California Press, 1972).

20. The role of prose, of course, requires its own study. Bandera and El Saffar have discussed the role of curiosity in the movement of narrative. See *Mimesis conflictiva* and Ruth El Saffar, *Distance and Control in Don Quixote: A Study in Narrative Technique* (Chapel Hill: University of North Carolina, 1975). Stephen Gilman, in a lecture given at Syracuse University, April 1979, studies the broken threads of narrative in *Don Quixote*, based on a reading of *DQ* I, 20 ("Los batanes").

21. Ernst Robert Curtius, *European Literature and the Latin Middle Ages* (New York: Harper and Row, 1963), pp. 159–62.

22. El Saffar, "*La Galatea* . . . ," p. 339; Avalle-Arce, "Introducción" to *La Galatea* (I, xxv).

Don Quixote (1605, 1615)

Cervantic Irony in *Don Quijote*: The Problem for Literary Criticism

Luis Murillo[*]

> . . . grave irony, a Cervantic species of pleasantry . . .
> — Sir Walter Scott (1821)[1]

The term irony was first applied to Cervantes and *Don Quijote* in England in the eighteenth century. We assume, in our contemporary criticism, that irony is a perfectly legitimate concept to apply to the Cervantic masterpiece, much as we assume that the proper way to read it, apprehend it and analyze it is to read it, apprehend it and analyze it as a novel. But irony as a *legitimate* critical concept for specifying our apprehension of certain effects that resolve an ulterior meaning with the explicit meaning of Cervantes' text is of relatively recent date. (Note that I stress the word *legitimate*.) In Spanish literary criticism we can be very precise as to the date when irony as a concept began to be applied to Cervantes and to *Don Quijote* in terms of a novel, and by whom. It was Menéndez y Pelayo in the years 1904 and 1905 who provided a synthetic concept of irony developed from his historical studies. We do not have an analytical study of Cervantic irony until Américo Castro provides one in 1941. This passage from Menéndez y Pelayo appears in three different places in his works; among them, significantly, at the close of volume one of *Orígenes de la novela* (1905):

> [Cervantes's work was not one of antithesis, nor of dry, prosaic denial, but rather it was one of purification and complementarity. He did not come to kill an ideal, but to transform and exalt it. He incorporated in his new work all there was of the poetic, noble and human in the chivalric, giving it all a higher meaning. All that there was of the quimerical, immoral and false, not exactly in the chivalric ideal but in the degenerations of it, was dissipated as if by magic before the classical serenity and benevolent irony of the sanest and most balanced of the Renaissance geniuses. In this way *Don Quixote* was the last of the romances of chivalry, the definitive and perfect one, the one

*Reprinted with permission from *Homenaje a Rodríguez-Moñino* (Madrid: Castalia, 1966), 2:21–27.

that concentrated with a luminous focus the diffuse poetic material, while at the same time raising to epic dignity the events of daily life. It thus became the first, never-surpassed, model of the modern realist novel.]

Don Marcelino [Menéndez y Pelayo's] immense authority and prestige established almost immediately this conception of Cervantes' achievement. If we examine the ideas expressed here we find the *benevolent irony* specified as an ingredient by which the ideals and literary content of chivalry are purified of degenerate and false elements. The objects of this irony, benevolent or merciful, are the degenerate narratives of chivalry; this is its negative side; but the ulterior intentions behind it are understood to be a purification and exaltation of the poetry, nobleness and humane sentiments of knight-errantry, and in the process, out of the parody of a degenerate form of art there results the new form that is the prototype for the modern realistic novel. I should like to draw your attention to two aspects of this irony as specified by Menéndez y Pelayo. The intentions of Cervantes are phrased in terms of a moral evaluation: they are the intentions of a Christian humanist influenced and enlightened by the spirit of classical antiquity. This evaluation is based on an historical treatment of literary and ideological currents in sixteenth-century Spain. But the historical perspective moves forward also to encompass the modern period in which Cervantes' masterpiece has served as a model for the realistic novel, the eighteenth and nineteenth centuries. Now, the impact of Cervantes' book on later writers in England, France, Germany, Italy, Russia and Spain can of course be studied in terms of tangential influences upon those writers and as something quite apart from the meaning it possessed for its first readers in the seventeenth century. But it is equally true that the successive changes in literary and social tastes, in ideas, sensibility and even psychological and metaphysical outlook in modern civilization since have changed and conditioned and shaped our estimates of Cervantes' intentions fully as much as they have influenced our evaluation of his effects. You will note that the passage of Menéndez y Pelayo is as much an historical statement as it is an esthetic one. The explanation of irony as a kind of catalyst destroying the old form of art and giving shape to the new is an esthetic notion based on the effects that Cervantes' narrative produces upon modern sensitivities in the aftermath of the great realistic novels of the nineteenth century. The synthesis of historical perspective and esthetic precept accounts for a large share of the critical validity of Menéndez y Pelayo's statements. So authoritative are they that they appear in fact to offer a concept of irony that is fully authenticated.

There is almost nothing in Spanish criticism on Cervantes before Menéndez y Pelayo to suggest that such a concept was in the making. The terms *ironía* and *irónico* had indeed been attributed to Cervantes by later eighteenth-century commentators like Vicente de los Ríos and Pellicer, but even their precept of a *"fina y picante ironía"* of a manner of satire had been ignored if not discredited by Juan Valera. To find the precedents for a concept of irony in the *Quijote* whose critical authenticity depends upon esthetic, biographical and historical considerations we must go to literary criticism and poetic theory outside of Spain, and to the works of literature that the influence of Cervantes' masterpiece gave rise to in the other European literatures. The concept of Cervantic irony acquired its use and meaning outside of Spain before 1905, but only in Spanish criticism since has it served the critic with a full degree of authenticity.

The English concept of "grave irony," the earliest application of irony to Cervantes, dates from about 1750. The term itself was not current in literary discussion much before then. Its use had been confined in the sixteenth and seventeenth centuries to the Rhetorics and Poetics. Its meaning as a trope or figure of rhetoric had been fixed in antiquity by the authority of Cicero and Quintilian. The "grave irony" that eighteenth-century poetic theory claimed for *Don Quijote* corresponded to a conception of the book as serious satire. The effects the book produced were interpreted as censoring and didactic, and these effects were sufficient for justifying the apperception of the author's intentions as those of mockery and ridicule. The laughter occasioned by the wit of a flawless and sustained mock (i.e., dissimulated) seriousness was the result of a decorous impersonality that had the effect of exposing the foibles of human nature in an engagement of controversial subjects. The irony of Cervantes constitutes the plane of a universal application of his ridicule of chivalry to the correction of foibles, humours and aberrations to which the human species is susceptible. "Grave irony" is both a conveyance of this ulterior meaning and an expression of the author's refined intellectual and moral qualities, his literary and social taste.

For the eighteenth century, irony was an incitement to controversy, to censure, to attack. But it was also apparent that Cervantes' refined qualities produced a positive effect that was not a consequence of the incitement to laughter, but a cause of it: a peculiar but charitable indulgence toward his characters. The impersonal manner of "grave irony" was a way of directing a satirical attack on a level of universal application that spared the characters of the book of hostile treatment at the hands of the author. Towards the close of the eighteenth century the English came to see this positive and non-hostile engagement of Cervantes' characters as *humour*. In *humour* they were conceived as the subjects of a satirical manner exposing the facts of human nature, but virtuous and lovable characters who in the eyes of the reader were never degraded. The effects of *humour* confirmed that the intentions of Cervantes were not hostile towards his characters.

One of the delicate points about the application of the term to Cervantes, and one of the points to be settled about the authenticity of its use, is the degree of conscious intention one presumes to lie behind the effect that conveys the ulterior and ironical meaning. In the eighteenth century it is applied to a manner of satirizing the illusory and fantastic excesses, the extravagances of men and society that are not in accord with reason and experience, in such a way that the ulterior significance of the fable or the narrative is universal. That is, that the manner or the means by which the meaning is conveyed is applicable to all rational beings. Irony applies to a mode and a conveyance of meaning that is impersonal, intellectual and universal. The reader reacting to an ironical effect and the author Cervantes engaged in conveying a didactic and ulterior meaning in the ridicule and parody of chivalry could meet on the plane of an ironical apprehension that confirmed the universality of a social or public art and ideas. The question of "conscious" intentions would not enter into the matter so long as it was assumed that the ironical effect conveyed a social and objective meaning. But nineteenth-century theories and interpretations of *Don Quijote* were to change all this.

The esthetic basis for attributing irony to Cervantes is owed to the theory of the German romantic movement. In relating irony to the literary form of the novel the German theorists were explaining the intentions of the novelist Cervantes according to their ideas about the creative process in the mind and imagination of the artist that brought forth symbolical works of art. In this case the critical authenticity of Cervantic irony is more theoretical than practical. The antitheses which Friedrich Schlegel, Schelling and Solger found in *Don Quijote* were explained in terms of a dialectical activity of the inner world of the romantic poet Cervantes. A contrast that in its outward, social and public aspects would have been interpreted earlier as a satirical contrast (an opposition between reason and folly and where the didactic effect depended upon an irreconcilable opposition) was now according to esthetic theory an opposition that could be reconciled by referring it to that theoretical point of unity where the finite and infinite are resolved in the issue of the higher unity of symbolism. But this was going considerably beyond a mere interpretation of literary intentions to a speculation on the activity of the artist in the subjective states of inspiration and execution of a work of art.

What has come to be called "romantic" irony in esthetics and literary criticism is in fact this awareness attributed to the artistic creator of dialectical opposites that in their play or conflict with one another provide for their resolution, reconciliation or synthesis. In Solger's theory of "artistic irony" this resolution is seen as the destruction of the "idea" whereby the "idea" is given finite form. One can distinguish by 1820, in the critical and literary use of the term, between irony in the satirical context which is didactic, public and social, and irony in the esthetic context which refers one to the dialectical activity of the creative process, and is subjective, "poetic," or "romantic." The first is the case in which the effects produced by Cervantes' narrative and his manner of telling it provoked a reader to explain his intentions in terms of didactic, social and moral purposes. The second is the case in which a reader attributed certain artistic and philosophical intentions to Cervantes and explained the book's effects in terms of these. In neither case is there a question of "conscious" motives or "unconscious" ones because no really personal or autobiographical point of view is assumed. In the early nineteenth century the historical explanation of Cervantes' purposes arrived at by literary scholarship applied only to the literature and institution of chivalry that we find as early as 1737 in Mayáns y Siscar.

The sensitivity and the critical mind of the nineteenth century looked for the authentication of "conscious" intentions in a subjective and psychological focus to the biographical portrait of Cervantes, framed by an attention to historical details that an advancing scholarship supplied. A romantic interpretation of *Don Quijote* and a positivistic application of it to the biography of Cervantes were not incompatible. Moreover, the biographical and historical approaches to the book authenticated one another mutually. It is now that a basis for attributing irony to Cervantes will be sought in the reconstructed facts of his biography. The multiple antitheses discovered in the book, illusion and reality, idealism and common sense, and so on (which might by themselves stand alone in a purely esthetical or philosophical interpretation) and the effects that their opposition provoked, were now interpreted in terms of Cervantes' personal ordeal and personal qualities of character. The effects the book produced upon modern sensibilities (pathos, melancholy, disillusion) could now be referred to personal feelings, and, in addition, as in the case of the French scholar Émile Chasles in 1866, to a positivistic interpretation of the subjective motives behind the social, moral and political criticism of Spain in Cervantes' time.

This is not the occasion for discussing the subject in detail. Let us say that it was not uncommon to interpret pathos, melancholy and disillusion as an expression of the author's personal sentiments and to find support for this reading in the account of the author's lifetime of misfortune and poverty. On the other hand, the man's character, his noble spirit and generous sentiments were evident in the sympathy and benevolence he showed toward his characters and towards the aspirations as well as failings of humanity. All these connotations, then, from the psychological to the moral and metaphysical, are gathered up by the term irony because this term, becoming very prominent in the *fin de siècle*, can be used (unlike *burla* or *ridicule* or *raillerie*) in multiple contexts that relate both positive and negative intentions to both negative and positive effects: dissimulation and benevolence, criticism and humor, from a personal and subjective degree to the more objective, impersonal and public.

The point to which all this leads is that the book itself at the close of the period of the great realistic novels now disclosed to its readers a critical but likewise imaginative representation of life approximating the plurality and complexity of life itself; the outer facets of life, actions and external reality, and the inner facets, psychological motives and the sources of personal values; and the consonance of these in dialogue; that is to say, that the book's form or style of representation is that of the novel, and this style or form is the originality of the *Quijote*.

This then is the situation when Menéndez y Pelayo writes the passage I quoted. In my opening remarks I called his concept of irony a synthetic one. By this I mean that while sanctioning the use of the term *ironía* he combined the three contexts in which nineteenth-century writers and critics had applied the term, the esthetical, historical and biographical contexts. In Spanish criticism, before Menéndez y Pelayo, the traditional terms were *burla* [ridicule] and *burlar* [to ridicule]; *hacer burla* [to make fun of] is a term Cervantes, or rather Cide Hamete, uses. The *Diccionario de la Real Academia* still defines irony as ["subtle and disguised ridicule"]. Now I think that when we speak of irony in *Don Quijote* we imply more than refined and dissimulated ridicule; we imply that we apprehend Cervantes in a sense other than ridicule or mockery, that he conveys a meaning to be apprehended on a level above or beyond the satirical denotations of *burla*. The first step in the recognition of this meaning is to perceive that the refinement of his manner conceals an ulterior aim which is both intellective and humane, critical but also benevolent and amiable toward the objects of his dissimulation. Thereupon the problem will become (for the critically sensitive) one of specifying this mode of apprehending the narrative and characters: how intentional or conscious are those effects perceived by us as the result of ulterior intentions? And how can we judge degrees of conscious and unconscious critical and moral objectives? The theory of the complete autonomy of the work of literature provides for the interpretation of the work as something quite apart from the biography of the author, and from the historical and ideological currents that may have determined it. The apperception of irony in this purely esthetical context is not in need of the critical legitimacy I feel is required for Cervantic irony in *Don Quijote*. The legitimacy is the prerequisite to a really analytical concept that we can apply. This mode of apprehension has had to be verified from both the historical and biographical contexts in addition to the esthetic, and this is what Menéndez y Pelayo accomplished and why his statements are so authoritative.

After Castro we may agree that the legitimate area for the critical apperception of irony lies in the analysis of the structure of the *Quijote* as a novel, but to advance beyond the point reached by Castro we need a greater critical refinement of the bases on which we authenticate our apperception of irony. The qualities of the book are such that we cannot completely dissever the effects that it provokes from the original intentions. Irony as a mode of apprehension correlating Cervantes' effects and intentions will exact from the literary critic a greater degree of discrimination for authenticating the biographical and historical bases on which to support esthetic categories.

Note

1. "In the comic part of their writings, we have already said, Fielding is preeminent in grave irony, a Cervantic species of pleasantry, in which Smollett is not equally successful." *Miscellaneous Prose Works*, III (Edinburgh, 1834), *Eminent Novelists*, I, pag. 180; [see also pages] 94, 95, 172.

Partial Magic in the *Quixote*   Jorge Luis Borges*

It is plausible that these observations may have been set forth at some time and, perhaps, many times; a discussion of their novelty interests me less than one of their possible truth.

Compared with other classic books (the *Iliad*, the *Aeneid*, the *Pharsalia*, Dante's *Commedia*, Shakespeare's tragedies and comedies), the *Quixote* is a realistic work; its realism, however, differs essentially from that practiced by the nineteenth century. Joseph Conrad could write that he excluded the supernatural from his work because to include it would seem a denial that the everyday was marvelous; I do not know if Miguel de Cervantes shared that intuition, but I do know that the form of the *Quixote* made him counterpose a real prosaic world to an imaginary poetic world. Conrad and Henry James wrote novels of reality because they judged reality to be poetic; for Cervantes the real and the poetic were antinomies. To the vast and vague geographies of the *Amadís*, he opposes the dusty roads and sordid wayside inns of Castille; imagine a novelist of our time centering attention for purposes of parody on some filling stations. Cervantes has created for us the poetry of seventeenth-century Spain, but neither that century nor that Spain were poetic for him; men like Unamuno or Azorín or Antonio Machado, who were deeply moved by any evocation of La Mancha, would have been incomprehensible to him. The plan of his book precluded the marvelous; the latter, however, had to figure in the novel, at least indirectly, just as crimes and a mystery in a parody of a detective story. Cervantes could not resort to talismans or enchantments, but he insinuated the supernatural in a subtle — and therefore more effective — manner. In his intimate being, Cervantes loved the supernatural. Paul Groussac observed in 1924: "With a deleble coloring of Latin and Italian, Cervantes' literary production derived mostly from the pastoral novel and the novel of chivalry, soothing fables and captivity." The *Quixote* is less an antidote for those fictions than it is a secret, nostalgic farewell.

Every novel is an ideal plane inserted into the realm of reality;

*Reprinted with permission from *Labyrinths: Selected Stories and Other Writings*, trans. James E. Irby (New York: New Directions Publishing Co., 1964), 193–96.

Cervantes takes pleasure in confusing the objective and the subjective, the world of the reader and the world of the book. In those chapters which argue whether the barber's basin is a helmet and the donkey's packsaddle a steed's fancy regalia, the problem is dealt with explicitly; other passages, as I have noted, insinuate this. In the sixth chapter of the first part, the priest and the barber inspect Don Quixote's library; astoundingly, one of the books examined is Cervantes' own *Galatea* and it turns out that the barber is a friend of the author and does not admire him very much, and says that he is more versed in misfortunes than in verses and that the book possesses some inventiveness, proposes a few ideas and concludes nothing. The barber, a dream or the form of a dream of Cervantes, passes judgment on Cervantes . . . It is also surprising to learn, at the beginning of the ninth chapter, that the entire novel has been translated from the Arabic and that Cervantes acquired the manuscript in the marketplace of Toledo and had it translated by a [Spanish Moor] whom he lodged in his house for more than a month and a half while the job was being finished. We think of Carlyle, who pretended that the *Sartor Resartus* was the fragmentary version of a work published in Germany by Doctor Diogenes Teufelsdroeckh; we think of the Spanish rabbi Moses of León, who composed the *Zohar* or *Book of Splendor* and divulged it as the work of a Palestinian rabbi of the second century.

This play of strange ambiguities culminates in the second part; the protagonists have read the first part, the protagonists of the *Quixote* are, at the same time, readers of the *Quixote*. Here is is inevitable to recall the case of Shakespeare, who includes on the stage of *Hamlet* another stage where a tragedy more or less like that of *Hamlet* is presented; the imperfect correspondence of the principal and secondary works lessens the efficacy of this inclusion. An artifice analogous to Cervantes', and even more astounding, figures in the *Ramayana*, the poem of Valmiki, which narrates the deeds of Rama and his war with the demons. In the last book, the sons of Rama, who do not know who their father is, seek shelter in a forest, where an ascetic teaches them to read. This teacher is, strangely enough, Valmiki; the book they study, the *Ramayana*. Rama orders a sacrifice of horses; Valmiki and his pupils attend this feast. The latter, accompanied by their lute, sing the *Ramayana*. Rama hears his own story, recognizes his own sons and then rewards the poet . . . Something similar is created by accident in the *Thousand and One Nights*. This collection of fantastic tales duplicates and reduplicates to the point of vertigo the ramifications of a central story in later and subordinate stories, but does not attempt to gradate its realities, and the effect (which should have been profound) is superficial, like a Persian carpet. The opening story of the series is well known: the terrible pledge of the king who every night marries a virgin who is then decapitated at dawn, and the resolution of Scheherazade, who distracts the king with her fables until a thousand and one nights have gone by and she shows him their son. The necessity of completing a thousand and one sections obliged the copyists of the work to make all manner of interpolations. None is more perturbing than that of the six hundred and second night, magical among all the nights. On that night, the king hears from the queen his own story. He hears the beginning of the story, which comprises all the others and also — monstrously — itself. Does the reader clearly grasp the vast possibility of this interpolation, the curious danger? That the queen may persist and the motionless king hear forever the truncated story of the *Thousand and One Nights*, now infinite and circular . . . The inventions of philosophy are no less fantastic than those of art: Josiah Royce, in the first volume of his work *The World and the Individual* (1899), has formulated the following: "Let us imagine that a portion of the soil of England has been levelled off perfectly and that on it a cartographer traces a map of England. The job is perfect; there is no detail of the soil of England, no matter how minute, that is not registered on the map; everything has there its correspondence. This map, in such a case, should contain a map of the map, which should contain a map of the map of the map, and so on to infinity."

Why does it disturb us that the map be included in the map and the thousand and one nights in the book of the *Thousand and One Nights*? Why does it disturb us that Don Quixote be a reader of the *Quixote* and Hamlet a spectator of *Hamlet*? I believe I have found the reason: these inversions suggest that if the characters of a fictional work can be readers or spectators, we, its readers or spectators, can be fictitious. In 1833, Carlyle observed that the history of the universe is an infinite sacred book that all men write and read and try to understand, and in which they are also written.

Oscillation in the Character of Sancho

Dámaso Alonso*

Perhaps regarding the evolution of a deception process there might not be a better example than our friend Sancho.

For a long time it was thought that of the two levels — realistic and idealistic — whose brilliant confluence makes the immortal work, Sancho was the prime representation of the realistic level. But in our time Unamuno and Papini have defended the thesis that the idealism of the knight pours down over Sancho and he thus enters the world of the phantasmagoric; i.e. that he is in his own way another Quixote. Doesn't he also leave his surroundings, his home, his family and his little piece of

*Reprinted with permission from *La novela cervantina* (Santander: Universidad internacional Menéndez Pelayo, 1969), 20–34. Translated for this volume by Nikki Beidleman.

property in order to attend to the visions of a madman? Does he not accompany him in his adventures and share in his fatigue and in his beatings? And for the poor squire, at the limits of the far-off horizon, like another enchanted Dulcinea, lies his ideal, the island, foreseen in all the pilgrimages (the mirages of the plain, always near fantasy and always far from his reach). Yes, Sancho is another knight of another ideal. And the true Sanchos, the "materialists," those incapable of dreaming and fantasizing are the priest and the barber, the housekeeper, the niece and, as the quintessence of one, the *bachiller* Sansón Carrasco, a man of letters in contact with the beauty and spirituality of the world, who does not comprehend anything about that white insanity that must have illuminated the universe. He even has the insolence to pretend to be him — rogue without faith and without ideals — knight of ideals, and he strives to destroy the fertile, the active, until he leaves the hero sprawled out powerless in the outskirts of Barcelona. Oh, how many Sansón Carrascos we know in the world of letters!

But the anti-Quixotes that I hate the most are the *Duques*, those of the genteel class who, in order to interrupt the empty idleness of their sterility, pretend to receive the knight errant honorably, then make him the object of their cruelest mockery. The great English essayist Charles Lamb used to say he could never forgive Cervantes for not having given one word of condemnation for the *Duques* on account of their abhorrent conduct.

The interpretation of Unamuno and Papini has brought to light various aspects of the *Quixote* and destroys certain erroneous ideas. Nevertheless, it is very simplistic and exaggerated. It doesn't penetrate deeply the character of Sancho. On the human side, Sancho is perhaps even more complex than his glorified companion.

Let's take a look at Sacho's psychology for a minute. And let's propose the idea that all of it is, in its unfolding, a long process of illusion and disillusion of that type that, as we said, is characteristic of the way souls are portrayed in Spanish literature, and which has among us a growing and uninterrupted heritage.

Sancho goes with Don Quixote motivated by greed since "at some time or another an adventure might occur that would win him in the twinkling of an eye some island, of which he would leave him governor." And one need only to think of the first encounter, with the windmills. Sancho always sees reality; Don Quixote always sees his mad fantasy. But the first process in Sancho's soul is that of meddling in the madness of his master. And when the blades of the mill, which Sancho has seen as really being the blades of a mill, had knocked the knight down, (at that particular moment) he was left convinced by the reasoning of his master. What a time to become convinced! "with God's help," replied Sancho, "I believe it all to be as your worship says."

Note his faith: he starts removing the clothes of the monk who was knocked down by Don Quixote because they strike him as legitimately being "spoils of the battle which his master had won," and when in the same adventure the basque gentleman is conquered by the illustrious man from La Mancha, Sancho rushes towards his master, kisses his hand, falls on his knees and says "Be so kind, my dear lord Don Quixote, as to make me governor of the island you have won in this dreadful fight; for however big it is, I feel strong enough to govern it as well as any man who ever governed islands in all the world."

He is crazy! He is also crazy (Yes: upon reaching this point it seems to us that Papini and Unamuno see him in his right light). At this point he has been conquered by the enchanted world of the tales of the knights errant. But there is no crazy man except Don Quixote that doesn't learn by his mistakes.

A new illusion: the balsam of Fierabras ("Fair Bras," according to Sancho's interpretation), that marvelous beverage that cures all wounds. Here we have the two battered heroes, beaten with sticks by the Yanguesans. Sancho says, "in a weak and piteous voice":

> "Don Quixote! Ah, Don Quixote!"
> "What is the matter, brother Sancho?" answered Don Quixote in the same faint and plaintive tones.
> "Well, sir," said Sancho Panza, "I should be glad if your worship could let me have two gulps of that drink of Fair Bras's, if you've got it handy. Perhaps it might be as good for broken bones as it is for wounds."
> — "Why," replied Don Quixote, "if I had some here, wretch that I am, what more could I want?"

At last, in the enchanted inn, across the confusion of a night of enamored princesses, lamps, Maritornes, coachmen of the Holy Brotherhood, and the mule team drivers, the two beaten heroes finally achieve enjoyment of the balsam of "Fair Bras." So strong is the unpalatable drink that it has on Don Quixote a cleansing effect. But in poor Sancho it produces nausea, fits of sweating and agonizing pains. And Don Quixote says:

> "I think, Sancho, that all this pain comes from your not being a knight; for it is my opinion that this liquor cannot be of service to any that are not."
> "If you worship knew that," replied Sancho, "the devil take me and my family, why did you let me taste it?"

Sancho still has faith in his master but he sees himself excluded from the world of fantasy and brutally pushed from the side of reality. And it doesn't surprise us that upon leaving the inn, tossed about and mocked, he rejects the balsam of Fair Bras and now shouts — let us note well — totally without respect for Don Quixote, "Has your worship forgotten, by any chance, that I am not a knight? . . . Keep your liquor in the devil's name and leave me alone."

He is sliding downhill, down on the side of disillusion. No; if his master wasn't able to aid him in the inn "it was something different from enchantment that stopped your getting over the yard wall or dismounting from Rocinante." Sancho now doesn't believe in enchantments; he therefore remains in the shadows, a rough creature of flesh and blood, far from the white ray of the ideal light.

And (two chapters further along) we get to the end of the process. Don Quixote and Sancho are sleeping in the middle of the countryside. The night is fearful. All of a sudden a frightening noise begins to sound. Don Quixote builds up his courage and decides to go out into a new adventure, and leaves his squire behind. But Sancho's blood is freezing in his veins with fear at the thought of being left alone in the middle of the night with that terrible noise! The sound of another world! He stealthily goes to his master's horse and ties up his legs. The knight kicks his horse with his spurs, but the horse can't move. "Heaven, moved by my begging and prayers, has ordered that Rocinante cannot move," says Sancho. What a crude trick to play on the knight! It is the first infidelity of the servant towards his master! It is the first time that Sancho shows his roguish side! Consider a summary of the process: Sancho leaves his home because of greed: although he sees the reality of the adventures, the reasoned fantasy of his master conquers him; he enters fully in the world of adventures. Up to this point the line ascends in the process of self-deception.

Past the balsam the movement is reverse: first of all, Sancho continues to believe the words of his master but he remains excluded from the world of fantasy because he is not a knight errant. In the second movement, Sancho no longer believes in the enchantments of his master. In the third phase Sancho comes to use the insanity of Don Quixote to deceive him; he deceives him precisely by acting out one of his enchantments. Sancho at this moment is not only outside of the fantastic world but falls within the roguish realm the way that Lazarillo did after receiving the blow in the head, and Guzmán when he was given the rotten eggs and spoiled meat. But good, noble Sancho will never be a permanent rogue.

Let us remember here the process of illusion and disillusion in the chapter of the *hidalgo* in *Lazarillo*. Lázaro, like Sancho, believes in his master when he starts out with him; he believes when he goes through the markets, like Sancho in the first adventures; he begins to stop believing when he feels unsatisfied hunger, like Sancho after the balsam of Fair Bras. And he ends up fooling his master, but fooling him out of compassion. Yet on this occasion Sancho is the heartless one, the true rogue.

But Sancho is to waiver between roguishness and idealism throughout the whole book, because what is characteristic of Sancho's soul is the way it reproduces the movement of illusion and disillusion, in waves, across all the pages of the book. We have seen his first innocence and his first disillusionment. When a man becomes disillusioned, he changes into a rogue. In the picaresque novel the hero quickly becomes disillusioned

(Lázaro with only the blow against the stone bull at the bridge of Salamanca), and now that his eyes are opened he will never recover his naivete. But Sancho, after many deceptions, returns time and time again to his original state of innocence; again he believes in his master.

Exactly towards the end of the first part, in the mist of that confusion of adventures which begins to weave in Sierra Morena and unravel in the enchanted inn / castle (Cardenio, Lucinda, Dorotea, Don Fernando, Clara, El Capitán Cautivo, Zoraida, Don Luis) Sancho passes through a period of great naivete and credulity. He very clearly sees the true threads within the pretended plot, that which is intending to lead them forth to the Kingdom of Princess Micomicona. He will see how she (in reality poor Dorotea) and her forgetful spouse go on kissing each other, whenever they have a chance, in whichever corner of the inn they can find. And thus he says to Don Quixote: ". . . I am positively certain that this lady, who calls herself Queen of the great Kingdom of Micomicona, is not more a queen than my mother; for if she was what she says she is, she wouldn't go kissing with somebody in this company every time anyone turns his head, and round every corner."

And he is so roguish at that moment that for the second time he deceives his master (making him believe that he truly brought the letter to Dulcinea del Toboso). But at the same time he has never seen closer at hand the promised island, which the existence of the Princess Micomicona could make real. It sometimes happens when a man is disillusioned, when he sees that the castle and the island are sinking, that he latches himself to it as if he wanted to prevent ruin by affirming or sustaining it by his own effort. Thus that is what I believe happens to Sancho at that moment. Cervantes observes it and also the cause, and he notes: "And Sancho was worse off awake than his master was asleep. Such did the promise affect him that his master had made to him." The characters of the work also note that insanity, and the barber says to him: "What, Sancho, are you of your master's fraternity, too? I swear to God I'm beginning to think you'll have to keep him company in his cage . . ."

It is well known how the second part of the *Quixote* is shaded in relation to the first; how the second part is less brilliant, less spirited and less fertile, but how it grows in human dimension; how the author now understands the greatness of the creatures which have come out through his hands; how (except for a few chapters) the slapstick tone is diminished; how he now feels not sympathy, but deep compassion for his knight and even for his squire. Upon feeling compassion he feels sadness.

It is not strange that, not far from the beginning of the second part, he would present Sancho completely translated into reality, that is to say sunken into a pit of disillusionment. And immediately the roguish attitude and the disastrous deception of the knight come forth. It is when Sancho, who has left Don Quixote in the outskirts of the "great city of El Toboso," directs himself to the town in search of the Princess Dulcinea. Here is a part of the long monologue of Sancho, seated at the foot of a tree, next to his gray donkey:

> — Now, let us learn, brother Sancho, where your worship is going. Are you going after some ass you have lost? No, certainly not. Then what are you going to look for? I am going to look, as you may say, for nothing, for a Princess, and in her the sun of beauty and all heaven besides. . . . Now, do you know her house? My master says it will be some royal palace or proud castle. And have you by any chance ever seen her? No, neither I nor my master have ever seen her. And if the people of El Toboso knew that you were here for the purpose of enticing away their Princess and disturbing their ladies, do you think it would be right and proper for them to come and give you such a beating as would grind your ribs to powder and not leave you a whole bone in your body? . . . for the Manchegans are honest people and very hot tempered, and they won't stand tickling from anyone . . . It's the Devil, the Devil himself who has put me into this business. The Devil and no other! . . . Well, now, there's a remedy for everything except death . . . I have seen from countless signs that this master of mine is a raving lunatic who ought to be tied up — and me, I can't be much better, for since I follow him and serve him . . . Well, he is mad — that he is — and it's the kind of madness that generally mistakes one thing for another, and thinks white black and black white . . . So it won't be very difficult to make him believe that the first peasant girl I run across about here is the lady Dulcinea. If he doesn't believe it I'll swear, and if he swears I'll outswear him, and if he sticks to it I shall stick to it harder, so that, come what may, my word shall always stand up to his . . . perhaps he'll think, as I fancy he will, that one of those wicked enchanters who he says have a grudge against him has changed her shape to vex and spite him.

And thus Dulcinea becomes enchanted, converted into a farm girl. Very famous is the encounter, and how the "dulcineated" farm girl falls from her donkey. When Don Quixote runs to catch her in his arms, she gets up herself, taking that job from him: "For, stepping back a little, she took a short run, and resting both her hands on the ass's rump, swung her body into the saddle, lighter than a hawk and sat astride like a man."

At which Sancho exclaimed: "By St. Roque, the lady, our mistress, is lighter than a falcon . . . : She was over the crupper of the saddle in one jump, and now without spurs she's making that hackney gallop like a zebra. And her maidens are not much behind her. They're all going like the wind."

These pits of disillusion dominate the Sancho of the second part. Cervantes tells us after the adventure of the enchanted boat: "For fool though he was, he was well enough aware that all, or most, of the knight's actions were extravagant, and he was looking for an opportunity of escaping and going home without entering into any reckonings or farewells with his master."

And the deceptions of the master continue: that of the cheese curds (*requesones*), that of the whipping for the disenchantment of Dulcinea. Now the thing that binds him to his master is human compassion. Thus he says to the Duchess: ". . . I should have left my master days ago if I had been wise. But that was my lot and my ill-luck. I can do nothing else; I have to follow him; we're of the same village; I've eaten his bread; I love him dearly; I am grateful to him; he gave me his ass-colts, and what is more, I'm faithful . . ." Good Sancho! Noble Sancho! No, Sancho is not a rogue.

In those same pages farther along in the work, when he still has another upsurge of illusion over the island, even that crumbles after seeing himself a hoax governor for a few days. And he leaves — the last illusion — the governorship and his old ideal without a complaint. Heroic Sancho, heroic in your good sense!

The formula of Unamuno and Papini is too simple: Sancho belongs neither to the world of the real (in which case he would be a rogue) nor to that of the phantasmagoric (then he would be a knight errant). What defines him is the state of oscillation, constantly passing from one level to the other, from illusion to disillusioned reality. He is a very realistic man; he is Man. Our hearts also have their idealistic islands, and we also serve them even to the point of insanity; they also crumble on us and we realize our folly, and are bitten momentarily by the demon of the roguish stance; but the island is shining again in the distance, and we advance towards it, oscillating always between the dream that cools our brow and the stones along the road that cut our feet.

Cervantes has painted the soul of Sancho without hurry and without concerning himself with the order of the brush strokes. The processes of his soul are as interwoven and complex as those of reality. And the creature is there, alive and eternal. One cannot find in the stiff, tight technique of Juan Ruiz, of the *Celestina*, in passages of *Lazarillo*, the painting of souls, this bringing to life of characters within an immense forest of adventures. Sancho will waiver in a human and real way throughout the book, with clashes and very natural contradictions of real character. The absence of visible artifice, the quickness of hand, the scattered bits of the aspects of the character remind me more of the psychological technique of the *Poema del Cid* (of course with very much more complex and eventful art).

But this is the heritage of Spanish realism that makes possible the serene, ample, and open mastery of Cervantes. In Cervantes, as in his predecessors, the *Poema del Cid*, the *Arcipreste de Hita*, the *Arcipreste de Talavera*, the *Celestina* and the *Lazarillo*, souls are bared by speaking. The comments of Cervantes himself are relatively few in the *Quixote*. The times in which the author tries to comment on the psychological reaction of his characters are few. It is necessary to add that even the scarce and indispensable indications of the circumstances (in contraposition to the short novels of the same Cervantes) are only minimally given in the *Quixote*. It thus results that the whole work is dramatized through the agreement and opposition of souls which become transparent to us through the dialogue.

The line of development of Spanish realism, of the realism of souls, is never broken. Its pinnacle of concentrated intensity is perhaps a few pages of the *Lazarillo*. The art of Cervantes is like an ample resting place, like a respite from the sharp note, a quiet corner in which the voice takes pleasure in singing more fully, and more serenely, of the binary world: of revery and truth.

The Reason of Don Quixote's Unreason
Charles Aubrun*

To find the reason of unreason is to measure the immeasurable, to ask the reason of error, to rationalize what seems at first to be irrational. Madness is never gratuitous and without a cause which explains it. There is no folly without its reasons. Don Quixote has not permanently lost his reason. On the contrary, he tries to rationalize his fundamental irrationality, which is in man's nature. He tries to make sense out of the verbiage ("razones") which Feliciano de Silva gives to one of his characters, a victim of love madness ("furioso"): "The reason for the unreason with which you treat my reason weakens my reason in such a way that with reason I complain of your beauty" (I, i).

It is then that he creates for himself, totally out of his imagination, a lady named Dulcinea, so that his reason can work on an excessive sentiment, mad love. He explains, "Your beauty is the cause of the wrong done to me, and of my madness as well. I demand redress."

He knows that it is necessary to practice excess in order to find his limits and know himself. By turning reason upside down, by exposing its other side, madness, Don Quixote bears witness, in his way, to the philosophic trend which would break down the extremes of logic, the "sophistries" ("sofisterías") of Aristotle's epigones,[1] the abstract mechanical rationalism of human reality.

Since it is necessary to be mad, Dulcinea will be the justification *a posteriori* of his extravagances; but she is certainly not the cause of them. Similarly the knights of the books who served him as example certainly fight in the name of their ladies. But it is to reform the world, to free it from the evil powers which corrupt it. When Don Quixote thinks of the greats of this world, those arrogant and unrestrained giants ("todos soberbios y descomedidos")[2], he loses his head. He can't contain himself, he is eager to cross swords with one of them: "[He was] driven to this by

*Reprinted with permission from *Homenaje a Casalduero* (Madrid: Gredos, 1972), 37–44. Translated for this volume by Louise K. Wornom and Ellen Lempera.

the thought of the loss the world suffered by his delay, considering the grievances he planned to redress, the wrongs he was to right, the injuries to amend, and the debts to pay." (I, 2)

Thus he wants to test himself in glorious combat against his own madness and against the madness of the world ". . . gold, which in this iron age of ours is valued so highly . . ." ["They did not know] those two words yours and mine . . ." ["there was then] no fraud, deceit or malice. Justice remained within her own proper purview and no one dared to confuse or offend her because of special favor or interest as now, when she is so debased, upset, and persecuted . . ." "and now, in this terrible age of ours . . ." (I, 2).

The "true" law, equal for all, foundation of all human society, is flouted by the powerful of the day;[3] nothing counts anymore today except wealth and property. So he undertakes to defend young ladies, to protect widows, to help orphans and the needy. He proposes to bring the world back to its first state, to the archetypal perfection of the golden age. If he fails, he will at least have borne witness, like Amadís and Palmerín, to the absolute values which remain incorruptible in our hearts.

Now Don Quixote's readings are nourished with his life experiences, experiences which he shares to a great extent with the people of his age, origin and social condition. The key to his obsessions, the reason for his attitudes toward other social classes, the cause, unknown to him, of his rages and his spontaneous indignation, the "razón de su sinrazón" must be sought and found in the fate suffered by the landed gentry between 1550 and 1600.

Literature and history concur to present us the same picture: country noblemen, served by a small number of faithful vassal peasants, suffer from the profound change which affects the economy and thus the social equilibrium. Lord Quixada or Quesada had to hang up the lance and shield inherited from his ancestors in the panoply of obsolete arms. About fifty years old at the beginning of the XVIIth century (like his creator Cervantes), he lives a half-life, the last of his line, with a young niece, a house-keeper, and a servant boy. For lack of the traditional rents in kind, the needs of the household absorb three quarters of his income.

He has been obliged to sell off numerous parcels of arable land. Having nothing else to do, he hunts, last privilege of his class; and then he reads, for he has bought the little library that we know about with his own cash. He reads to the point of drying up his brain.

In short the man doesn't have much to lose when, breaking with his mediocrity and full of complaints against the new society, he sallies forth to his adventures. As for his neighbor, promoted to squire, he has everything to gain. The peasant is poor; he has been promised marvels, even the governorship of an island. Whether the adventure succeeds or fails, he will have escaped for a short time from the hard and not very profitable work of the land; and he is assured of not starving to death, his master having saved a small nest-egg. Some younger noblemen embark for the Indies; other peasants emigrate toward the cities. Quixada and Panza have chosen to live their adventure in their native country and even, if the opportunity comes up, in the rest of the kingdom of Castille. Why wouldn't the world beyond their village be more or less similar to the one described in the books of chivalry, in romanesque tales or in the fabulous stories reported in true royal chronicles? It suffices to intelligently interpret the texts so that their similarity with present situations appears.

Don Quixote has a sense of the universality and permanence of human things; he will not be fooled by the different appearances they take according to circumstances, time and place. People themselves are only the avatars of those who have preceded them "You ought to know, mister don Rodrigo de Narvaez, that this beautiful Xarifa I have been referring to is not the lovely Dulcinea del Toboso" (I, 5).

Let us not argue against his opinion that it is here a question of fictitious characters. Fiction is never an effect of art. However fantastic it may appear, it fulfills a basic need of our soul; it expresses our real feelings when elsewhere they are repressed, inhibited.

Now, our two men are going to clash head on with a new society, hateful, despite appearances, in which the ever-present agents of the devil have donned masks as beautiful as they are difficult to tear off. In olden times the knight-errant would go along dangerous and poorly–marked roads, from castle to castle, "from absolute values to absolute values." Recently, since a network of roads with posting-houses and inns facilitates the traffic of goods and businessmen, he no longer finds a sure refuge where he can be refreshed. In Spain everything has started to move (except in a remote corner of La Mancha which it is much better *not* to name). On the road he only meets muleteers, rogues, actors, "henchmen" of justice, and noblemen of a new type, more rich than generous.

Don Quixote, a villager living in a past idealized by his readings, assimilates this strange new world to the world of evil giants and dwarfs where cursed enchanters set up ambushes in the paths of lovers and champions. Thus come looming up in his path the objects of his obsessions and all the causes, personified according to his need, of his own wretchedness and public misfortunes.

We shall limit ourselves here to comment on three of his first adventures. Besides, if these among the others have captured the attention of the work's readers, it is doubtless because, full of significance, these adventures stir in them the deeply–hidden and unconscious memory or apprehension of three typical experiences, which none of them, none of us, has been able or would be able to avoid. These are the battle against the windmills, the attack upon a flock of sheep, and the uproar over the fulling-mills.

Lord Quixada used to own wheat fields in La Mancha. Now, an innovation upsets the agricultural economy of the country: the windmill, which makes the peasant the tributary of the miller. The old *aceña*, the paddle-wheel mill located on some narrow and capricious stream, sufficed until then for the village. But one always needs more flour to feed the expanding cities and to provide for the needs of the kingdom of Spain. La Mancha started to bristle with gigantic towers fitted with turning wings. Don Quixote counts thirty or forty of them in the countryside. Windmills altered not only the landscape, but also traditional life.[4] These giants are the origin of the decline and poverty of the *hidalgos*. The knight, mad with a suppressed rage, rushes out on his mount, spear in hand, to knock them down: "Though you wield more arms than the giant Briareus, you'll pay for it." (I, 8). Alas, they are the stronger. One doesn't stop "progress", one doesn't hold up the march of time; one is dashed to pieces, one will always be broken by the arms of the windmills. Cervantes, inventor of this profound fable, knows this from experience. He himself, in his youth, wanting to be faithful to the noble ideals of the past, had broken body and spirit to save them at Lepanto, in Algiers and Spain. He wanted to humble the insolence of their enemies, Turkish or Christian. He laughs now at his hero as he laughs at himself. Let us note this in passing: this laughter of a man before his own reflection in the mirror of memory and of conscience, this is indeed a new sentiment which has just appeared in literature: humor.

When Cervantes flung his hero against the windmills, did he have the set purpose to symbolize the noble and ridiculous assault of tradition against change, the heroic rear-guard combat of the old manorial regime — with its tributes in kind — against the system of the merchants — founded on dealings and money? The question is pointless. It is reported that Rimbaud's mother, who had read one of his poems, asked her son what he meant by that. The poet answered, "What is important is not what I meant, but what *that says*."

The intentions of Cervantes and even the hidden processes of his thought are one thing, which pertains to the study of mentalities, the history of ideas, the psychology of the unconscious, etc. Black words on white paper in their order with their connotations, their recall of one another, and the infinity of suggestions which emanate from their forms and their content, these are another thing. They pertain to literary criticism, or discipline.

We shall confine ourselves to the words. Don Quixote does not lay the blame on rocks with fantastic silhouettes, on trees twisted like ghosts, or on parts of walls. He charges an enormous structure where one grinds grain, his grain, the wheat of La Mancha. It is enough to make one lose one's head; his unreason is not without reason. Certain millers, some newly rich, had been able to adapt to the new state of things, to "adjust."[5] Lord Quesada refuses to abjure, to disavow the social condition which his ancestors had transmitted to him. The bones of Don Quixote are dashed to pieces on the arms of the windmill.

On the way to his adventures, a fortuitous encounter will again unleash his rancor. Far ahead of the plain, a cloud of dust is rising (I, 18). It is a huge flock of sheep with its shepherds and dogs. Don Quixote sees an army there composed of numerous nations ("de diversas e innumerables gentes"). In effect, every year transhumance brought together the cattle of numerous owners ("pastores") in a *cabaña*. At this, Sancho points out to his master another similar cloud at the other end of the horizon. Don Quixote sees it as a second army; he even imagines that the two troops are going to wage battle. In his confused mind this is a transfer of the hostility attributed to the two *cabañas* that made up the celebrated Mesta, the very powerful corporation of cattlebreeders. His imagination races, always in the direction inspired by his reading. In the two forces he sees "cristianos" on one side and "moros" on the other. And he counts the noblemen who command the numerous companies.[6]

Now we know what the exorbitant privileges acquired over the centuries by Castilian "shepherds" cost the agrarian economy of Spain. In 1568 their Honorable Council ("Honorable Concejo") even succeeded in exempting itself from the control of the Crown, and in having its "chief distributor" administer justice as well.[7]

One of the traditional routes of transhumance passed to the south of La Mancha. The right of pasturage ruined farming there. Peasants deserted the country for the cities. Two among them, the nobleman Quesada and the peasant Sancho, preferred a more arduous and glamorous adventure. In their wandering one day, they met shepherds with their two flocks, who were one of the causes of their impoverishment. Foolishly, Don Quixote sided with one against the other. Both of them agreed to stone him with their slings. Then Sancho counted the teeth of the foolhardy "peasant": there remained only two and a piece of a third.[8] "Then didn't you see that those were sheep?" "Did I not tell you, Don Quixote, to turn back, that it was not armies you were going to attack, but flocks of sheep?" (I, 18).

Indeed, all the peasant could see was some animals ravaging the land, whereas the nobleman saw in the cloud of dust the gigantic figures of the powerful grazing their flocks in the wheat fields of the small agrarian republic. The cloud dissipates; all that is left is innocent cattle: "This one who pursues me . . . has turned the enemy squadrons into flocks of sheep." Which of the two companions is hallucinating, Don Quixote or Sancho?

For the triumphant Mesta this encounter with an aggressive crack-pot is purely accidental. The "shepherds" do not want to cause the death of the "peasants," even if they are stubborn. "The shepherds then came to him, and believing that they had killed him, hurriedly gathered up their flocks and took the dead sheep, which were about seven in number, and without further inquiry, they left."

Scarcely more than seven dead sheep: this maniac is not much of a threat to the new society. As long as the Don Quixotes attack the most obvious causes of their misfortunes, as long as they do not challenge the new socio-economic system, its original cause, and as long as they do not become aware of it,[9] the powerful need not worry about them.

The fulling-mill adventure is no less meaningful. It is pitch black; the place is deserted and it is windy (I, 20). Against the background roar of a large waterfull, one hears a frightful din recurring at regular intervals. Don Quixote braces himself to face danger, maybe death. Sancho becomes frantic: he manages to restrain his master by shackling Rocinante. But at dawn, the fearless knight marches straight to the hamlet from where the noise originated. He discovers six fulling hammers: "When Don Quixote saw what it was he became speechless and blushed from head to foot with signs of being embarassed."

Sancho does not refrain from laughing. Forgetting his previous wrath, his master also bursts out laughing; but he does not permit his servant to make fun of him any longer. Besides, the two companions are very "reasonable"; says one: "I admit that I have laughed too much." "I don't deny that what has happened to us is laughable, but it should not be told to anyone since not everyone is so discreet as to know how to interpret it rightly," says the other.

Thus the knight reduces excess to moderation, finds the "razón de la sinrazón": such is his golden rule.

And yet Cervantes chose to tell this adventure; a ridiculous one even in the eyes of his hero; a humiliating and in no way glorious one, as had been, all things considered, the adventures of the windmills and of the flocks of La Mesta. For unlike these contrivances of the devil, the fuller, perhaps newly introduced in La Mancha, is not responsible for the landed gentry's poverty. It does not even compete with the village weavers, for all it does is dress their cloth, put the finishing touch on the product of their humble, traditional industry. Don Quixote can mock it as a useless refinement, a luxury. He does not consider it a cowardly and abject creation (or creature) ("cobardes y viles criaturas", I, 8), a monstrous enemy of the old order, the divine order.

He is not carried away by his imagination; his temper, usually so quick, subsides as soon as his senses and common sense can reassure him. Our knight-errant of the year 1600 does not want to do away with the fullers any more than he wants to abolish the new inns. He is not trying to wipe the new roads of the king off the map of Spain. In the new world he can spontaneously distinguish the insignificant from the harmful. Since he is not senseless, he can see in the things and beings of his time mere "repetitions" of the things and beings of the past, neither more nor less useful or harmful. This is precisely the role of the enlightened and efficient knight: to be able to recognize true essence beyond appearances, and to distinguish between good and evil every day and on all occasions.

So, just as Dulcinea was called Jarifa in former times, a windmill is a new giant (Briaria), and a despotic Castilian shepherd is basically no different from Alifanfarón, the powerful heretic. But a fuller remains what it is: a fuller.

There are many adventures in Cervantes' novel. Only the first ones can sometimes be explained by socio-economic motives. This is because in the first chapters of his story, Lord Quesada, who has just broken with his previous life, his natural milieu, his village, appears particularly eager to fight the enemies who diminished his personal status and brought misfortune upon his community. His mood, ordinarily so calm, is deeply altered. He loses his grip. Rosinante bolts. In his character of a thwarted *hidalgo*, the knights of the Round Table, the twelve peers of France and the nine heros of Fame come to life again.

Later on in the novel, Quesada will free himself from his class, his personal concerns and his bookish culture. He will take on the obsessions and the aspirations of all men of good will. He will become the true, the eternal Don Quixote.

Notes

1. "that Aristotle himself wouldn't understand" (I, 1).

2. A single exception, the giant Morgante, who appeared to be "affable and well-bred." Might this be the Duke of Béjar, to whom the work is dedicated?

3. The giants. See F. Olmas, *Cervantes en su época*, Madrid, 1968.

4. Is this related to a new technique, that of the set of wings, changeable according to the wind, which came from the Netherlands?

5. Their relative prosperity was at its peak between 1570 and 1580 as attested by the *Relaciones*, scrupulous research conducted in those years at the behest of Phillip II. It did not last beyond 1600.

6. Would there be a key here, and would the named characters be disguises for real livestock owners? Rodríguez Marín (*D.Q.*, Appendix XIV, edition 1947–1949) reveals part of it: Pentapolín, Duke of Osuna; Miulina, Duchess of Medinasidonia; Espartafilardo, Count of Niebla.

7. Stock-raising declined starting from about 1550; this is precisely why the threatened breeders proved to be more demanding of public powers. Besides, regarding sheep at La Mesta, regarding two empires, how could the reader in 1605 not think of its two *cabañas*?

8. In a very similar adventure, Cervantes lost the use of his left hand.

9. Today, psychologists would call this de-dialectization and mistaken consciousness.

Sierra Morena as Labyrinth: From Wildness to Christian Knighthood

Javier Herrero*

Emile V. Telle, in his monumental *Érasme de Rotterdam et le septième sacrament*, asserts that the true origin of the Reformation should be found, rather than in the controversies on the nature of grace, in the passionate arguments about celibacy and marriage, in the strong movement away from monasticism towards philogamy and secular life. Marriage, then, and human love, the enduring affection which cements the unity of the family, are at the core of the religious revolution: "One could—and I beg to be excused for the metaphor—compare all questions relating to marriage to the beams which, passing through the magnifying glass of the seventh sacrament, concentrate in the hearth of marriage, and start the fire of religious revolution".[1] No matter how one evaluates the merits of Telle's thesis, he is undeniably right in asserting that human, secular love, as opposed to both the mystical traditions of monasticism and the aristocratic conventions of courtly love, is one of the central themes of sixteenth-century culture. It is true that Neo-platonism, associated with the tradition of courtly love, was still the accepted poetic and artistic vehicle for aristocratic sentiment; but through the influence of Christian humanism, and as an expression of the strength of the new bourgeoisie, the preoccupations with secular life and, above all, marriage, replaced the stylized conventions of chivalry and the austere ideals of monasticism.

It is not surprising, then, to see that Cervantes, who so faithfully reflected the spiritual movements of his time, made of love (and marriage) one of the two central themes of *Don Quijote* (the other being adventure). The theme of marriage in fact links the stories interpolated in *Don Quijote*, Part I. In the intertwined stories of Cardenio-Luscinda and Fernando-Dorotea, Cervantes aims to show the destructive power of the passions hidden under the trappings of love, and to extol the virtues of love and marriage as conceived by the Christian humanists. Weakness, ambition and, above all, lust, twist human destinies, separate lovers, impose the will and desires of the powerful upon the helpless. This is the condition of suffering humanity in the Age of Iron, so different from the peaceful and trusting one of the Age of Gold:

> [Then simple and beautiful country lasses did wander from vale to vale and from oak grove to oak grove. . . . Then the amorous conceits of the simple soul were decorated in the same simplicity in which they were conceived. . . . Young ladies and honesty went wherever they wanted, as I have said, alone and with dignity, without fear that another's misbehavior and lascivious desire would offend them . . . and now, in these hated times, no one is safe, even if they are hidden and enclosed in

*Reprinted with permission from *Forum for Modern Language Studies* 17 (1981):55–67.

a new labyrinth, like that of Crete, because even there, through the cracks or through the air, with the persistence of its cursed efforts, the amorous plague reaches them and causes them to give up their seclusion to their ruin.] (I, 11)[2]

One of the main characteristics, then, of our Age of Iron is the ["amorous plague"]. Lust is the Minotaur which transforms life into a labyrinth. Dorotea is carefully guarded by her parents; Luscinda is Cardenio's bride and should have been protected by their mutual love, and later by the remote convent in which her family hid her; but Fernando's power and lust penetrated and polluted every dark recess. Only Providence, by transforming him from the diabolical Minotaur into a Christian knight, could save his victims from their doom. But lust is not the only mortal enemy of true, Christian love. Equally dangerous is the Renaissance ideal in which courtly, Petrarchan and Neoplatonic elements combine to produce an artificial concept of love and woman. Of course, this ideal woman, and the devotion of her adoring lover, is the object of special irony in don Quijote's cult of Dulcinea; but the destructive force of Renaissance love is the object of many other attacks in the book: Grisóstomo's suicide and Camila's death are the direct consequence of the adoration of woman and of the lover's search for superhuman perfection.[3] In the interpolated stories Cardenio and Luscinda love each other under the delusion of heroism learnt from the novels of chivalry, and especially from the *Amadís*. Death is better than life without the beloved; Luscinda will stab herself with a dagger rather than marry Fernando; Cardenio will kill Fernando before surrendering Luscinda. But they are human beings, not literary copies of knightly heroes: Luscinda yields to family pressures and Cardenio to fear. Again, only through grace dispensed by Providence, and after being purified and fortified by suffering, will they overcome their weaknesses and become worthy of each other. Love, Cervantes is telling us, is conquered; and is conquered precisely by overcoming our human failures. In part, human beings love each other, not because they are perfect, but in spite of their imperfections. A far cry, indeed, from the mystical description of love given by Bembo in the fourth book of Castiglione's *Il Cortigiano*.

Sierra Morena is Cervantes' labyrinth. The treacherous love of don Fernando for Luscinda and his lust for Dorotea have created a confusion in their lives (and in Cardenio's, Luscinda's lover) which has brought them to despair, madness, and almost death. The story is presented to the reader *in medias res*. Cardenio is first seen by don Quijote jumping like a goat from rock to rock, in the thick of Sierra Morena, and metaphorically nude: his loins are covered with the remains of torn breeches and he lives inside a tree. When later on we meet Dorotea, she is sitting by the bank of a stream, still dressed as a young peasant. Her clothes are also torn, and she immediately stands and lets her hair fall free to cover her body. Rising from the water, her feet and legs bare, and covered with the radiant blondness of her locks, she appears figuratively as a Venus image, or as Edward Dudley has suggested, as a pagan nymph.[4] The nudity (or appearance of nudity) of Cardenio and Dorotea and their immersion in their natural background, *inside* the trees and *within* the water, are the poetic expression of their loss of social ties and civilized norms, and of their reduction to a level of animal existence, a fusion with the instinctive, amoral, natural forces. Such a state can be considered as a fall from grace to Nature, or in less theological terms, a loss of ethos, of civilization.[5] This fall is experienced by these victims of love as an unbearable anguish; they both enter the story with expressions of loneliness and despair and of longing for death.

Two images dominate this desolate world. One is its natural environment: the vision of narrow valleys surrounded by steep slopes of forest is a *topos* which, as opposed to the harmonic landscape of the *locus amoenus*, expresses anguish, violence, and war.[6] The second image, superimposed upon the first, is the great classical myth of the labyrinth.[7] We have already quoted don Quijote's comparison of life in the Age of Iron to Crete's labyrinth. Later on, through don Quijote's expression, Sierra Morena itself is figuratively linked to the *Labyrinth of Theseus*. As the Athenian hero used a thread to guide himself through its confusion, Sancho leaves behind branches of bushes to find his way through it: ["Moreover the best thing for you to do so that you don't stray too far and get lost is to cut some branches from the many there are around here and place them every few feet along the way until you reach the clearing. They will serve you as signs and markers so that you can find me when you return, imitating the thread of Perseus' labyrinth"] (I, 25).[8]

The image of the labyrinth signifies the moral confusion of several lives twisted into the wrong paths through their sins. This meaning is made clear in the expressions of several characters. Fernando, after his conversion, ["gave thanks to heaven for the blessings received and for having lifted him out of that intricate labyrinth in which he had come so close to losing reputation and soul"] (I, 37).

Between the beginning and the ending of these stories Cervantes interpolated two narratives: "The Tale of the Man of Foolish Curiosity," and don Quijote's battle with the wineskins. In "The Tale of the Man of Foolish Curiosity," thematically closely related to the other interpolated stories,[9] Anselmo, husband of the beautiful Camila, is creating a maze out of the relationships of love (which links him to his wife) and of friendship (which binds him to his friend Lotario). An insane jealousy moves him to propose an "impertinent" experiment to his friend. Lotario refers to the moral confusion of Anselmo, which threatens to twist all their lives out of their right paths, as ["the labyrinth which you have entered and from which you want me to take you"] (I, 33). Of course, by yielding to his friend's wishes he himself will enter the labyrinth which, in their case, brings them all to destruction. In both cases we see that the fall from love and reason to irrational passions of lust, pride, and jealousy, diverts men from the truth, from the morally right direction, and, by confounding their ways, creates mistrust, confrontation, violence, and (if divine Providence does not intervene) eventually death.

The Minotaur of this labyrinth is, of course, the Prince of Darkness. The Great Rebel, the Devil himself, is the irrational power of confusion, the mainspring of violence and chaos. Cervantes states this clearly at the end of the interpolated stories. Peace reigns finally in the inn: love and friendship govern and link all the characters with sweet bonds. The devil then intervenes in a final effort to destroy this harmony: ["the devil, who does not sleep, ordered it so that in that very moment the barber, from whom Don Quixote took Mambrino's helmet, entered the inn . . ."] (I, 44). The well-known episode of the argument and fight about the true nature of the helmet (the bone of contention being whether it is a helmet or a barber's basin) takes place. At the end of it the inn has become again a ["chaos, and labyrinth of confusion"] (I, 45). Reason triumphs again through the good offices of the priest and a judge who has come to the inn recently (that is to say, through the combined powers of divine and human justice). But the Devil makes a final effort to pit against these forces of love his violent impulses of hatred: to recreate the labyrinth: ["But upon seeing himself marked and disdained, and seeing the little he had gained from throwing everyone into such a confused labyrinth, the enemy of harmony and rival of peace decided over again to try his hand, stirring up new battles and restlessness"] (I, 45).

The Devil, of course, will be defeated finally and love and peace will triumph. But Cervantes has made his point very clear; the chief giant from whom his followers obtain their terrifying power is the Minotaur, who brings his victims to the darkness of the labyrinth, there to devour them; that is to say, to confuse and inflame them in such a way that they destroy each other with the claws and fangs of jealousy, lust and hatred.

Sierra Morena, then, is the emblem of Hell. The characters who inhabit it live in moral wildness and emotional desolation. The image of the labyrinth expresses the ethical and religious roots of such a state: men convert their lives into Hell by straying from the right path. The main agent of confusion in the story is Fernando, who is moved by lust and pride, thus becoming the evil giant who storms through the other's lives and hurts and destroys them all with the hurricane of his unleashed passions. But all the other characters had weaknesses which contributed to the resulting confusion. The labyrinth image clearly reveals the social character of Cervantes' view of moral and Christian life: Fernando's sins not only twist his own spiritual path, but through the complicity and lack of sincerity of his companions (that is, by generating social evil) they throw his victims' lives into confusion also and create general chaos, moral darkness, and misery.

But Cardenio and Dorotea are not alone in having been reduced by love to a state of wildness; don Quijote, too, is suffering from love and has cast off his armour and his civilian clothes until he also becomes a naked beast, jumping from rock to rock in a mocking parody of Cardenio. It is true that he is playacting, while his companions feel their distress deeply, but this does not make him different from a moral standpoint. He has been forced to enter Sierra Morena because of his attack on the guards of the galley slaves. Once in the thick of the Sierra he has decided that it might be easier to win glory by imitating the penance of Amadis than by endeavoring to succeed in great adventures which seem either to elude him, or to end with terrible beatings. He shares with Cardenio and Dorotea a view of the world colored by the literature of chivalry and an imitation of Beltenebros which in him at first is acted and then profoundly lived. Errors, passions and sins have brought all the characters, to put it in Fernando's words, ["at the point of losing reputation and soul"]; in fact to the "purgatory" of Sierra Morena.[10]

It is certainly not accidental that a priest is the agent who will bring them all out of the purgatory and the labyrinth of the Sierra and back to society and morality.[11] The priest, accompanied by the barber, had left don Quijote's village in order to find him and bring him back to his house and, if possible, to sanity. On their way the two searchers come across Sancho, who had been dispatched by don Quijote to El Toboso to inform Dulcinea of his master's penance and to ask for her blessings. They take Sancho to the inn of Juan Palomeque el Zurdo (where don Quijote and his squire had created so much confusion earlier in the story) and there the priest thinks up a plot which will allow them, not only to lure don Quijote out of Sierra Morena, but to bring him safely home. Surprisingly, it will be a novel of chivalry (and a lie) that will initiate the redemption of all the straying souls.

The priest proposes that they present don Quijote with an adventure which will lead him to take action. He disguises himself as a princess, a damsel in distress, who comes from a far away kingdom to ask the help of the famous knight. The barber, properly transformed beyond recognition, plays the part of his squire. Guided by Sancho they go to the Sierra in search of don Quijote. On their way, they find Cardenio and Dorotea, who tell them their stories. On hearing of the priest's plans, Dorotea offers to play the role of the damsel asking for the help of don Quijote's famous arm. She will take the name of Princess Micomicona.

From this moment the beast-like victims of love who were lost in Sierra Morena begin their return to civilization. On hearing of the distress of Dorotea, Cardenio finds the courage, which he had lacked hitherto, to confront the agent of their common woes, the tyrannical Fernando, and he determines to become a "Christian Knight":

> [I am the unhappy Cardenio, brought to my present state by the same one who put you in yours. You find me broken, naked, without any human solace, and, what is worse, completely without reason. . . .

> I came to this remote place with the intention of ending here my life.
> But . . . it still could be that heaven has waiting for us both something
> better than we, in the midst of our troubles, can imagine. . . . I swear
> to you on the oath of a Christian and a gentleman that I will not
> foresake you until I see you in the arms of Fernando.] (I, 29)

In these words of Cardenio we find the general outline of the "wild"
characters' progress toward sanity and happiness. Let us consider Cardenio's situation: (1) his present state is of total deprivation: of clothes
(naked); of company (without human comfort); without reason; he is, not
surprisingly, filled with a desire to die; (2) he intends to fight for Dorotea's
happiness and, in so doing, he will act as a gentleman and a Christian; (3)
but he does not exclusively trust his own strength; if he succeeds, it will be
with God's help: trust in Heaven is the way by which a wild man can
become, not merely a knight, but a Christian knight.

The first stage of this progress is to abandon nakedness, the image of
animality; and this is done through a story of chivalry and under the
priest's guidance. The story, which dominates the whole development of
these episodes, contains the stock elements of the genre. Princess Micomicona, of the kingdom of Micomicón, is the daughter of a magician king—
Tinacrio the Wise Man—and the queen Jaramilla. By means of his science
the king finds out that some day the princess will be an orphan, and a
terrible giant, Pandafilando de la Fosca Vista (so called because he squints
to frighten people) will usurp the kingdom. The king further prophesied
that only one knight could defeat the giant, the famous Spaniard don
Quijote de la Mancha.

The story is a metaphor of Dorotea's predicament. Critics have noted
that Pandafilando is a transparent illusion to don Fernando, and the
destruction of her kingdom the image of her seduction and ruin. In fact,
Cervantes who, as Oscar Mendel pointed out, does not like to leave us in
doubt as to his intentions,[12] says that much:

> [Sancho heard all this, with no little anguish in his heart, consider-
> ing that all his hopes for a governorship were going up in smoke, and
> that the beautiful princess Micomicona had turned into Dorotea, and
> the giant into Fernando.] (I, 34)

We shall try to show that the metaphoric character of the story is even
more precise, and that the king Tinacrio stands for a Divine Providence
using don Quijote's courage and generosity as an unwitting instrument of
its designs. Dorotea's exhortation to don Quijote at the end of the episode
is not only an ironical version of the adventure, but, through its irony, a
valid commentary on it:

> [And so, my master, let your goodness give back honor to the father who
> engendered me, and take him for a wise and prudent man since in his
> wisdom he found such a true and easy way to remedy my disgrace. I
> think that if it were not for you, sir, I would never have managed to have

the luck I have, and in this I speak the truth as the good gentlemen present will testify.] (I, 37)

But this will be seen, I hope, at the end of my argument; at present we must go back to the analysis of our character's progress.

Under the influence of the Micomicona story, and with the good purpose of enticing don Quijote out of the Sierra towards his home, Dorotea acquires the first mark of social progress: the dress. To disguise herself as Micomicona Dorotea opens a bag, where she kept an elegant dress and her jewelry (taken along when she left her house), and adorns herself with the rich attire which used to be hers. By playing a dignified role in a novel of chivalry she is becoming herself. At the same time the priest, in an almost sacramental way, bestows on Cardenio the first marks of his return to social decorum: [". . . the priest . . . , with scissors that he carried in a case, quickly cut the beard off of Cardenio, dressed him in a brown cape he had brought with him, and gave him a black jacket"] (I, 29). Thus transformed, they begin their return to sanity, which consists of a joint pilgrimage to the inn where the complex and orderly unraveling of their labyrinthine paths will take place. As soon as they arrive, don Quijote retires to rest; this is not surprising, since he has spent several days in the Sierra. Three important and interrelated events follow: (1) in his own room, don Quijote, in a dream, fights against the giant Pandafilando and beheads him; (2) the reading of the novel "The Tale of Foolish Curiosity" takes place; (3) don Fernando arrives, having abducted Luscinda from the nunnery. Only the first and third ones will concern us here.

The battle of the wineskins is the most important deed of don Quijote in the inn, and, by placing it in the center of the interpolated stories, it is clear that Cervantes meant for it to be highly significant. Thematically, it is the major event in the imaginary adventures of don Quijote, since it is the only time he succeeds, if only in a dream, in defeating a member of ["that generation of giants, all of whom are arrogant and disrespectful"] (I, 1). In a previous encounter, face to face, with a colossal giant, the enchanter Frestón had transformed the monster into a windmill, and don Quijote had been ignominiously defeated. But in the present case the battle is especially meaningful because a princess, Micomicona, has come from a remote kingdom to search for this valiant champion. He is not, as in the field of Montiel, alone in the deadly encounter: the princess, her squire, Cardenio, the priest, are all awaiting the outcome of the battle. A careful study of this episode would take us far from our present purpose. Let us, then, refer here simply to its structural function in the interpolated stories. In this battle the courage of the knight finds its climax: he meets the terrible Pandafilando, faces him without a moment of hesitation, and attacks him regardless of the mortal danger of the unequal fight. That the battle is imaginary is, of course, irrelevant. By penetrating the wildness of Sierra Morena in amorous penance, and by assuming the burden of

Micomicona's request and of the terrible combat, don Quijote has acted as the main agent in the rescue of the disgruntled victims of love from Sierra Morena's labyrinth.

The main agent of men's restoration from sin and abjection to virtue and dignity is for Cervantes, not surprisingly, the action of Divine Providence through the means of the priest and don Quijote. The analysis of the denouement seems to make this quite clear. In the development of the stories we are examining Cervantes will point at the true ways of love: by them giants are transformed into Christian knights, and damsels in distress into honest wives. In fact, recalling the initial description of the characters' wildness in Sierra Morena, we can say that they, in the end, are raised from animality to human dignity.

The rest of the Cardenio-Luscinda, Fernando-Dorotea story is as follows: after don Quijote's battle with the wineskins Cardenio stays in his room to watch over the knight's sleep, and the other characters remain in the inn, Dorotea sitting in a chair by don Quijote's door, her face covered with a veil. Soon after four gentlemen arrive at the inn, bringing with them a most lovely lady, seemingly a prisoner. They are don Fernando and three companions, who have kidnapped Luscinda from the nunnery where she had taken refuge. Inside the inn, she is deposited in a chair near Dorotea. Luscinda, of course, is upset and looks ill; Dorotea, full of sympathy, offers her help; Luscinda remains dejected, and don Fernando says that it is useless to try to help her because she is ungrateful, and it is also better that she does not answer because she does not speak the truth. To this Luscinda replies that her truth makes him false. Hearing these voices, Cardenio rises with a start in don Quijote's room: he has recognized them. Luscinda also recognizes him, gets up and tries to run into the room, but she is stopped by don Fernando, who clasps her in his arms from behind and prevents her from joining Cardenio. Dorotea recognizes don Fernando and faints, but recovering, kneels at his feet and asks him to recognize the truth of their union and act as a Christian knight:

> [You cannot belong to the beautiful Luscinda, because you are mine, and she cannot be yours because she belongs to Cardenio . . . And if this is so—as it is—and if you are as much a Christian as you are a gentleman, why do you delay making me happy at the end as you did at the beginning? . . . I am your true and legitimate wife. . . . Whether you like it or not I am your wife. Your words are witness . . . your signature will be witness, and heaven, whom you called in witness to what you promised me, will also serve as witness.] (I, 36)

After a long pause in which don Fernando fights between lust and duty, he opens his arms and set Luscinda free. Cardenio, who had remained behind don Fernando, finally gathers enough courage to face him and

> [every fear set aside and venturing everything, he ran to hold up Luscinda, and, taking her in his arms he told her: If merciful heaven

desires that you have rest, loyal, firm and honest wife of mine, I think there is no place where you will feel more sure than in these arms that now receive you and that once before received you when fortune wished it that you could call yourself mine.] (I, 36)

Let us consider some significant elements in Dorotea's and Cardenio's remarks. Dorotea has said that Luscinda cannot belong to Fernando because she belongs to Cardenio and Fernando belongs to her (["you are mine"]; ["she is Cardenio's"]); and a few lines earlier she had said that ["You wanted me to be yours, and you wanted it in such a way that even if now you wished it were not so, it would not be possible for you to stop being mine"] (I, 36). She explains that she is his wife and as witness she has his words, a written document ["your signature"], and "Heaven" to whom he appealed as a witness ["heaven, whom you called in witness to what your promised me"]. What he had promised, in fact, was to become her legal husband and had called as a witness, not only Heaven, but an image of Our Lady, and finally Dorotea's maid, as a human witness who could testify in court. Let us look at his oath: ["taking an image [of our Lady] which was in the bedroom, Fernando placed it as witness of our marriage. With most effective and justly extraordinary words he gave his word to be my husband"] (I, 28). It is true that *esposo* can be "betrothed" as well as "husband"; but we must remember that at the time of the writing of the *Quijote* (immediately after the Council of Trent) the dispensation of the sacrament of marriage was undergoing a considerable change. After, as before Trent, the ministers of the sacrament of marriage were the bride and bridegroom. The external ceremonies had only the value of social confirmation of the spiritual act of marriage which consisted in the solemn expression of the will of the parties and which was sealed by consummation. But it is obvious that such a state of affairs could produce great confusion, and Trent made the formal intervention of the Church a necessary requisite for the validity of marriage.[13] *What Dorotea is saying really is that don Fernando is her husband, and that is the truth that he finally accepts.*[14] But we are told more; we are unmistakenly led to realize that Luscinda also has married Cardenio and that their marriage has been consummated.[15] It is true that we had been initially misled by a remark of Cardenio's which asserted that their relationship had been wholly innocent: ["the furthest that my boldness went was to take, almost by force, one of her white hands and lift it to my lips"] (I, 27). But that is the expression of a gentleman talking about a lady; Cervantes leaves no doubt about the real state of affairs and, if anything, his insistence is almost excessive. Cardenio can enter her house, when she is forced to marry don Fernando, because ["I knew all its entrances and exits very well"]; during the ceremony Cardenio exclaims: ["Oh Luscinda, Luscinda! Look at what you're doing: consider what you owe me; see that you are mine and ought not to belong to another!"] (I, 27). And this assertion is confirmed by

Luscinda herself, who as we have seen, had written a letter before her wedding (and hid it in her bodice) stating that ["she could not be Fernando's, because she was Cardenio's"] (I, 28); in explaining to Dorotea that they can still have hope in Heaven's help, Cardenio says that ["Luscinda cannot marry Fernando because she belongs to me"] (I, 29). That their marriage was consummated is clear by the assertion of Cardenio (quoted above) in which he proclaimed unguardedly, in a moment of great emotion when he takes Luscinda from the arms of don Fernando into his own: ["these arms that now receive you and that once before received you when fortune wished it that you would call yourself mine"]. In this context we now fully understand the strength of Dorotea's assertion that don Fernando cannot undo what Heaven has done: ["You have at your feet your wife, and she whom you wanted for a wife is in the arms of her husband. Consider if it will be well for you, or even possible to undo what heaven has done"] (I, 36). This is the truth that don Fernando has finally faced.

The story proceeds with the grace of a ballet where the spiritual progress is marked by successive symbolic steps: we have seen Luscinda imprisoned in don Fernando's arms; she tries to join Cardenio, who hides behind don Fernando; Dorotea kneels at the feet of don Fernando; vanquished by the love of Dorotea, don Fernando frees Luscinda who faints; Cardenio gets up his courage and turns around and faces don Fernando and embraces Luscinda. At this moment a strong feeling of pride overwhelms don Fernando and Hell is on the brink of regaining its prey; possessed by jealous fury, don Fernando puts his hand on his sword. Everybody prays now that don Fernando will accept the truth; but it is the priest who finally vanquishes his obstinacy with his Christian exhortation. He argues that ["only death could separate Luscinda and Cardenio"], that don Fernando "must vanquish himself" and that ["if he valued himself as a Christian and a gentleman, he could do no other than to fulfill his promise"] (I, 36). Don Fernando yields: ["It was a matter of lowering himself and embracing Dorotea"]. And this symbolic descent culminates in the reconciliation with Cardenio and Luscinda; they too kneel at his feet, but he raises them to his level and embraces them too. We see clearly that the spiritual movement has been completed by don Fernando's descent from lust and pride to a Christian humility and fraternity by which he raises his victims to the level of his affection and, now reunited in love, a common embrace is possible. The giant is dead, and the true man, the Christian gentleman, has replaced him.

But, which powers have brought about the conversion? Has it been the beauty, the tears, the truths of Dorotea? The priest's persuasion? They certainly all have a part in it; but the text leaves no doubt that all these elements, together with don Quijote, have been but the instruments of Providence. As Leo Spitzer proved in a memorable article, which dealt with other of the interpolated stories, God is the supreme Agent in the work of love which brings about the triumph of Christian charity over the torments of ill-directed passions.[16] While men and women have been acting through the impulse of their passions, which brought them to the labyrinth of Sierra Morena, not a reference has been made by Cervantes to Heaven's will; but as soon as Cardenio meets Dorotea and is told that don Fernando did not take Luscinda with him, he expresses hope that Heaven has decreed their salvation. From that moment on, their destinies began to escape from the darkness and confusion of the labyrinth. At the inn, the *locus* of social reunion and consequently of the transition from wildness to civilization, Luscinda, having been released by don Fernando in the scene just described, exclaims: ["See how Heaven, by strange and hidden ways, has placed my true husband before me. You know by a thousand costly experiences that only death would be sufficient to erase him from my memory"]. Immediately, and in the long scene of reconciliation, all the participants claim that their meeting in the inn is not accidental, but, on the contrary, the work of Providence: ["not by accident, as it seemed, but by the particular providence of Heaven, had all those come together in that place where least they expected it"]. Don Fernando claims that, if Dorotea and he had been separated, ["perhaps it has been by order of Heaven, so that by my seeing in you the faithfulness with which you love me, I would learn to honor you as you deserve"] (I, 36). And it is Don Fernando himself who gives final credit to Providence for the full extent of the Grace received. Referring to the abduction of Luscinda, he says: ["and it was thus that, accompanied by tears and silence, they had arrived at that inn, which was for him like reaching Heaven, in which all the misadventures of earth find their ending and are resolved"] (I, 36). And immediately afterwards, he proceeds: ["Fernando gave thanks to Heaven for the blessings received, and for having lifted him out of that intricate labyrinth in which he had come so close to losing reputation and soul"] (I, 37). Only by escaping from the diabolical labyrinth, then, can the human abode become an image of the celestial one.

Against a sentimental and a Neoplatonic tradition which made of woman a goddess, Cervantes takes the side of the conjugal love presented by Erasmus and Vives as the Christian ideal which allows man not only to enjoy the legitimate pleasure of the sexual union, but to help each other to fight against the inevitable weakness and imperfection of the human condition. By emphasizing the social, civilizing aspects of marriage, Cervantes, as Bataillon and Márquez Villanueva have pointed out, was closer to the new doctrines of reform than to the Renaissance ideals of love; indeed, with his attacks on the pastoral and by the story of "The Man of Foolish Curiosity," Cervantes is precisely marking his distance from the great aristocratic tradition of the Renaissance and joining the new, to a great extent bourgeois, Christianity which descended to the South of Europe from the Low Countries. In opposition to Amadís, Palmerín, Belianís, etc., the new bourgeois lover is not a knight but a Christian gentleman. Such love, as we have seen, has two elements. It is Christian, and the activity of Providence and the priest show the role that God and His Church play in its growth. But it is also gentlemanly: both Cardenio and don Fernando become through love not only Christians, but Christian gentlemen. Courtly love brings the knight to madness; but Christian love saves him. Such a rescue is metaphorically expressed in our story by the great classical myth of the labyrinth. Lost in the wilderness of Sierra Morena, their lives twisted into the intricate maze of the labyrinth, on the brink of being devoured by the Minotaur of lust and madness, Cardenio, Luscinda, Dorotea, and Fernando are finally rescued by don Quijote's courageous battle and by the civilizing force of an Erasmian Church. Divine Providence, in fact, has provided, as Ariadne, the saving thread.

Notes

1. Émile V. Telle, *Érasme de Rotterdam et le septième sacrement. Étude d'Évangélisme matrimonial au XVI siècle et contribution a la biographie intellectuelle d'Érasme* (Genève: Librairie E. Droz, 1954), p. 263.
> Normally the historian of the pre-Reformation, accustomed since Montesquieu to the determinism of supposed "causes," would expect that the open war between Sainte-Siege and the protesters should break out over the subject of the seventh and not the fourth sacrament, and if it were possible to conceive a sixteenth century without the monk of Wittenberg, it would be possible to imagine a Reformation which had been at its origin pro-marriage and anti-monastic.
>
> In great measure, it is in the light of the discussions regarding the sacrament of marriage that the anti-sacramental doctrine of the Protestants — that will culminate in Calvinist determinism — is forged between 1516 and 1536. One could — if I am permitted the metaphor — compare all the questions having anything at all to do with marriage to light rays which, passing through the lens of the seventh sacrament, would bend to the "hearth" of marriage, and would light the fire of the religious revolution.

The translation is my own. A very useful study is Robert V. Piluso's *Amor, matrimonio y honra en Cervantes* (New York: Las Américas, 1967).

2. All quotations from *El ingenioso hidalgo don Quijote de la Mancha*, ed. Luis Andrés Murillo (Madrid: Castalia, 1978).

3. For Cervantes' attack on Renaissance ideals of love see Javier Herrero, "Arcadia's Inferno: Cervantes' Attack for Pastoral," *Bulletin of Hispanic Studies*, 55 (1978), 289–299, and bibliography there included.

4. Edward Dudley, "The Wild Man Goes Baroque" in *The Wild Man Within*, ed. Edward Dudley and Maximillian E. Novak (Pittsburgh: University of Pittsburgh Press, 1972), p. 118.

5. Peter Dunn, "Two Classical Myths in *Don Quijote*", *Renaissance and Reformation*, IX (1972), 3–4.

6. For a historical development of the *topos*, see Ernst R. Curtius, *European Literature and the Latin Middle Ages* (Princetown: Bollinger Series, 1973), pp. 198–202; see also Márquez Villanueva, *Personajes y temas del "Quijote"* (Madrid: Taurus, 1978), pp. 39–43.

7. As far as I know, there does not exist a study of the myth of the labyrinth in the Spanish baroque, although it plays a very important part in its iconology, especially in Calderón. The labyrinth in Classical literature has been studied by W. F. Jackson Knight in

Cumaean Gates (Oxford: Basil Blackwell, 1936); in English Renaissance (Spencer) by Angus Fletcher: *The Prophetic Moment* (Chicago: Chicago University Press, 1971). The classical work for a general study of the myth of the labyrinth in Western culture is G. R. Hocke's *Die Welt als Labyrinth* (Hamburg: Rowholt, 1957).

8. In I, 25, Cervantes mentions the thread of the "Perseus labyrinth". It remained like this in the three Cuesta editions, although later editions corrected to "Theseus." That carelessness is shown by the fact that in I, 48 (p. 574 of Murillo) he writes about "a labyrinth of fantasies from which you cannot escape even if you have Theseus' rope." See Murillo, p. 317, note 67.

9. The thematic and structural unity of the interpolated stories is now generally accepted. Major articles on this subject have been: E. C. Riley, "Episodio novela y aventura en *Don Quijote*", *Anales Cervantinos*, 5 (1955–1956), 209–30; R. Immerwahr, "Structural Symmetry in the Episodic Narrative of *Don Quijote*, Part One", *Comparative Literature*, 10 (1958), 121–35; Edward Dudley, "Don Quijote as Magus: The Rhetoric of Interpolation", *Bulletin of Hispanic Studies*, 49 (1972), 355–68. There is considerable critical literature on the relationship between "La novela del curioso impertinente" and the interpolated stories. Classic studies are B. W. Wardropper, "The Pertinence of El curioso impertinente,", *PMLA*, 52 (1957), 587–600, and Juan Bautista Avalle-Arce, *Deslindes Cervantinos* (Madrid: Edhigar S. A., 1961), pp. 121–235.

10. The labyrinth-hell interpretation of Sierra Morena is confirmed by Sancho and don Quijote here: Sancho calls Sierra Morena a "purgatory," to which Don Quijote replies that it would be better to call it "Hell." (I, 25).

11. Ruth El Saffar has seen clearly that the priest is the controlling force in don Quijote's return: *Distance and Control in "Don Quijote,"* North Carolina Studies in the Romance Languages and Literatures, No. 147 (Chapel Hill: Publication of the Department of Romance Languages, 1975), p. 66. But he is also instrumental in changing Cardenio and Dorotea from their wild appearance to a civilized demeanour.

12. Oscar Mandel, "The Function of the Norm in *Don Quixote*," *Modern Philology*, 55 (1957), 156–57.

13. Since the Reformation had converted the social aspect of marriage into an essential element, it is not surprising that there was a strong party at Trent which was afraid that the new attitude, which carried the day, could be seen as a concession to the Protestants and a weakening of the sacrament. See in this respect Marcel Bataillon, "Cervantes y el matrimonio cristiano," *Varia lección de clásicos castellanos* (Madrid: Gredos, 1964), pp. 238–55. The acrimony of these disputes can be easily understood if we recall that the Church had uniformly accepted the sacramental validity of the clandestine marriage followed by consummation. The problems created by marriages without witnesses (bigamy, inheritance, secrecy, etc.) was the cause of their condemnation by the *Fuero Juzgo*, *Siete Partidas y Leyes de Toro*, and finally, of course, by Trent's famous *Tametsi* decree (November 11, 1563) which became law in Spain by Philip the Second's *Pragmática* of 12 July 1564. That the *pragmática* was only partially obeyed is shown by Spanish Golden Age theater and novel. A good study of this question in Piluso, pp. 63–73.

14. The validity of Fernando's marriage to Dorotea has been established beyond doubt by the critics; see Márquez Villanueva, p. 32, and bibliography there quoted; also Piluso, pp. 73–77. As Piluso and Márquez Villanueva make clear, Dorotea was attracted to Fernando; showed remarkable lucidity and energy to direct Fernando's passion towards the clandestine marriage; was sexually aroused at the time and desired its consummation; and, as could be expected from a woman of her temper, she enjoyed it.

15. The marriage of Cardenio and Luscinda is, of course, much less clearly stated than the one of Fernando and Dorotea. However, I trust that the analysis offered in my paper validates my assertion. The relationship between this timid pair is extraordinarily complex and deserves even more attention than the considerable one already given it. Especially

puzzling is Cardenio's flouting of Luscinda's charms to Fernando, which provokes the crisis in their interrelationship: see Cesareo Bandera, *Mimesis conflictiva* (Madrid: Gredos, 1975), pp. 71–111.

16. Leo Spitzer, "Perspectivismo lingüístico en *El Quijote*", *Lingüística e historia literaria* (Madrid: Gredos, 1968), pp. 135–87.

Don Quixote: Story or History?   Bruce W. Wardropper*

Although today we call *Don Quixote* a novel, Cervantes did not. The modern Spanish word "*novela*" did not yet exist in the sense of an extended work of prose fiction; it could be applied only to the short story of Italian origin. The other family of words used to designate longer prose fiction derived from Latin "*romance*"; in France "*roman*" covered fictional romance, but in Spain the equivalent word "*romance*" had been pre-empted for other purposes.[1] There was thus no appelation for the early Spanish romance or novel. The chivalric and pastoral romances were called "*books*"; the sentimental romances, "*tratados*," or treatises; Francisco Delicado's *La lozana andaluza*, a "*retrato*," or portrait; the picaresque works, "lives." On his title pages Cervantes carefully refrains from saying what his work is: "*The Ingenious Gentlemen Don Quixote de La Mancha*" "*The Second Part of the Ingenious Gentleman Don Quixote de la Mancha*." The friend who advises him, in the prologue to Part I, about the preliminaries to his work calls it simply a "book." If, as the friend assumes, *Don Quixote* is essentially a parody of the [books of chivalry], one would think that the term designating the original would be the best to apply to the parody. But Cervantes seldom uses it in the body of his text. He prefers to call his book an "*historià*," by which, as we shall see, he means, not a story, but a history. We know, of course, that he is fooling us: *Don Quixote* may be a romance, or a novel, or a story, but it is certainly not a history. We have to deal, then, with a story masquerading as history, with a work claiming to be historically true within its external framework of fiction. The study of *Don Quixote*, it seems to me, must begin with this paradox.

The problem of the spurious historicity of the work is usually stated in terms of the Aristotelian principles of the universality of poetry and the particularity of history. "The difference between the historian and the poet," says Aristotle, "is not the difference between writing in verse or prose; the work of Herodotus could be put into verse, and it would be just as much a history in verse as it is in prose. The difference is that the one tells what has happened, and the other the kind of things that would happen. It follows therefore that poetry is more philosophical and of higher value than history; for poetry unifies more, whereas history

*Reprinted with permission from *Modern Philology* 63 (1965):1–11.

agglomerates."[2] This approach to *Don Quixote* — adopted wholeheartedly in Américo Castro's *El pensamiento de Cervantes* (Madrid, 1925) and more cautiously in E. C. Riley's *Cervantes's Theory of the Novel* (Oxford, 1962) — would seem at first sight to be sound. El Pinciano, whom Cervantes had certainly read, expounded this doctrine in his *Filosofía antigua poética* (1596),[3] and Cervantes himself has his characters in *Don Quixote* discuss literature from this Aristotelian point of view.[4] In terms of sixteenth-century aesthetics it might be said that history is natural, since it narrates events as they occurred, each one emerging by the logic of nature from those which preceded it,[5] while a story is artistic — *"artificiosa"* — since in it events are made to happen in a peculiarly satisfactory way.[6] In *Don Quixote* Cervantes both manipulates the adventures to achieve an artistic end and allows each adventure to spring naturally from what has gone before. One is left with the conclusion that the work is at the same time poetry and history, that it is, to use Castro's critical imagery, a watershed from which the two slopes, the "poetic slope" and the "historical slope," may be contemplated.[7] The difficulty with the Aristotelian approach is that it does not explain so much the work as some of the theory behind the work.

My own approach derives not from such theoretical considerations but from the history of literature and the history of history. This historical method, old-fashioned as it is, may be made to shed light on the form and the thematic sense of Cervantes' masterpiece.

Cervantes, then, seldom refers to his book as anything but an "historia." Does he perhaps mean by this term what we call a story? The word could, even in the early years of the seventeenth century, be used to designate fiction. Don Quixote himself uses it in this sense on one occasion: ["you have told one of the most original fables, tales or histories that anyone in the world could have thought up"] (I, xx). Against this quotation, however, one could set hundreds in which the word means what historians mean by history. This is clearly the sense in which Cervantes normally uses the word. Cervantes (or his alter ego, the fictitious historian Cide Hamete Benengeli) describes this history with a variety of adjectives: ["simple," "grand," "curious," "strange," "pleasing," "delightful," "modern," "original," "invented"]. But the one used over and over again is "true." *Don Quixote* is a true history. We tend to discount these assertions as playful irony, or we disregard them altogether as a convention of the time, like the true plays that were no such thing.[8] But are we justified in ignoring even an ironic clue to the nature of the book? Some historical perspective will help us answer the question.

English, alone among the Indo-European languages, draws a clear (though not absolute) distinction between history, the narration of true events, and story, the narration of imagined events.[9] Both words have the same Greco-Latin etymon. Other tongues use a single word — *histoire, historia, storia, Geschichte* — to denote both kinds of narrations of events.

A bifurcation must have occurred in the semantic development of antique *historia*, permitting the word to embrace both the actual and the fictional. The linguistic bifurcation corresponded to a development, or rather to repeated developments, in literary history. In the second and third centuries A.D., for example, the *Erotici Graeci* wrote several imaginary histories: the most famous, Heliodorus' *Historia Aethiopica*, was, despite its apparently scholarly title, one of the most far-fetched pieces of fiction the world has known. It is important to realize that the Alexandrian romance, the only considerable body of prose fiction in antiquity, emerged not from epic poetry but from historiography. Although this step-child of history found favor, it was barely conscious of its debt to historical writing, and its false claims to be truthful irked intellectuals and scholars alike. Because the fictional history of the ancients abstained from irony, it never attained the dignity of the novel. Lucian found it necessary to parody this absurd type of romance in his ironically entitled *Vera historia*, just as in modern times Cervantes would parody ironically another kind of romance.[10] Lucian's *Vera historia* was, in some respects, the *Don Quixote* of its culture.

The same bifurcation of *historia* took place in the Romance territory of medieval and Renaissance Europe. At first the classical distinction between prose and poetry was scrupulously observed: poetry — whether epic, lyric, or dramatic — was for fiction; prose was used to expound unimaginative thought — on astrology, theology or gemmology — but, above all, it was used for historical narrative. The rise of the novel is explained in traditional scholarship as a prosification of the epic, with important generic mutations resulting from the shift from male hearer to female reader, from market place to boudoir, from public performance to intimate reading.[11] Strictly speaking, however, this explanation covers only the idealized fiction of the romance: stories of chivalry, of Troy, of Alexander the Great, and, much later, of shepherds — in short, stories of Never-Never-Land.[12] In the meantime, the folk were telling their tales, orally and in prose. And similar, though more didactic, tales were imported from the Orient and written down in Latin or in the vernacular for the benefit of sermon-writers and others in search of edifying moral illustrations. Medieval prose fiction — if we exclude the work of an innovator like Boccaccio — consisted of romances, folktales, and *exempla*. It is confusing to relate any of these kinds of writing to the modern novel. The novel has its roots in historiography.[13]

The earliest chroniclers could not entirely suppress their imagination. Historical *lacunae* were filled with original inventions or with prosified epics, which are by definition products of the imagination.[14] It is the tragedy of historiography that the historian can never operate on a purely factual or intellectual plane: he imagines motives; he imagines conversations; he imagines what his sources neglect to tell him. To a greater or lesser degree all history merely pretends to be history.[15] And now, in the later Renaissance, we have a new factor: some works of fiction, such as the *Lazarillo de Tormes* and *Don Quixote*, also pretend to be history.

Prose-writing contained thus a moral dilemma. Did an author have a right to tamper with what he believed to be true by injecting into it the fancies of his imagination? Did he, on the other hand, have a right to present the flights of his imagination as the truth? The imagination, the dimension of poetry, was the lying faculty of the mind. By the sixteenth century fiction, whether in poetry or prose, was unequivocally called lying; the ascetic critics of the Counter-Reformation, Garcilaso and Montemayor were morally reprehensible liars who planted the seeds of error in fertile young minds.[16] The poetic mode, since it was expressly designed for this pleasant lying, at least deceived no one. Prose, however, the vehicle for legal documents, for sermons, for history, was considered to have been abused by those who made it carry the falsehood of fiction. The dangers contained in fictional prose were greater. How was the reader of prose to know when the historian, or the story-teller, was telling a truth or a lie? A reader is more easily misled when the safeguards of convention have been removed. It follows that the moral responsibility of the prose-writer is greater than that of the poet. But there is an aesthetic consequence of this analysis that is of far greater significance to us today. The problems entailed in writing prose fiction are themselves admirable subjects for prose fiction. The prosaic mode supplies a ready-made allegory for the moral dilemma of man, who must live in a world where the boundaries between truth and falsehood are imprecise.

It was the great merit of the Spanish baroque that its writers of fiction, in both prose and verse, having understood the analogy between their professional dilemma and their readers' dilemma, exploited it to the full. This continuing discussion revolved around the words *engaño* ["deception"] and *desengaño* ["disillusion"], ["truth"] and ["falsehood"]. In the *letrillas* of Góngora, the plays of Calderón, and the *sueños* of Quevedo clear-cut answers are given to man's baffling predicament; he is handed a thread with which to make his way through the *confusión*, the *laberinto* of this world. It is as though these writers imposed their orderly artistic solution on an existential quandary. By its nature, however, history abstains from organizing and rationalizing the chaos and unreason of the world of men; it reflects faithfully the reigning confusion. Cervantes – a "historian" and a novelist – was inevitably less dogmatic than were contemporary artists, less sure of the line separating truth and error. *Don Quixote* does not disentangle the story from the history, but points its telescope at the ill-defined frontier itself. It presents the evidence for the uncertainty of truth and says to the reader: "You be the judge." ["You, reader, since you are prudent, judge according to how it seems to you"], says Cide Hamete Benengeli in a marginal note, after casting doubt on the authenticity of the Cave of Montesinos episode (II, xxiv). This awareness of the ill-defined frontier between history and story, between truth and lie, between reality and fiction is what constitutes Cervantes' *Don Quixote*, is what constitutes the novel as distinct from the romance. The novel is the most self-conscious, the most introverted of literary genres.[17] Unlike the Alexandrian romance, it is sensitive to its origins in historiography and aware of the need to handle its claim to historical accuracy with massive doses of irony.

Cervantes' expression of the novelistic self-consciousness is complex. Because his subject matter is fictional, he must have recourse to a variety of devices to persuade, and if possible to convince, his reader that Don Quixote actually lived and actually did those things he is reported to have done. We have already noticed the reiterated claims that the history is true. But there is more to it than this. The realism of the inns and road of La Mancha,[18] the perfect credibility of characters like Maritornes or Don Diego de Miranda, the guaranteed historicity of the bandit Roque Guinart—such details as these captivate the reader's will to disbelieve. The references to the Annals of La Mancha and to its Archives, to the manuscript found in Toledo, to the lead box full of verses discovered during the razing of a hermitage, the intrusions of the historian Cide Hamete and of his translator amount to the creation of a vast historical apparatus which gives to each and every chapter the illusion of being historically verifiable. The questions raised by the translator about the possibly apocryphal nature of Sancho's conversation with his wife or of Don Quixote's descent into the cave only serve to impart a sense of historical accuracy to all the rest of the narrative. Finally, thanks to the providential intervention of Avellaneda, the historical truth of Cervantes' Don Quixote is vindicated against the false claims of the fictional Don Quixote who appears in Avellaneda's spurious Second Part.[19] The "real," the "historical" Don Quixote is made, as it were, to stand up and identify himself.[20] The reader of *Don Quixote* does not really want to believe that the story is history; the author must therefore wear down his critical resistance.

What has Cervantes accomplished in making his story pass for history? The easy, or neo-Aristotelian, answer is that he has achieved verisimilitude.[21] But he has done much more than this: he has obliterated the dividing-line between the actual and the potential, the real and the imaginary, the historical and the fictional, the true and the false. To the extent that he has been successful, he has eliminated the critical scrutiny of evidence. He has written a novel, the first novel, a novel about the problem involved in writing a novel.

In just such a destruction of the critical faculty, in just such a failure to discriminate between history and story, lies the cause of Don Quixote's madness. It is not so much the reading of too many books of chivalry that drives him mad; it is the misreading, the misinterpretation of them that causes his insanity.[22] Juan de Valdés, Saint Theresa, Saint Ignatius of Loyola remained perfectly sane after devouring all the chivalrous romances they could lay their hands on.[23] Don Quixote went mad because he could not differentiate between events that actually had happened to living people and events that had happened in the imagination of some author to people who were equally figments of his imagination. Don Quixote thought that, although the Cid Ruy Díaz was a very good knight, he could not hold a candle to Amadís, the Knight of the Burning Sword.[24] He confused the factual dimension with the imaginary dimension, history with story.

Cervantes, in seeking to undermine the reader's critical faculty, is carrying a mimesis to its logical end; he is trying to make his reader participate in his hero's madness. Quite apart from the moral impropriety of trying to make a fellow human being lose his wits, one might wonder whether this objective was feasible. It surely was, to a degree. Anyone who has conducted a seminar on *Don Quixote* knows that intelligent students turn a little mad when they discuss this book. This mild form of insanity, one is tempted to think, is a part of the human condition. Certainly nearly all the characters in *Don Quixote*—excepting only the Caballero del Verde Gabán, the Duke's chaplain, and a very few others—are tainted with this form of *dementia*, which consists in the inability to distinguish the fictional from the real.[25] And we have all asked ourselves at one time or another: "Did such-and-such a thing really happen or did I only imagine it?" This kind of madness is particularly prevalent among the literate.[26] Historical truth is by no means as certain as we would like it to be. Did our modern knight-errant, Lawrence of Arabia, perform the heroic deeds with which history credits him, or are his detractors right in seeing him as an imposter? Is Jean-Jacques Rousseau or literary history more to be believed in the question whether he put his children into a foundling home? The literate man reads both history and story. Historians make their histories read like novels, and novelists make their novels read like histories. Writers—scholars and artists alike—conspire to loosen man's grip on reality, to conduct him to the fringe of madness. The intellectual, the reader of books, is bound to ask himself repeatedly: "What is reality?" or even "What is truth?" Jesting Pilate may have been more in earnest than we realize.

The illiterate man has the same problem but feels it less intensely. He too has moments when he does not know if "he dreamed it all" or if "it really happened." But, since for him the experience is not corroborated by the testimony of a thousand books, he takes this human weakness more for granted. Accordingly, he is more certain of his grasp on reality. The illiterate Sancho Panza, in Part I, does not doubt that Don Quixote's armies are sheep and his giants, windmills. But with something remote from his experience, the fulling-mills pounding away in the dark, he is face to face with the noumenal; he feels the awesome fear of the unknown which the intellectual derives from his books. In Part II, after having consorted intimately with the literate Don Quixote, some of the intellectual's anxieties about truth have rubbed off on him. Though, by misrepresenting an ugly peasant girl as the mistress of his master's thoughts, he has personally enchanted Dulcinea, he will be convinced by the Duchess' words and his self-flagellation that the randomly chosen wench is indeed Dulcinea. He knows the truth and yet doubts that he does.[27] Within Cervantes' fictional world he cannot distinguish between history and story, between the reality of a country girl seen with his own eyes and the lie he has told about her. The text assures us that in Part II Sancho becomes as mad as his master. His madness, it should be observed, has the same cause and is of the same kind.

Cervantes' preoccupation with the problems of historical truth and its cognition was induced, I believe, by the crisis being undergone by the historian's art. If medieval chroniclers had innocently — perhaps unwittingly — blended fiction into their narrations of events, since the fifteenth century historians had been busily engaged in the deliberate falsification of history. Pedro de Corral, in the *Crónica sarracina*, which he wrote about 1430, was so inventive that his contemporary Fernán Pérez de Guzmán said that rather than a chronicle ["it could better be called a falsehood or an open lie"].[28] Modern critics, more charitably but less accurately, call the work the first Spanish historical novel.[29] The important fact is that it pretended to be history and was accepted as such by later historians. The work was printed in 1499 and ran through a large number of editions down to Cervantes' day. Pedro de Corral started a vogue for what has been called ["the novel and invented history"].[30]

This vogue drove scholars crazy. Humanistic historians like Jerónimo de Zurita (1512–80) and Ambrosio de Morales (1513–91) made a valiant attempt to sift the truth from the lie. By studying their sources carefully, doing research in archives, adducing new kinds of evidence like medals, inscriptions, and monuments, they restored to history some of its lost dignity. They paved the way for the greatest and most reliable of Golden Age historians, Father Juan de Mariana. But these conscientious efforts to ascertain the truth of history scarcely stemmed the tide of false historiography: they may even have planted new ideas in the minds of the counterfeiters.

The discovery in the Sacro Monte of Granada, between 1588 and 1595, of the so-called "*Libros plúmbeos*," or "Leaden Books," revealed the most monstrous attempt to rewrite history before the compilation of the *Soviet Encyclopaedia*. In Ticknor's words, these metallic plates

> when deciphered, seemed to offer materials for defending the favorite doctrine of the Spanish Church on the Immaculate Conception, and for establishing the great corner-stone of Spanish ecclesiastical history, the coming to Spain of the Apostle James, the patron saint of the country. This gross forgery was received for authentic history by Phillip II., Phillip III., and Phillip IV., each of whom, in a council of state . . . , solemnly adjudged it to be such; so that, at one period of the discussions,

some persons believed the "Leaden Books" would be admitted into the Canon of the Scriptures.[31]

Another great imposture was what cultural history knows as the *falsos cronicones*, a series of fragments of chronicles circulated from 1594 in manuscript and printed in 1610.[32] They purported to have been written by Flavius Lucius Dexter, Marcus Maximus, Heleca, and other primitive Christians and contained important and wholly new statements concerning the early civil and ecclesiastical history of Spain. Flattering fictions were fitted to recognized facts, as if both rested on the same authority; new saints were given to churches inadequately provided for in this department of hagiology; a dignified origin was traced for noble families that had before been unable to boast of their founders; and a multitude of Christian conquests and achievements were hinted at or recorded which gratified the pride of the whole nation the more because they had never till then been heard of.[33]

Belief in these forgeries was very persistent. As late as the eighteenth century some overcredulous writers were still citing the *Libros plúmbeos* and the *falsos cronicones* as authorities for alleged historical facts. The Roman church—around the middle of the seventeenth century—had indeed declared that the Leaden Books were counterfeits, and an obedient Spain had for the most part reluctantly given up accepting the story they told as history. The false chronicles were harder to dispose of. A lively controversy over their authenticity raged for the better part of a century. Their author, the Jesuit Father Higuera of Toledo, himself had the audacity to express his doubts concerning their veracity. As early as 1595 Juan Bautista Pérez, the Bishop of Segorbe, exposed the whole fraud. In spite of this, as late as 1667–75 Gregorio de Argáiz, "a man of much worthless learning,"[34] published six large folio volumes in defence of the *falsos cronicones*. The *coup de grâce* had really been given them, nevertheless, in 1652, when the great bibliographer Nicolás Antonio began his *Historias fabulosas* a book which, although never finished, left no doubt as to the extent and nature of Father Higuera's fraud.

If scholars were baffled by the reams of imaginary history pouring from Spanish presses, what was the layman to think? If he was naive, like the innkeeper in *Don Quixote*, he believed in the historical accuracy of the forgeries on the grounds that they had been printed by royal license. If he was skeptical, like Cervantes, he reserved judgment and pondered on the difficulty of sorting out historical fact from fictional fraud. And if, again like Cervantes, he had a free, inquiring mind—what Cervantes called *"curiosidad"*—he reflected on the human dilemma posed by the uncertain frontier separating story and history.

I like to think that some of the inspiration for *Don Quixote* may have come from yet another example of spurious history: Miguel de Luna's *True History of King Rodrigo, Composed by Albucácim Tarif.*[35] Part I of this "true history" appeared in Granada in 1592 and Part II in 1600, ["three years before and five after the false discovery of the leaden books which filled the Sacred Mount of that city with fantasy martyrs"], comments Menéndez Pidal significantly.[36] Miguel de Luna, the official Arabic interpreter to Phillip II, had the gall to dedicate to his sovereign this egregious example of intellectual dishonesty. He claimed to be merely the translator of a work written in the eighth century by Albucácim Tarif, a Moor alleged to have had access to King Roderick's archives and to letters written by Florinda and Don Pelayo. To give his work an air of authenticity Luna entered into the margins the alleged Arabic original of words he had supposedly found difficult to translate.[37] Given the fraudulent nature of his undertaking, he comes perilously close to blasphemy when in his preface he has Albucácim invoke God's help: ["one God the creator and maker of all things created in this world . . . , to whom I humbly plead that he give me help so that *without any kind of imagining* I can tell *with clear and open truth* the story of the events of the war of Spain"].[38] God is called upon to bear witness to the truth of this fake history. The new light Luna (or Albucácim) shed on the Arabic conquest of Spain served to illuminate countless histories written later by well-meaning but unwary historians.[39] I cannot, of course, prove that Cervantes saw in Albucácim the progenitor of Cide Hamete Benengeli, but the point is that, at the time he was composing *Don Quixote*, such liberties were being taken with history. Cervantes does with pleasant irony what Luna does with the deadly seriousness of a forger.[40] A whole generation had lost its respect for historical truth.

Along with this fictionalizing and falsifying of history went a fundamental change in the role of the historian. In genuine histories the author retreats modestly behind his narrative, appearing, if at all, only in the prologue, where he customarily reviews his qualifications to write the book. Fiction, even the pre-novelesque romance, is more self-conscious than history; the author cannot conceal himself. In a romance of chivalry, like the *Amadís de Gaula*, the old jongleuresque parenthetical address to the listeners still shines through the chinks in the narration: ["as you have heard," "the dwarf whom you heard," "which would be long to relate"]. In the sentimental romance, *La cárcel de Amor*, El Autor plays an important part in the story.[41] In *La lozana andaluza* the author appears in a series of self-portraits as the painter, the transcriber of observed reality.[42] With the *Lazarillo de Tormes*, a feigned autobiography, the fictional author has become the actual subject of the history, even though the real author conceals himself behind a veil of anonymity. In the pastoral romance the author hides behind his narrative, but the narrative and the characters that people it reflect his own personal experiences and problems. Cervantes, who in *Don Quixote* is writing the first novel, must complicate enormously the role played by the author. He intervenes in the events to tell the reader what to believe, to steer him away from total madness with the phrase ["and that is the truth"].[43] He invents a pseudo-historian whose credibility is alternately impugned and defended. And this pseudo-historian plays a part in the novel second only to those of the protagonists, Don Quixote and Sancho. This novel, then, is a fake history in which the historian assumes even greater importance than the author in a romance. The novel, emerging from false history, turns out to be far more self-conscious than the old-fashioned romance.

The most puzzling question is why Cervantes, in unknowingly inventing the novel, hit upon this dubious subject matter of the *falso cronicón*. One answer is that he was a satirist. If the overt target of his satire is the romances of chivalry, it can hardly be the principal one. His chief butt was man's gullibility — gullibility about alleged historical facts. But, as we have seen, he chose to satirize human credulity in a dangerous way: by encouraging, by seeking to some extent to cultivate, in his reader the very defect he was ridiculing. Why did he tread such dangerous ground? He did so, I believe, because he was — in older aesthetic terms — imitating the human dilemma. Today we would say that he was re-creating the human dilemma, casting it into artistic form. Man, notwithstanding the catechism, does not in his heart believe truth to be categorical; he resists the dualistic tendencies of ecclesiastical orthodoxy. He does not choose between good and evil, as the moralists say, but between greater and lesser goods and between greater and lesser evils. Similarly, he does not choose between truth and falsehood, but between higher and lower truths and between white and black lies. This is how Cervantes viewed man's situation. Everything in the human condition is for him a matter of nuance. We have seen how, in this respect, he differs fundamentally from the dogmatic writers of the baroque: Calderón, Quevedo,[44] Gracián. *Don Quixote* is, among other things, a tremendous protest against the moralistic assurance of Counter-Reformation Spain. It is in these terms that I would rephrase Américo Castro's brilliant insight associated with the term Cervantine hypocrisy.[45] Despite the furor[46] aroused by this unfortunately formulated catch phrase, there was some truth in it. "Ironic protest against dogmatic oversimplification" might be a better way to put it. Irony is the form Cervantes' protest against Tridentine dogmatism had to take; it was wholly appropriate to his serious sense of the complexity of the moral world which was being masked. Play with historical truth, like all play, has a serious basis.

Cervantes took such a risk — the risk of disseminating a madness he deplored — because in this common madness was the evidence for a truth about man's world which the Counter-Reformation was suppressing. The truth, far from being simple, is complex and ultimately unascertainable in all its complexity. One cannot apprehend the whole truth; one can only get glimpses of partial truth. This is the great lesson of historiography, if not of history itself. Hence Cervantes' book is, as we say, "open." The [madman] is also [sane]. Who can say when Don Quixote's lucid intervals begin and end?[47] Should we sympathize with a village priest whose good intentions, love of his friend and desire for his cure are negated by his fondness for play-acting? Should we condemn a Puritanical chaplain whose dour mien and inhuman severity make him one of the most unpleasant characters in the book, when he alone, of all the members of the Duke's household, protests against the baiting of a madman for the entertainment of the idle rich? These characters — all of Cervantes' characters — are compounds of antithetical qualities. This is the human reality he was seeking to convey. And the work itself — a fusion of chivalric, sentimental, pastoral, picaresque fiction, of short stories and poems — reflects this many-sided makeup of man. Hybridization is the artistic means chosen to present Cervantes' sense of the complexity of truth.

X *Don Quixote*, a compendium of all previous literary genres, implies the further elimination of ill-defined frontiers, just as it blurs the boundary between history and story. This is the primary intuition on which Cervantes constructs his novel. To understand this intuition is to see the answer to the most baffling question one can ask about the work: why is it that across the ages no two people have been able to agree on the meaning of *Don Quixote?* X

Notes

*This paper was originally presented orally in an abbreviated form, before the Romance Section of the MLA convention in New York on December 28, 1964.

1. The word meant "vernacular" or "ballad." [Modern Philology, August, 1965]

2. Aristotle, *On the Art of Fiction*, trans. L. J. Potts (Cambridge, 1953) p. 29.

3. López Pinciano, *Fiilosophía antigua poética*, ed. Alfredo Carballo Picazo (3 vols., Madrid, 1953), I, 203–4, 206, 265–68; III, 165–67.

4. Especially in chaps. lxvii and lxviii of Part I. But for some reservations about the genuineness of Cervantes' Aristotelianism in these chapters see my "Cervantes' Theory of the Drama," *MP*, LII (1955), 217–21.

5. Raymond S. Willis, Jr., in his admirable structural study *The Phantom Chapters of the "Quixote"* (New York, 1953), pp. 98–100, argues that the phrase "history says" which serves to restore fluidity to apparent dislocations of the narrative, relates to a Platonic idea of Don Quixote's history, which is mythical, perfect, and whole.

6. See my "The Pertinence of *El curioso impertinente*," *PMLA*, LXXII (1957), 587–600.

7. *El pensamiento de Cervantes*, p. 30. Aubrey G. F. Bell, in his *Cervantes* (Norman, Oklahoma, 1947), p. 88, writes, "*Don Quixote* is both true and imaginary; it is a *historia verdadera* and it is a *historia imaginada* (I, 22). Cervantes bends his whole genius to reconcile the two worlds."

8. Some authors, of course, saw nothing transcendental, nothing more than an amusing convention, in fiction's claim to historical truth. The fictional hero of the *Estebanillo González* advises his reader that his autobiography "is not the *false* one of Guzmán de Alfarache, nor the *fantastic* one of Lazarillo de Tormes, nor the *supposed* one of the Knight of La Tenaza, but the *true* story" (*BAE*, XXXIII, 286; italics mine).

9. The distinction is clear enough for all practical purposes, but it should not be

forgotten that we tend to blur it at times. A child's book may be called *The Story of Ancient Rome* (for *The History*); H. G. Wells could write the (fictional) *History of Mr. Polly*.

10. It is interesting to note that for El Pinciano the romances of chivalry are modern Milesian tales: ["fictions which lack imitation and verisimilitude are not fables but foolishness, like some of those that they used to call Milesian, now called books of chivalry, which contain events beyond any good imitation and semblance of truth"] (edition cited, II, 8).

11. See, e.g., Karl Vossler, "La novela en los pueblos románicos, "in his *Formas literarias en los pueblos románicos* (Austral), pp. 91–106.

12. I observe in this paper the distinction between romance and novel habitually drawn in the eighteenth century and redefined for ours by Northrop Frye in his *Anatomy of Criticism* (Princeton, 1957), pp. 304–7.

13. Frye sees the connection between the novel and history, but he thinks of the novel as a romance *moving toward* historiographical form: "The novel tends rather to expand into a fictional approach to history. The soundness of Fielding's instinct in calling *Tom Jones* a history is confirmed by the general rule that the larger the scheme of a novel becomes, the more obviously its historical nature appears" (op. cit., p. 307). Philip Stevick ("Fielding and the Meaning of History," *PMLA*, LXXIX [1964], 561–68) is not concerned with the novel as history; he is interested in the intellectual history which shaped Fielding's understanding of the historical process.

14. Cf. Pero Mexía, *Historia del Emperador Carlos V*, ed. J. de Mata Cariazo (Madrid, 1945), p. 7: ["The old historians who wrote the lives and histories of the great princes and kings all tried and worked to give lineages and origins which would be high and illustrious, sometimes faking them when they were not content with what they knew, and using for this effect poetic fables, making both the birth and the upbringing of some of them very strange and mysterious"]. It is often asserted, following Menéndez Pidal, that the Spanish epic is historically exact. Too often this assertion leads scholars to ignore its essential poetry, its dependence on the human imagination. It was left to Pedro Salinas ("La vuelta al esposo," in his *Ensayos de literatura hispánica* [Madrid, 1958], pp. 45–57) and to Leo Spitzer ("Sobre el carácter histórico del *Cantar de Myo Cid*," in his *Romanische Literaturstudien* [Tubingen, 1959], pp. 647–63) to rectify the erroneous conclusions drawn from Menéndez Pidal's well-known theory.

15. My colleague Richard L. Predmore (*El mundo del "Quixote"* [Madrid, 1958], p. 21) makes the excellent point that Cervantes insists on "the contrast . . . between life and any effort to register it with exactitude."

16. Cf. Pedro Malón de Chaide, prologue to *The Conversion of the Magdalene*: ["What are the books of love, the *Dianas* and Boscanes and Garcialasos, the songs of fabulous lies and stories of the likes of *Amadís*, *Florisel* and *Don Belianis*, and the fleet of similar portents such as one finds written, but a knife in the hands of a madman when they are given to the young?"] (*BAE*, XXVII, 279).

17. Excellent illustrations of the novel's self-awareness may be found in detective stories, which must repeat *ad nauseam* traditional formulas. For example, in Agatha Christie's *The Body in the Library*, Colonel Bantry, having been told of the crime committed in his house, assumes that his wife has imagined it as a result of her addiction to detective fiction, "*Bodies*," he says, "are always being found in libraries in books. I've never known a case in real life." In the same work a nine-year-old boy asks Superintendent Harper: "Do you like detective stories? I do. I read them all, and I've got autographs from Dorothy Sayers and Agatha Christie and Dickson Carr and H. C. Bailey." The mention of the author's name is, in this degenerate form of the novel, the equivalent of the appearance of "a certain Saavedra" in *Don Quixote*!

18. The roads are in fact evoked rather than described, as Flaubert pointed out: ["How one sees those Spanish highways which are never described!"]

19. Avellaneda's *Don Quixote* also purports to have been written by a pseudo-historian,

Alisolán, ["a historian no less modern than honest"]. But Avallaneda, unlike Cervantes, falls into the most crass relativism in his attitude to the truth of fictional history: ["In some ways this is different from his [Cervantes'] first part, since my inclinations are also the opposite of his. *In matters of opinion regarding history,* his is as authentic as this one, and *every person can choose what seems best to him*"] (prologue; italics mine.)

20. Cervantes' problem is the reverse of that of the historical novelist. The reader of a historical novel believes in the historical foundation of the plot, and accepts uncritically the unhistorical accretions.

21. It is interesting to compare the Aristotelian Canon of Toledo's defence of *verisimilitude* — ["The lie is better to the degree that it seems true"]; ["verisimilitude and . . . the limitation in which the perfection of what is written consists"] (I, xlvii) — with the "historian" Cide Hamete's passionate espousal of *truth*; ["he wrote them [the madnesses of Don Quixote] in the same way that he [Don Quixote] did them, without adding or subtracting from the story one atom of truth, and without accepting any objections they might impose on him for being a liar"] (II, x). A different view of the relation of history to truth and verisimilitude appears in the *Elogio,* written by Alonso de Barros, of Mateo Alemán's *Guzmán de Alfarache.* There it is said that Alemán had, by his success in cultivating verisimilitude, earned the title of historian: ["for his admirable order and observance of the verisimilar in the story the author has happily acquired the name and office of historian"] (*BAE,* III, 187).

22. This explanation of Don Quixote's madness may seem to contradict Cervantes' statement that "because of his little sleeping and much reading his brain dried up and he lost his wits" (I, 1). In fact, it is wholly consistent with both implications of the statement: (1) that the hidalgo read too much and (2) that he was physiologically prone to insanity. Other statements in the first chapter — and in the rest of the novel — add to this basic information the fact that he confused history with story.

23. Américo Castro produces evidence of the imitation of books by Saints Theresa and Ignatius ("La palabra escrita y el *Quixote*" in *Semblanzas y estudios españoles* [Princeton, 1956], pp. 259–60. But apart from the fact that the latter ["lived in his youth very much in accord with the spirit of the chivalric books"], they imitated books of devotion, not of fiction. Ignatius, in his youth, adopted the noble ideals of the fictional knights; he did not try to perform noble deeds.

24. I, i. Another beautiful example of Don Quixote's confusing of fiction and history is given in his own confused words after he has slashed Maese Pedro's puppets: ["it seemed to me that everything that happened here happened just as it did: that Melisendra was Melisendra; Don Gayferos, Don Gayferos; Marsilio, Marsilio, and Charlemagne, Charlemagne"] (II, XXVI). In each case the first mention of a name refers to the fictional character, and the second, to the historical character.

25. Almost all the literate characters (and semiliterate ones like the innkeeper) are avid readers of books of chivalry. There are many shades in their acceptance of the fictional as real. The village priest tells the innkeeper that Don Felixmarte and Don Cirongilio are imaginary: ["it is all confection and invention of the idle minds who made them up for the sake, as you say, of passing away the time"] (I, xxxii). For his part, the innkeeper is sure they are historical. The Canon of Toledo sometimes lets his guard down: ["for my part I say that when I read them, so long as I don't remind myself that they are all lies and frivolity, they give me some pleasure"] (I, xlix).

26. Leo Spitzer, while not concerned with history as such, stressed the importance of the book as the major issue discussed in *Don Quixote:* "a theme which informs the whole novel is the problem of the reality of literature" ("Perspectivism in the *Don Quixote,*" in his *Linguistics and Literary History* [Princeton, 1948], p. 51). See also his lecture "On the Significance of *Don Quixote,*" MLN, LXXVII (1962), 113–29.

27. The parallel experience for Don Quixote is the vision of the Cave of Montesinos: he *thinks he knows* what he saw, and yet *doubts* that he does (as a result of Sancho's skepticism, Maese Pedro's monkey's equivocal oracies, etc.). This statement of the nature of truth and its cognition differs somewhat from previously enunciated theories; prismatic truth, objective truth, perspectivism. Truth is presented paradoxically or ambiguously in *Don Quixote*: one has it and at the same time does not have it. The root of the problem is historical truth, which mankind both possesses and does not possess. This paradoxical view of truth harmonizes, I believe, with the thesis so persuasively sustained by Manuel Durán in *La ambigüedad en el "Quijote"* (Xalapa, 1960).

28. *Generaciones y semblanzas*, in *BAE*, LXVIII, 697.

29. Cf. Marcelino Menédez Pelayo, *Orígenes de la novela* (Buenos Aires, 1943), III, 171, and Ramón Mendéndez Pidal, *Floresta de leyendas heroicas españolas* (Clásicos Castellanos), I, lxxxix.

30. Alonso Zamora Vicente, in *Diccionario de literatura española* (Madrid, 1953), p. 764.

31. George Ticknor, *History of Spanish Literature* (4th ed., Boston, 1879), p. 215, n. 15.

32. See J. Godoy Alcántara, *Historia crítica de los falsos cronicones* (Madrid, 1868).

33. See Ludwig Pfandl, *Historia de la literatura nacional española en la edad de oro* (Barcelona, 1952), pp. 590–92.

34. Ticknor, *loc. cit.*

35. The full title of the "seventh edition" (Madrid, [1676]), which I consulted in the library of Duke University, follows: [*True / History / of King Rodrigo, / in Which is Considered / the Principal Reason for the Loss of Spain and the Conquest / Which Was Made of it by Miramamolen Almanzor, / Who was King of Africa and the Arab World; / And the Life of King Jacob Almanzor / Written by the Wise Alcayde Albucácim Tarif, / of the Arab Nation. / Newly Translated from the Arabic Language by Miguel de Luna, Near / Granada, Translator of the King our Lord*]. Menéndez Pelayo (*op, cit.* III, 185, n. 2) says: "There are at least nine editions of this book, which is still commonly found in Spain. Almost all the catalogues of rare books begin with it."

36. *Op. cit.*, II, xliii.

37. E.g., ["The Arab calls the royal ceptre harimalmulq"] (edition cited, p. 4). The marginalia also give careful consideration to dates, which are liberally translated from the hegira to the Gothic "it was Cesar's" and to the Christian *Anno Domini*. Some marginal comments sound like the translator's comments on Cide Hamete's "history"; apropos of a letter supposedly written by Queen Anagilda to King Roderick Luna writes: ["This letter was translated by Abentarique, from Spanish into Arabic, and now it has been translated again, back into Spanish from Arabic, and it was found in the chambers of the King Don Rodrigo in the city of Córdoba"] (p. 8).

38. Pp. 1–2. Italics mine.

39. Cf. Menéndez Pelayo, *op, cit.*, III, 186: "it achieved such scandalous notoriety, many taking it for true history, and others using it as a source of poetry."

40. Cf. R. Menéndez Pidal, *op. cit.*, II, xliv: ["The only concern of Miguel de Luna seems to be to publish a stupendous discovery which will validate him in his role as learned Arabist. Thus he insists on disfiguring or contradicting the most accepted historical traditions, so as to give his story endless novelty. Every forger has a little that is disturbing, but Luna has a lot; his inventions confuse and dizzy the reader, like those of a madman, since they unbalance and contradict for no reason everything that we are accustomed by tradition to take as well known"].

41. See my "Allegory and the Role of El Autor in the *Cárcel de Amor*," *PQ*, XXXI

(1952), 39–44.

42. See my "La novela como retrato: el arte de Francisco Delicado," *NRFH*, VII (1953), 475–88.

43. Cf. Richard L. Predmore, "El problema de la realidad en el *Quijote*," *NRFH*, VII (1953), 489–98.

44. Evidence that the monolithic facade of conformity could on a rare occasion be pierced by an existential anguish was brilliantly adduced for the dogmatic Quevedo by Carlos Blanco Aguinaga, in "Dos sonetos del siglo XVII: Amor-locura en Quevedo y sor Juana," *MLN*, LXXVII (1962) 145–62.

45. In *El pensamiento de Cervantes* Castro made the statement (which he later recanted) that "Cervantes is a skillful hypocrite" (p. 244). A less forceful phrase on p. 240 expresses the same idea more subtly and in more acceptable terms: "Cervantes was a great disimulator, who covered over with irony and skill opinions and ideas contrary to those usually accepted."

46. Summarized by Otis H. Green, "A Critical Survey of Scholarship in the Field of Spanish Renaissance Literature, 1914–1944," *SP* XLIV (1947), 254, n. 120.

47. Don Diego de Miranda's poet son uses this phrase: "he is a man of mad moments, spaced with intervals of lucidity" (II, xviii).

The Narrator in *Don Quijote*: Maese Pedro's Puppet Show

George Haley[*]

In the chivalric romances, Cervantes found a subject ripe for parody and, with it, a way of telling stories that called for the same treatment.[1] He made them both serve the ends of comic enjoyment and instruction in *Don Quijote*. But in the course of poking fun at the narrative technique of the chivalric novelists, Cervantes used and enlarged it with such skill that, in his hands, the overworked devices became expressive instruments once more. Through his ingenious manipulation of one of the chivalric novelist's favorite devices, the fictitious author, Cervantes was able to set before the reader a novel viewed in the round and depicted in the process of becoming: the dynamic interplay of a story, its dramatized tellers and its dramatized readers. It is this aspect of *Don Quijote* that I should like to consider.

Alongside the supposed history of Don Quijote's adventures, Cervantes' novel presents a supplementary story with a different set of characters and something of a development of its own. This is the story of how Don Quijote's adventures came to be known and set down, a record of the written stages through which it is claimed they have passed on their way to Cervantes' book. It traces the way in which a fragment becomes a complete story, a process that most novelists follow, if at all, in separate notebooks or diaries. But in *Don Quijote*, this process brought to light has

*Reprinted with permission from *MLN* 80 (1965):145–65.

become an integral part of the finished novel. As it unfolds in the margin of Don Quijote's adventures, this secondary tale develops its own entanglements and moments of suspense that have little to do with Don Quijote's insane understanding but everything to do with whether the account of it will be completed and become a book.

The characters in this corollary tale are all involved in the mechanics of telling and transmitting Don Quijote's story. Their adventures, not as violent as Don Quijote's but no less exciting for that, are the search for source materials in Manchegan archives, the creation of a continuous narrative from fragmentary and sometimes overlapping sources, the translation of the continuous narrative from Arabic to Castilian, the recasting of the translation and the publication of the revision, with intrusive commentary at every stage.

There is, first, the unidentified "I" who begins the narrative and introduces Don Quijote, only to confess at the end of the eighth chapter that he must surrender his office and leave Don Quijote with his sword poised in the air because his sources have given out. He is followed by a "segundo autor" who takes over the "I" and the narrative with a description of his experience as a frustrated reader of the first eight chapters who was left impatient to know how the story ends. He did not wait long, he tells us, for chance led him to the original Arabic manuscript of Don Quijote's story in the market at Toledo. But the discovery creates a new problem and another moment of suspense: how to read the manuscript? This difficulty is also soon resolved after he calls in a Morisco to render the text into Castilian. Don Quijote's adventures can now proceed.

At the point where the second author concludes this autobiographical detective story and returns to Don Quijote with his sword still poised in the air, what he offers the reader is his rendition of the Morisco translator's version of the Arabic original. It is here that the author of the original manuscript appears: Cide Hamete Benengeli, Moor and chronicler in the first instance of Don Quijote's high deeds. Cide Hamete is a contradictory figure, as E. C. Riley has clearly shown. He is part wizard because of his omniscience, which does not keep him from using documentary sources; part historian because of his devotion to the truth as he sees it, though he is a Moor and therefore a liar by definition, according to the Christian second author; and he is part poet because of his expressed concern with artistic selection, invention and adornment.

With the appearance of the Moorish chronicler, the focus shifts from the hunt for sources to the labor of composition, and the story of the narration of *Don Quijote* becomes essentially the story of Cide Hamete's telling, with numerous overt reminders of the refracting presence of the other intermediaries. It may be pieced together from Cide Hamete's comments to the reader: his evaluation of Don Quijote's behavior, his professional confidences concerning the task of narration with its pitfalls and satisfactions, his personal revelations.

As the novel progresses, Cide Hamete's narrative task turns into a mission as militant as the knightly career of his hero. Before the novel is done, an adversary befitting a man of letters will take up the challenge issued in Ariosto's words at the end of Part One: "Forse altri canterà con miglior plettro." This adversary was Avellaneda, who published a spurious continuation of *Don Quijote* while Cervantes was still at work on his own Second Part. Cide Hamete duly takes notice of this effrontery in the novel, brandishes his pen and engages the challenger in a duel of words.

Cide Hamete's story comes to an end when, after describing Don Quijote's death, he turns his attention away from both his subject and his reader, who have shared it until then, to bid farewell to his pen. In putting aside his writer's instrument, which has also served as a weapon, he provides an appropriate sequel to the hero's surrender of the sword as arms and letters meet for the last time in the work. The parody of this ritual act is a suitable valediction to the story of Don Quijote, in which has been told the story of how it came to be written. But while Don Quijote's mission has given way to defeat and disillusionment, the chronicler's toil ends in triumph, the distinctly literary triumph of a narrative brought successfully to completion.

One intermediary remains. This is the agent overlooked by those who like to equate the second author with Cervantes. He is the shadowy figure who materializes at the end of Chapter viii to join the first author's fragment to the second author's contribution and appears again in the final chapter of Part One to supply the concluding remarks. He is the intermediary furthest removed from Don Quijote's adventures and at the same time closest both to the book and to the reader. It is this intermediary, in fact, who formulates the relationship between the implied author and the ideal reader when he transmits the second author's request that the reader give the story ["the same credit as intelligent men usually give to those books of chivalry which are so highly valued in the world"] (I, lii).

The virtuoso display of this palimpsest reveals Cervantes' interest in experimenting with the techniques of telling in ways that only an artist sure of his power would dare. Consummate rhetorician that he is, Cervantes demonstrates a complementary concern with the effect of a story upon its readers, which leads him to dramatize the act of reading as well. Each of the intermediaries who work at telling and transmitting Don Quijote's story functions, at the same time, as a critical reader of a previous version of that story. In all of these cases, narration is conceived of as much in terms of the writer's preparation, reading critically and selecting, as in terms of telling. Yet none of the intermediaries forgets the reader who follows him in the series. Cide Hamete, in the first instance, addresses himself to a hypothetical reader. The translator is that reader made explicit within the novel, and he in turn directs his translation and comments to his reader, the second author who hired him to execute the translation. The second author is a fusion of both Cide Hamete's hypothetical reader and the translator's actual reader, and he likewise addresses himself to a hypothetical reader in his adaptation. Through the good offices of the last intermediary, the second author's hypothetical reader becomes the hypothetical reader of Cervantes' book, who would seem to subsume all of the others except for one difficulty. All of the intermediaries foreshadow coming events. They have read the story before they begin to recount it. They are second-time readers. The reader postulated by Cervantes' book, on the other hand, is a first-time reader for whom the effects that depend upon progressive inference are expressly designed, as we shall soon see.

Within the story of Don Quijote's adventures, the interplay of story, teller and reader is repeated on a smaller scale and in a different mode with countless variations. I should now like to examine one such variation which provides perhaps the most vivid illustration of this interplay in action, for in it, teller and story and listener are all literally dramatized. This is the episode of Maese Pedro's puppet show, for which folk tradition supplied the original legend and determined the basic features of its treatment as a puppet play. Cervantes had already transformed this popular art form into an examination of illusionism in the *Entremés del retablo de las maravillas*. In Maese Pedro's puppet show, Cervantes probes the same aesthetic problem more deeply from another angle of vision.

Maese Pedro arrives at the inn with his "talking" ape and puppet show just as the lance-carrier concludes his story of the two aldermen who search the woods for a lost donkey. The aldermen bray antiphonally with such skill that they confuse each other's imitation with the real thing and repeatedly mistake one another, not without reason, for the donkey. The stranger's unusual narrative will later have a sequel in which Don Quijote and Sancho Panza participate. But for the moment, it serves the more immediate purpose of preparing the company gathered at the inn for Maese Pedro's equally unusual display. After hearing the lance-carrier tell of the marvels of the braying aldermen, Don Quijote and the rest of the "senate and audience" shift effortlessly to the first part of Maese Pedro's show, which offers a reverse parallel in the form of a talking ape.

The story of the donkey-like aldermen and the demonstration of the man-like ape together constitute a carefully graduated introduction to Maese Pedro's puppet show. These complementary cases of mimicry mark successive stages in a process of dehumanization that culminates in the representation of the legend of Gaiferos and Melisendra by inanimate dolls made of paste. They constitute, at the same time, stages of increasing elaborateness in a gradual progression from simple mimicry to a more complex kind of imitation presented in a rudimentary work of art. That Cervantes intended Maese Pedro's puppet show to be seen as the climax of such a progression becomes even more clear later, when the reader learns that only on this one occasion does Maese Pedro observe this order of performance (["the first thing he did was to present his puppet show, sometimes showing one story, sometimes another, but all happy, joyful, and well known. After the show, he would offer for consideration the abilities of his monkey . . ."] [II, xxvii]).

The audience that begins by listening to the story of the braying aldermen's innocent mutual deception based on mimicry and then allows itself to be partially taken in by the more elaborately mounted fraud of the talking ape is thus in a proper frame of mind for a more highly articulated mimetic illusion when the puppet play begins. Having been desensitized by a charlatan's mummery, it is now fully primed for an artist's magic.

The candles on the puppet stage are blazing. They outline what Ortega calls ["the frontier of two spiritual continents"]. Maese Pedro takes his place behind the scenes. His assistant, pointer in hand, stations himself alongside the stage. Don Quijote, Sancho and the rest of the audience are waiting expectantly. The assistant begins to speak, but no sound comes forth. His speech has been suspended by Cide Hamete, who intervenes at this moment and thus reminds us that we are reading a story he is telling, that we are gazing at the spectacle of another audience gazing at a spectacle. We are promised that what the assistant tells will be both heard and seen either by the one who hears the assistant, the spectator at the inn, or by the one who sees the next chapter, the reader of the book: ["that which will be heard or seen by him who hears or sees the next chapter"]. The ironic "or" here has the force of "and." The audience seated in the room at the inn has been subtly expanded to encompass the reader explicitly, even though that audience forms part of the show in the reader's more comprehensive view.

There is a further delay, for a chapter ends, again reminding the reader that this is not only a story but also a book. A new chapter begins with a verse, like the novel itself, but this one is a composite quotation from Vergil: ["They all fell silent, Tyrians and Trojans"]. This audience, no less heterogeneous than the one that heard Aeneas relate the fall of Troy, is composed of a would-be knight-errant, his squire, an innkeeper, a page, someone's cousin, others. It is composed not only of characters in a story but of readers of a book, and it is still waiting in silence for a puppet play that will suggest more than one parallel with the destruction of Troy before it is over. Trumpets and artillery sound. The assistant again begins to speak. This time there is no interference. His words now begin to flow and the story unfolds before characters and reader alike.

That story is the legend of Gaiferos and Melisendra, drawn from Spainish ballads of the pseudo-Carolingian cycle. Although the puppet play has no formal title, it is more than once described as the ["Liberation of Melisendra"] in deference to its traditional ending, which is altered in a curious way in this performance. According to the assistant, the "Liberation of Melisendra" is a true history with a pedigree that can be traced through Spanish ballads back to French chronicles. The assistant alludes to certain authors who have had a hand in the compilation of this "true" history, but he mentions none of them by name and offers only ballad quotations as proof of the historicity of his account.

The story is a simple one. It begins in the middle of things, which is not surprising. In this performance, it ends in the same fashion, which is surprising or at least worthy of note. The peerless Melisendra, wife of Gaiferos, is held captive by the Moors in Spain. Urged on by [Charlemagne], Melisendra's ["reputed father"], Gaiferos travels to Spain incognito and manages to communicate with Melisendra in her tower. Melisendra finally recognizes her husband and together they escape, pursued by the Moors. While the original legend follows them through Gaiferos' defeat of the Moorish pursuers to a triumphant arrival in Paris, Maese Pedro's version of the "true" history comes to an abrupt end just as the Moors begin the chase.

Maese Pedro's assistant has no name. He is simply the ["young man"] or the ["servant"] until it is time for the puppet show, when three different yet related terms are used to designate his various functions in the spectacle: *intérprete, declarador, trujamán*. He is, etymologically as well as functionally, a mediator, a clarifier, a translator. The assistant stands alongside the stage, yet he is a central figure in the spectacle. His physical position shows that he is not part of the play, yet the operation he performs from the sidelines is essential to it. The pointer he holds calls attention in a graphic way not only to the puppets as they enter but also to his office as "interpreter and declarer." Since the puppets he points out enact the ["mysteries of such a tableau"] (note the reminder, rich in connotations here, of the ecclesiastical origin of the name for the puppet stage), there is even the suggestion that his use of the wand will involve magic of a sort. And indeed it does, for the pointer enables him to cross over the footlights vicariously while he stands in the offstage world. Most narrators are Janus-like creatures. The assistant epitomizes this double nature as he watches the physical movements of the puppets and translates them into words at the same time as he gauges the effect of both movements and words upon the audience.

The most striking feature of Maese Pedro's puppet show is its hybrid form. As the story is acted out by puppets, it is being narrated by the assistant. Telling and showing are simultaneous here, and the puppet play is both a narrative act and a dramatic spectacle at the same time. The talking ape needed an interpreter to translate its soundless mimicry into oracular speech. The deciding factor of the illusion's power was words, which made credible what the spectators had seen the moment after they had seen it: an ape supposedly talking. So it is with the puppet's gestures too, despite Maese Pedro's injunction just before the show: " '*operibus credite, et non verbis.*' " ["Believe words, not deeds."] Cervantes' reader has no choice but to depend upon the words.

Yet the words themselves of the puppet play are not in the dramatic mode that even puppet plays require. The puppets do not have voices, let alone individual voices, supplied by the puppeteer. They do not even speak in the whistles which were commonly used for puppet speech in Cervantes' time, as J. E. Varey tells us. There is no dialogue in this play, which offers only two utterances supposedly issuing from the puppet characters. Both examples are quotations from ballads in which the characters do speak for themselves. But in this context, even these examples of direct discourse are so overladen with narrative preface — ["so the story goes"] ["the words of the conversation that passed between them are given in the ballad . . . but I will not repeat it now, for prolixity often breeds boredom"] — that the dramatic nature of this speech is, if not lost, greatly overshadowed by the teller's narrative style.

The assistant's temporal confusion shows the same thing in a different way, recalling once more the ballads, in which it occurs for different reasons. He begins his narrative of the events unfolding on the puppet stage in the present, the tense of all drama. But as the play proceeds, the assistant occasionally shifts into the imperfect, usually used to describe events evolving in the past and here a sign that narrative style is asserting itself over drama. Though the play is still in progress, the assistant sometimes even lapses into the preterit, the tense of completed history or of legend, but certainly not of a dramatic performance in the act of taking place.

The assistant's constant exhortations — ["see over there"] ["Look, gentlemen"] ["Turn your eyes"] — do call attention to the visible activity on the stage, but they also remind the audience that it is being directed in its theatrical experience by a figure who does not ordinarily appear in a dramatic performance unless it be this most special kind: a narrator external to the events being enacted. So that even for the audience at the inn, who can "see" what Cervantes' reader must infer, the spectacle is at least as much a narrative experience as it is a dramatic one.

The assistant is a relentlessly minute narrator who leaves various important questions unanswered but revels in explaining the obvious. In his search for the illusion of history, he dwells, as the balladeers had sometimes done, on domestic and unheroic trivia. This gives an irreverent, not to say plebeian, view of the story of an emperor's daughter and her no less noble knight: the quarrel between father-in-law [Charlemagne] and son-in-law Gaiferos, who would rather play chess than rescue his wife from infidels; the request to borrow cousin Roland's sword, which he here refuses to loan to cousin Gaiferos, contrary to the known ballads; the kiss stolen by the Moor from the lips of Melisendra, who spits in disgust and dries her mouth on her sleeve; the clumsy descent from the tower, during which Melisendra's skirt catches on the balcony railing and the princess is left unceremoniously hanging in mid-air by her petticoats.

Like all the narrators mentioned so far, the assistant does not confine himself to narrating events which have first been ordered by someone else. He renders them with commentary. Sometimes his parenthetical remarks are designed to support his claim to historical authenticity either by relating the world of his story to the world of his audience, or by defining the materials of the spectacle, or both: ["in the city of Sansueña, as they used to call the city now known as Zaragoza"] ["it is supposed that it is one of the towers of the castle of Zaragoza, which now is called the Aljafería . . ."]. Yet when the assistant points out an innovation in this particular version of the story, he admits to the spectator that an element of *poesis* has crept into the supposedly factual account: ["Now behold a new incident, the likes of which you have probably never seen before"].

The assistant also indulges in the purely personal aside that allows the spectator to see clearly where the narrator's sympathy lies and to be influenced in his reaction accordingly. His personal commentary twice threatens to turn into long-winded digression and its effect upon the immediate audience can be assessed from the criticism it provokes. I shall consider the criticisms later.

In the assistant, then, Cervantes presents a narrator who is both part of the performance and part of the creative act and is also the ideal spectator. What of the audience in this spectacle? The mute crowd of Tyrians and Trojans finds a voice in Don Quijote, who is the principal spectator not only by virtue of being the hero of the story, but also because he is the one member of the group who makes his reactions known. Don Quijote is the spectator dramatized, and the effect of the play upon him is what the reader is meant to notice.

Because of his madness, Don Quijote cannot clearly distinguish literature from life. He is convinced that the heroes of romance were once people of flesh and blood and that the account of their deeds given in chivalric novels is history. This conviction is what determines his reaction to the puppet play. Taking the narrator at his word, which requires little or no adjustment, Don Quijote readily accepts the premise that the legend of Gaiferos and Melisendra is history. His remarks show that he prefers to have it treated as such.

When the assistant digresses in order to express his moral indignation against the Moors' dispatch in punishing culprits, Don Quijote breaks into the narrative to remind him: ["Boy, boy . . . go straight ahead with your story, and do not go on curves or tangents; for it requires much proof and corroboration to bring a truth to light"].

Later, when the interpreter describes the city of Zaragoza drowned in the pealing of bells, Don Quijote again interrupts the narrative (as well as Maese Pedro's sound effects) to correct the facts. He argues not so much with the narrator as, over the narrator's head, with the playwright himself: ["That's not right! . . . In this matter of the bells Master Peter is much mistaken, for they do not use bells among the Moors, but kettle-drums and a kind of instrument like our clarion, and this about ringing the bells in Sansueña is most certainly utter nonsense"].

Annoyed by the narrator's digression before, Don Quijote here provides one himself. He apparently supplies historical proof as well. Maese Pedro, from behind the scenes, defends himself and orders his assistant to get on with the story. When the assistant does continue, he repeats the description of Sansueña. But this time he incorporates Don Quijote's correction into the narrative. It begins to seem that the spectator not only experiences the effect of the play but also exerts his effect upon it in turn. The spectator who participates in the telling is an appropriate partner for a narrator who leads the viewing. This is a retable of marvels indeed.

The last time that Don Quijote interrupts the puppet play, it is to make the spectator's effect upon the spectacle felt in a literal way. Having corrected the narrator's style, having altered the narrative, interrupting both action and illusion each time, he now intervenes physically. Aroused by the description of the Moorish cavalcade and the offstage ringing of bells (for Maese Pedro has not corrected the sound effects), Don Quijote makes his final commitment to the illusion onstage. In his imagination, the puppets have become not only historical beings, but living people whose lives extend forward into a future still to be lived rather than backward into an already determined past. On the pathetic premise that he can alter the course of what he considers history come alive, Don Quijote attacks the Moorish pursuers. He is innocent of the knowledge that the happy escape of Gaiferos and Melisendra is guaranteed not by irreversible history but rather by unalterable legend. In either case, their fate is beyond Don Quijote's power. His noble intentions blindly carried out once more produce contrary results. Luckily, it is only the puppets who suffer. Unable to accept art as art, even in a puppet show where the illusion is minimal, Don Quijote attempts to invade the impenetrable world of fiction. This effort is as vain as his many attempts to impose the world of fiction upon the ordinary lives of men. The disaster that follows is the total destruction of the puppet play and the puppets by the one spectator who demonstrates, in destroying them, how completely he had fallen under their spell. He will realize his mistake too late.

It is now time to take a closer look at Maese Pedro, the itinerant mountebank. His puppets are dehumanized miniatures of human actors, and he himself may be considered a caricature of the *autor* of Spanish Renaissance tradition, the theatrical impresario who both managed his troupe of actors and wrote plays for them to perform. Maese Pedro has created his version of the "Liberation of Melisendra" by combining a number of scenes from different versions of an old ballad into a continuous story, not without adding a few strokes of his own. He is, in the most literal sense, the prime mover of the puppet play that he animates on his marvelous retable. The strings that lead from his hands to the puppets' limbs (J. E. Varey shows that Cervantes' description is based, to a large extent if not exclusively, on puppets with strings) are the tangible signs of his connection with their movements and with the play's action. The very explicitness of this link between author and puppet must have influenced Cervantes to use in this episode a puppet play rather than a more conventional play with human actors, which Avallaneda treated so unimaginatively in that strikingly similar episode of his spurious Second Part.

Maese Pedro, serving as his own barker, urges the spectators to take their seats and promises Don Quijote: ["This show of mine contains sixty thousand marvels. I tell your worship, Don Quijote, that it is one of the rarest spectacles in the whole world. But deeds, not words! Let's get to work, for time is drawing on, and we have a lot to do, to tell and to show"]. Do and tell and show. Thus does the creator describe the spectacle. The mechanics of the performance are as important as the story itself. The telling, as we have already seen, is deputed to the assistant. The showing is the function of both the assistant, who points out, and Maese Pedro, who figures forth. But the doing will be Maese Pedro's task alone, and on this all else depends. The Latin epigram is not without its irony in this context, where telling stems from showing, words from actions, the whole from Maese Pedro's hands.

After his barker's prologue, Maese Pedro disappears behind the scenes. Most playwrights are content to remain there in silence. Even Pirandello, in that famous case which both Castro and Livingstone have compared to this one, prefers to observe from the wings the struggle of his characters towards an identity, a play and an author. But Maese Pedro is not content to limit himself to so passive a role and to allow his play to speak for itself. He remains hidden, one might say immanent, yet his participation as author in the play is as fully dramatized as the narrator's and spectator's.

Maese Pedro, like his spectator, breaks into the play to offer his commentary on the narrative in progress. When Don Quijote bids the assistant develop the story along a straight line, Maese Pedro seconds the advice: ["Boy, don't go in for flourishes, but do what this gentleman says, which will be best. Go on with your plain song and don't stray off into counterpoint, for that's the way the strings get broken"]. It is not often that a playwright is in a position to overhear the spectator, let alone take sides with him, while the play is in progress. In doing so here, he seems to disagree with the assistant's stylistic falsification of his intentions. The assistant, merely a deputy, must obey.

At the point where the assistant harangues the fleeing lovers, ["Go in peace, oh peerless pair of true lovers! . . ."] Maese Pedro interrupts the overblown periods to deliver from behind the scenes (as though he were speaking from out of a cloud) a second lesson in the art of storytelling even as the story is being told: ["Plainness, boy! Don't soar so high, for all affectation is bad!"]. Again he introduces into the performance an element that does not belong there.

Maese Pedro's longest comment occurs when he hears himself criticized for ringing bells in Sansueña. This time he not only intrudes into the sacrosanct precinct of the story but gives himself away besides. The creator controlling the puppets speaks to both spectator and storyteller. He injects into the play a truly gratuitous element, a confession of his own insincerity, his materialistic credo where even an artistic one spoken directly by him would be out of place: ["Don't worry about trifles, Don Quijote, or expect perfection, for you'll never find it. Don't they perform countless comedies almost every day, in these parts, full of innumerable improbabilities and absurdities? But for all that they have a successful run not only with applause but with admiration and all? Go on, boy, and let them speak, for so long as I fill my bag they can act as many improbabilities as there are motes in the sun"]. Maese Pedro is again at variance with his deputized narrator. He has just confessed that he does not believe in the kind of historical integrity that his assistant in vain claims for the play. Nor does he defend the inaccuracy by dismissing it as the kind of trivial detail that does not matter — in poetry. Who but Don Quijote could remain spellbound after this cynical admission? For though this may well be the truth behind many a creation, to say so in the creation itself is to undermine the illusion at its very source.

With Don Quijote's violent intrusion into the puppet play, the ending of this version of the legend of the liberation of Melisendra is drastically altered. Instead of witnessing the triumphant return to Paris, the audience at the inn sees, rather, the destruction of the paraphernalia of Maese Pedro's production, very nearly of Maese Pedro himself. It is only in what might be called this last act, a finale which neither the legend nor Maese Pedro had envisaged, that the reaction of the rest of the audience is mentioned: ["The crowd of spectators was in an uproar, the ape fled up the inn's roof, the student was frightened, the page in a panic, and even Sancho Panza himself in a terrible alarm, as he affirmed after the storm had passed, because he had never before seen his master in such an outrageous temper"].

The fear of the rest of the audience, which in Sancho's case will give way to pity as well, suggests that for them the history of the "Liberation of Melisendra" in its unforeseen denouement has turned into something akin to a Senecan tragedy. In this last act of the spectacle, it is the puppeteer on whom the audience focuses its attention. After the violent intrusion of the outside world, the creator stands in the foreground, surrounded by his mutilated creatures and his retable. Maese Pedro is hardly a tragic figure in the Aristotelian mold, yet he is pathetic as he laments the loss of his paraphernalia, of his livelihood. His lament for his lost possessions moves towards the kind of larger context that all elegies seek. It begins as a gloss of the ballad in which King Rodrigo mourns the loss of his kingdom. Maese Pedro, as owner of a puppet theater, was also lord of kings and emperors a moment ago. Yet now he is reduced to nothing. Maese Pedro's figurative language is an echo of the theatrical metaphors that have been commonplaces since Antiquity, as Curtius points out. Even Sancho is familiar with them through his preacher. But despite the fact that this language uttered by an impostor is disproportionate to the situation and applied to a mere puppet show, it does evoke serious overtones. The very way that Maese Pedro moves from puppet stage to kingdom recalls the steps described by that other conjurer, Prospero, in his enlargement from "the baseless fabric of this vision" through the "cloud-capped towers" to "the great globe itself." For, cynical though his motives are, Maese Pedro is the creator of the puppet play. And even though he does so at the same time that he asks Don Quijote to pay damages, he nevertheless defines his relationship to the creatures, now relics, who enacted *misterios* on his marvelous retable: ["And these relics lying on this hard and barren ground, how were they scattered and annihilated but by the invincible strength of that powerful arm? And whose were their bodies but mine? And how did I support myself if not by them?"] The maimed puppets, even though for mercenary reasons, are after all so many of Maese Pedro's bodies, other selves that are a little more solid, perhaps, than those spirits of Prospero's who vanish into thin air. They are the creatures used by this greedy demiurge to create his false illusions. Yet Maese Pedro is only a demiurge, a subordinate creator, and his broken little world is contained within the larger one governed by Cide Hamete, who is about to give a more complete account of the puppeteer.

The implied reader, with whom the reader of Cervantes' book is meant to identify, enjoys the advantage of distance and superior knowledge over Maese Pedro's audience as well as over the creator and narrator of the puppet play. He knows that the story of Gaiferos and Melisendra is a fiction and is therefore impervious to the assistant's protestations of historical truth. He sees the fiction in turn as a burlesque of a legend and of chivalric material in general. He watches while the play is cut up into divisions that are travesties of acts not because of any inner necessity but because during this caricature of a dramatic performance a spectator and the playwright keep interrupting the narrator and breaking the continuity. He notes, in a way that that audience seems to, the creator's destructive admission of insincerity. All of these things amount to what Brecht might call the "alienation effect" (*Verfremdungsefekte*) and keep him from falling under the spell of Maese Pedro's illusion. He merely watches others being gulled by a charlatan.

But although the reader experiences the spectacle from this superior vantage point, he is at the same time surpassed in knowledge by the chronicler and the intermediaries, who have one further secret to reveal. While the reader may not succumb to the marvels of Maese Pedro's retable, he unwittingly falls victim to another illusion mounted by Cide Hamete and sustained by the intermediaries.

After witnessing the destruction of Maese Pedro's puppet show and sharing, to some extent, Sancho's sympathy for its creator's loss, the reader looks upon Don Quijote's payment of damages as a fair recompense for the puppeteer's vanished livelihood. It is right that the madman, who could not see the play for what it was, should pay for the equipment he destroyed. Don Quijote himself eventually admits the justice of it. But just after this sympathy is aroused, the reader is told something about Maese Pedro that affects his view. He learns that Maese Pedro is not Maese Pedro at all, but Ginés de Pasamonte, whose acquaintance he had made before. In case he does not remember, the chronicler reminds him that this is the same villainous Ginés who had repaid with a volley of stones Don Quijote's kindness in freeing him from a chain gang. The same Ginés who, after that, had stolen Sancho's donkey and thus wrought an injustice not only upon Sancho but also upon the author of the book, who had to take criticism for the fact that the printer had omitted the passage in Part One where the theft is described.

Maese Pedro is an impostor in his own life also and the disguise has been penetrated. The reader has been deceived, then enlightened by the chronicler. The other intermediaries concur in the deception by maintaining Cide Hamete's arrangement of events in their retelling. Theoretically, any one of them might have pointed out the disguise at the beginning and thus spared the reader from squandering his sympathy.

The reader has just been shown how easy it is to be taken in by one illusion at the very moment that he might be satisfied with himself for not having been taken in by another. This knowledge, won at his own expense, is not soon forgotten. It is essential for him to be armed with it if he is to understand Cervantes' novel properly. The reader's newly sharpened wariness is immediately applied to the explanation of Maese Pedro's identity itself. The Moorish chronicler is responsible for the unmasking. He swears an oath on it like a true Christian. The second author reports verbatim a literal translation of the oath and passes on the Morisco translator's explanation that ["Cide Hamete's swearing as a Catholic Christian, he being a Moor as he doubtless was, meant that just as the Catholic Christian when he swears, swears, or should swear the truth, so he would tell the truth, as if he had sworn like a Catholic Christian . . ."] (II, xxvii). But how can the reader trust such a strange oath sworn by a Moor who is suspect and explained by a no less suspect Morisco? That the reader remembers to ask such a question is in itself a protection against the kind of ingenuous belief that Don Quijote has just shown in the puppet show, a necessary protection against the continuing blend of clarification and mystification he finds in *Don Quijote*.

With the final discovery of Maese Pedro's identity, the reader is at last in a position to see the episode of the puppet show from the vantage point of the chronicler, however unreliable that vantage point may be. After he has seen the entire novel, he perceives in addition certain mutually illuminating coincidences between the part and the whole. It is to these that I now turn.

Ginés de Pasamonte is as much a literary man as he is a criminal. He is an author, though an unpublished one. This point he made when he first appears in the chain gang episode of Part One, where he and Don Quijote discuss the autobiography he wrote with his own thumbs: *La vida de Ginés de Pasamonte*. The information that he had composed a thick volume describing his crimes is repeated, lest it be overlooked, in the explanation of the Maese Pedro disguise. In the puppet show, Pasamonte works in a different medium. No longer the first-person narrator of an autobiographical narrative which can presumably claim to be historical, he is here the creator of "The Liberation of Melisendra" which, disguised as Maese Pedro, he animates but which he leaves to a narrator to tell. Ginés de Pasamonte, has, in other words, first assumed a fictitious identity, the Maese Pedro disguise, and then surrendered the actual telling of his hybrid creation to his assistant because that is what this art form demands. When he intervenes in the performance, it is because his narrator or spectator gets out of hand, but he intervenes as Maese Pedro, a character created by him in the living play which is his life now that he is living it as another.

What, if not something very close in principle to this, has Cervantes done in his disposition of the narrative scheme of *Don Quijote?* Cide Hamete once confesses (II, xliv) that speaking ["through the mouths of so few people"] is an unbearable effort for him. So, too, it is for Cervantes, who, rather than narrate the novel in his own person, not only delegates the role of author of the supposed history to Cide Hamete but also adds both a translator and interpreters to interpret and declare — translate and narrate — the story. The relationship between the author-criminal Ginés de Pasamonte bears to the puppeteer Maese Pedro, and he in turn to the assistant is, in its essentials, the same as that which Cervantes bears to the chronicler Cide Hamete and he in turn to his translator and interpreters. Ginés de Pasamonte, the historical self who is the subject of his autobiography, has no place in Maese Pedro's puppet show. Nor has Cervantes left an explicit place for himself as author in *Don Quijote*. His purpose in excluding himself from the novel (except as just another reference in his characters' conversation) was not to elude ultimate authorial responsibility, as many seem still to believe, but rather to render his creation artistically self-sufficient.

Only with reference to this plural *dédoublement*, so intricately constructed, can the reader of *Don Quijote* understand the full implication of the remark that Cervantes utters as author in his own voice in the Prologue to Part One: ["But I, though in appearance Don Quijote's father, am really his stepfather . . ."].

The novel as a whole even has its counterparts to Don Quijote who interrupts and corrects Maese Pedro's puppet play and to the assistant who watches both play and audience while he tells the story. These are the intermediaries who are simultaneously dramatized readers and intruding narrators. The discrepancies between puppeteer and assistant, between action and words, are in the novel inaccuracies of translation: ["They say that in the real original of this history it states that when Cide Hamete came to write this chapter, his interpreter did not translate it as it was written . . ."] (II, xliv).

There are, finally, other striking similarities between the whole and the part. These have to do with the story. "The Liberation of Melisendra" is a tissue of ballads. So, also, is *Don Quijote* in the early chapters of Part One. According to Menéndez Pidal, a short burlesque of ballads is all that Cervantes intended to produce until he discovered the possibilities latent in the material and enlarged his scope to include romances of chivalry. The irreverent treatment of Gaiferos and Melisendra echoes the chronicler's mock-heroic view of Don Quijote and Dulcinea, and certain coincidences of detail seem designed to make the connection explicit. Melisendra, captive in the Moorish palace, must be rescued by Gaiferos, just as Dulcinea, prisoner of a wizard's spell, as Don Quijote believes, must be rescued from the Cave of Montesinos by Don Quijote — or rather, disenchanted by Sancho, who is just as unwilling to flagellate himself as Gaiferos is to leave his chess game. Melisendra's leap onto the croup of Gaifero's horse, where she sat ["astride like a man"], invites comparison with the earlier episode in which the country lass (Dulcinea, according to Sancho) falls from her mount and takes a running leap into the saddle, where ["she sat astride like a man"] (II, x). All that is made of Melisendra's *faldellín* in the descent from the tower recalls the *faldellín* (and it was this very garment) that the same country lass Dulcinea had already offered Don Quijote as collateral for a loan in the Cave of Montesinos. These similarities are enough to account for Don Quijote's empathy with the fleeing lovers in the puppet show, though only his madness is responsible for transforming empathy into belief and belief into overt action.

Maese Pedro's puppet show is, then, an analogue to the novel as a whole, not merely because the burlesque legend that Maese Pedro recreates with puppets is a *reductio ad absurdum* of the same chivalric material that Cervantes burlesques through his characters, but also because it reproduces on a miniature scale the same basic relationships among storyteller, story and audience that are discernible in the novel's overall scheme. Yet analogy does not imply absolute identity, and the discrepancies in this case are as meaningful as the correspondences.

Maese Pedro's puppet show is the creation of a charlatan with no purpose but to delude the unwary for money, whereas *Don Quijote* is the creation of a writer who aspires to a higher kind of entertainment aimed at instructing the reader as well as delighting him. Maese Pedro addresses himself to ignorant, superstitious folk and to a benign madman, while *Don Quijote* is directed towards an implied reader who is educable and potentially prudent. In Maese Pedro's show a spectator is carried away by the illusion; but in Cervantes' novel, the constant alienation effects prevent him from remaining spellbound for very long.

It is established from the very beginning of the novel that Don Quijote's madness is caused by an overdose of fiction and shows up most clearly whenever fiction, especially the chivalric romance, comes into play. The novel follows his repeated attempts and failures to revive the chivalric romance in the most literal way: by living it and urging others to follow his example for more than their own amusement at a madman's antics. In the puppet show, Don Quijote comes face to face with fiction presented as history. He reacts predictably, as we have seen, because he is a madman. But Cervantes' reader is prudent, or at least will be when Cervantes has done with him, and the puppet show reminds him of this fact once again, this time in an analogue with implications that concern his reading of the whole novel.

Cervantes' expressed purpose, if not necessarily his only one, in writing *Don Quijote* is to discredit the chivalric romances. He says so several times in a variety of voices. Speaking as author in his own voice in the Prologue to Part One, he seconds the advice offered by the friend who bursts into the study to deliver the harangue that Cervantes turns into the Prologue itself: ["In fact, seek to overthrow the ill-based fabric of these books of chivalry abhored by so many yet praised by so many more . . ."] This sentiment is repeated at the end of the novel by another of Cervantes' many second selves. Cide Hamete claims that ["my sole objective has been to arouse men's contempt for all the feigned and absurd stories of knight-errantry, whose credit this tale of my genuine Don Quijote has already shaken, and which will undoubtedly soon tumble to the ground"] (II, lxxiv). The reader has learned to be wary of such "true histories," and Maese Pedro's puppet show has helped make him so.

Yet one must read these statements with caution. *Don Quijote* contains evidence of the delight which the chivalric novel provided for many readers. The [Curate] and the [Barber] spare several romances from the bonfire. Those that escape the holocaust are spared because one or another technical excellence outweighs in the judges' eyes the extravagance of the stories they have to tell. The [Canon of] Toledo disapproves of chivalric romances in general, yet confesses that he has enjoyed reading some and has even tried his hand at writing a fragment of one. These characters and others like them are, despite their foibles, people in whom discretion is shown to override whatever human failings they may have. In this, they resemble the reader that Cervantes has molded in the process of telling his story: the discreet reader who learns to be wary through experience and for whom Don Quijote's unrestrained participation in the puppet play stands as an example to be shunned.

In proposing to discredit the chivalric novel, Cervantes does not suggest that we not read chivalric novels, but only that we read them properly for what they are, outlandish and sometimes beautiful lies, fiction rather than history. In order to achieve this end, he shows the reader how such fictions masquerading as histories are put together by laying bare their inner workings. Starting with one such invented history written by an unreliable Moorish chronicler, then emphasizing the unreliability by showing how the possibility of error and the impossibility of verification are multiplied with each stage in the transmission of the account to the book, he provides an object lesson in how fiction is created with the very techniques used in the writing of history, itself an ambiguous word in Spanish.

The reader, if he did not know this before, can see the process demonstrated with variations again and again. He witnesses the illusion of life-like history alternately created and torn down before his eyes. He therefore cannot take the illusion at face value unless he is as mad as Don Quijote. The very presentation ensures his alienation, for Cervantes knows that belief can only interfere with, even destroy, the reader's perception of the bittersweet humor and the rhetorical purpose which it serves. But the techniques of alienation, at the same time that they interfere with identification and belief, direct the reader's attention inevitably towards the artificial nature of the invention itself, soliciting his admiration (as Cervantes through his characters often does in so many words) and above all his appreciation of the fiction as fiction. The friend of the Prologue to Part One put it this way: ["Also aim that the reading of your story makes the melancholy laugh, and the merry laugh louder; that the simpleton is not vexed, that the intelligent admire your invention, the serious do not despise it, nor the prudent withhold their praise"]. The invention is the handiwork of the novelist. In taking it exactly for what it is, the reader reciprocates the creator's virtuosity with an appropriate aesthetic response.

Note

1. This lecture was first delivered on November 12, 1964, for the University of Chicago's Festival of Shakespeare and the Renaissance, and repeated at Bryn Mawr College on March 9, 1965. The material here presented forms part of a longer study in which it will appear in a somewhat revised form. Therefore, no attempt has been made to alter it for the present purpose.

All quotations from the *Quijote* are drawn from Francisco Rodríguez Marín's *Nueva edición crítica* (Madrid, 1947–1949). Only those passages not found in the Prologue or in the Maese Pedro episode itself (II, xxv–xxvi) are identified by Part and Chapter.

The critical and scholarly works referred to in the text are, in this order: E. C. Riley, *Cervantes' Theory of the Novel* (Oxford, 1962), esp. pp. 205–212; José Ortega y Gasset, *Meditaciones del Quijote*, in *Obras completas*, I (Madrid, 1946), 380; J. E. Varey, *Historia de los títeres en España* (Madrid, 1957), esp. pp. 232–237; Américo Castro, "Cervantes y Pirandello," in *Santa Teresa y otros ensayos* (Santander, 1929), pp. 219–231; Leon Livingstone, "Interior Duplication and the Problem of Form in the Modern Spanish Novel," *PMLA*, LXXIII (1958), 397; Ernst Robert Curtius, *European Literature and the Latin Middle Ages*, tr. by Willard R. Trask, Bollingen Series, XXXVI (New York, 1953), 138–144; Ramón Menéndez Pidal, *Un aspecto en la elaboración del "Quijote"* (Madrid, 1924).

Doubles
Marthe Robert*

The subject of the quixotic novel embodies the multiple aspects of an underlying conflict between the fictional and the real, the flesh-and-blood hero and the paper hero, the new and the old; and the highly traditional method of imitation seems admirably suited to develop these oppositions on every possible level of the narrative. Imitation, and even its clichés, serves the special purpose of the quixotic novel by establishing the connections between the *current* imitator and his *past* model, and by furnishing a crude but immediately intelligible summary of the complex relations between the living and the dead, the real and the imaginary, the past and the present, the true and the false. As a simple method of invention, imitation can be considered as a language without words, a dumb-show expressing directly many more ideas, feelings, beliefs, and judgments than one could include in a long treatise. Morality, aesthetics, literary conceptions, are all displayed simultaneously in a kind of serio-comic theater, where literature, and finally language itself, fatefully grapples with the centuries.

Shrewd as he is, Don Quixote recognizes the immense advantage to be gained from a technique offering so many new resources for his own hidden designs. He understands that indeed nothing is better suited to his enterprise than the extreme posture of imitation, which corresponds precisely to the demands of his literary passion and provides him with a practical, as well as a strict, rule of conduct. So he decides to "sally forth," not, as we are too often inclined to believe, to battle windmills, but to obey in full consciousness the self-appointed vocation of imitator.

The most radical quixotic act, then, is never the accomplishment of some personal ambition, but on the contrary, the imitation of an ideal fixed by tradition, indeed by literary convention, and consequently stripped of all originality. Don Quixote is not inspired to invent his faith or his own actions; he is rather guided by an imitation whose rule is clearly dictated to him by his favorite author. He is therefore profoundly irritated each time his companions, for whom literature means nothing, treat him like an eccentric, a vulgar redresser of wrongs moved only by the derangement of his fantastical mind. " 'Have I not told you,' " he explains to Sancho at the critical moment of his madness, " 'that I mean to imitate Amadís by playing the part of a desperate and raving madman, thus imitating Orlando at the same time . . . ? . . . So, Sancho my friend, do not waste time in advising me to forego so rare, so felicitous, and so unheard of an imitation as this. Mad I am and mad I must be . . .' " (I,25). With a precision, a clarity, and in spite of his anger, a patience characteristic of the authority of a master, Don Quixote explains his

*Reprinted with permission from *The Old and the New: From "Don Quixote" to Kafka*, trans. Carol Cosman (Berkeley: University of California, 1977), 11–21.

madness in a way that, to be sure, will never convince priests and barbers, but that the reader, and particularly the serious critic, must acknowledge. Thus, despite appearances that arbitrarily obscure his simplest features, Don Quixote is not in the least at odds with Cervantes, who decreed that the novelist must employ "only imitation in what he writes; the more perfect the imitation, the better the writing will be." Surely Cervantes could not disavow a hero whose conduct conforms so perfectly to the very principle of his own technique. Whatever differences the commentators imagine they can prove, Don Quixote's rare, felicitous, and unheard of imitation makes such differences largely unimportant and convinces us that essentially author and hero are in absolute agreement.

When imitation imposes a way of writing on the novelist and a way of living on the hero, it creates a functional identity between these two similar and disparate figures that tells us more than any external circumstance about the true extent of their relation. Indeed, the usual assumptions of biographical and psychological criticism are not very helpful in distinguishing the precise affinities between Don Quixote and Cervantes, the Land-Surveyor and Kafka. Although these conventional critical methods can reveal certain common features—Cervantes' passion for chivalric novels, Kafka's exile—they are unable to explain the kind of astonishing mutation by which the author transforms himself, making his own features entirely unrecognizable. From this point of view, the quixotic work can be distinguished from the romantic novel in which the hero takes shape from an image of the author touched up for the requirements of poetic transposition but still recognizable; and it can be distinguished as well from the naturalistic or realistic novel in which the author, supposedly separate from his creatures, is content to describe them and judge them without being personally implicated in their actions. The critics of quixotism clash principally over this problematic nature of the hero who, produced by a radical metamorphosis, both *is* and *is not* the author in a way that continually disguises his real origin.

Unable to measure a fixed distance between the author and his novelistic surrogate, most interpretations propose either a simple identification or a clear opposition. In Kafka's case, either the author is automatically taken for his hero, or inversely, there is no consideration of the metamorphosis that from the very outset transforms Kafka irreversibly into K. Don Quixote, on the other hand, is most often taken for a caricature, not of Cervantes himself, which would still be conceivable, but of character types seen objectively from the outside by the penetrating but finally banal vision of a moralist. On the basis of such interpretations, the hero is soon deprived of a good part of his own existence. If K. is entirely identified with Kafka, he is no longer treated as a fictional character but rather is lifted out of the novel, the only place where his acts have any importance, and granted an absolutely autonomous life of his own for which the author is scarcely considered responsible. Similarly, Don

Quixote becomes a perfectly independent person whose greatness, intelligence, and genius far surpass the assumed intentions of Cervantes, who is accused of unconsciousness and even stupidity by his most passionate admirers. It is only another step (one that celebrated critics do not hesitate to take) to the suggestion that the quixotic author does not know what he is doing, that he is unworthy of his own genius and crushed by it. Although a similar suggestion might be justified in other cases (however dubious it might be to anyone who would not confuse unconsciousness with stupidity), certainly in the case of *Don Quixote* such a notion is not very clear or economical. It uselessly creates a new paradox by which the partisans of Don Quixote forever confront the partisans of Cervantes![1]

We are asked to choose sides on the basis of the few details of biographical information and of psychological analysis presented in the text. But the adventurous life of Cervantes does not correspond to Don Quixote's, and Kafka, whatever he might have suffered, was not a vagabond. Clearly, nothing in the text itself suffices to span the enormous gulf separating the novelist's real personality from his fictional mask. The narrative tells us rather that the hero, a born imitator, defines himself by a function clearly analogous to literature, which, whatever its subject, pretends only to reproduce, represent, and imitate some real or supposedly real aspect of life. Mimesis, which is the point of departure for all literary creation, and even for all art, here offers proof of the creator's solidarity with his creature, otherwise rather difficult to establish, since the same texts can equally serve to exaggerate or entirely ignore this solidarity. Within the narrative itself, imitation represents an equivalent to the very act of writing and clarifies the extent to which author and hero are separate and yet absolutely united in their common cause.

Therefore, since Cervantes has no intention of confusing his fictional character with himself, it is useless to ask him either to repudiate or to accept responsibility for all of Don Quixote's notions. Cervantes only intends to delegate his *literary* functions to his protagonist, to give him the right to represent the writer's condition, which he urgently needs to understand for himself. Cervantes splits himself off from Don Quixote and thereby mirrors the split he perceives inside himself between the ordinary man and the bizarre being who, instead of living, stops right in the middle of things to describe them. From this separation, which is a conjuration, or perhaps an exorcism, the secret novel is born whose thread is woven into the fabric of the visible text. In this half-hidden novel, Don Quixote shoulders the responsibility for his author's condition: he becomes the writer incarnate, absolute and alienated, freed from any compromise with life and therefore from the latent conflict between the writer's vocation and reality. Abstracted from everything that is not purely literal, Don Quixote is a monstrosity: at best a buffoon, at worst a madman. He is both the caricature and the idealization of Cervantes, his fear and his hope, proof of his simplicity and perhaps, too, the deepest cause of his sadness.

We can see then that the "modernity" justly credited to Cervantes is not primarily a matter of realism, if realism is understood narrowly as the crude description of the customs of an epoch. Rather this "modernity" lies in the camouflaged presence of the author in his own work, which, for the first time, affirms and develops a meaningful doubling, an image of precisely the same conflict that art engenders in the modern consciousness. The real concern is *art*, not a particular artist presented in the guise of a writer-protagonist who speaks as a professional, an obvious mouthpiece for the author, simply revealing his inner debates or his theories. Nothing is more truly alien to the quixotic hero than that image of a particular novelist or fictional artist, familiar since Balzac and Zola, who, having missed his calling for strictly personal reasons, sees literature or art as a form of his fate. Don Quixote is not interested in these crises. He is moved, worried, and perpetually amazed by the literary phenomenon itself: the banal and marvelous fact that books have always existed, in some fashion, with people who write them and others who read them. He is fascinated by the existence of an unlimited legacy that belongs to all men, whether they recognize it or not. And he is struck by the surprising role of language, which is always both excessive and inadequate. These considerations create the special situation from which all writers, by definition, profit and suffer, a situation whose anomalies can be perceived only by an extraordinarily discerning or a childishly naïve intelligence.

In order to put into novelistic play such a sum of ruthless questions and naïve confusions, Cervantes has recourse to a characteristically modern method. He splits the artist in two, depriving him of the prestige that makes him too attractive and at the same time continually preventing him from fulfilling his vocation. As the child of this schism, Don Quixote carries literature inside himself like an incurable wound. If he writes poems on occasion, and if, by way of compensation, he indiscriminately *christens* beings and things, appropriating the most personal privilege of the poet, he does not write the work he dreams of. In this he is very like the modern writer whose mysteriously baffling vocation remains unfulfilled: "Many a time he was tempted to take up his pen and literally finish the tale as had been promised, and he undoubtedly would have done so, and would have succeeded at it very well, if his thoughts had not been constantly occupied with other things of greater moment" (I,1). From the second page of the book, we understand why Don Quixote cannot appear in his own adventures adorned with the name and prestige of the writer: his postponed vocation obliges him to show a certain discretion on this point. Later, when the final consequences of the "other things of greater moment" that keep him from writing have developed, his descendants, bound by quixotic honesty, will lose even this literary dilettantism by which Cervantes permits Don Quixote to betray himself.

In his style of life and speech, his habits, and his appearance, the Land-Surveyor no longer has anything to remind him of literature, not even remotely. He is left — and this is enough to justify his role — with only the dubious social condition of the writer and the immoderate ambitions that make him, depending on the case, either dangerous or absurd. Whereas Don Quixote lives his ungratified passion for literature to the full, the Land-Surveyor is no more than an allusion to a supposedly exact art (land-surveying), which he hasn't the means to practice and which is not, in any case, in much demand. As a failed writer, the last quixotic hero is an imposter, a shrewd adventurer who demands a following but does not offer the slightest justification for his exorbitant pretensions. True, his madness has not changed, but unfortunately it makes him dangerous, or at the very least, suspect.

Thanks to the doubling that reveals a certain functional correspondence between the novelist and the hero, the novel can develop without the aid of rhetoric: "pro" and "con" are not discussed but made manifest and translated into action. At issue here are not exactly ideas, but contradictory tendencies, deep-rooted and equally active, which can neither suppress nor mutually accept each other, and therefore ask us to respect them together and, if possible, to set them free. Just as the multiple oppositions embodied in the pair "hero-author" cannot always be superimposed, the play of antitheses repeats itself through all the characters in the narrative, which is literally populated with *doubles*. The inseparable quixotic pair, Don Quixote and Sancho, the two assistants and the Land-Surveyor, issue from a secondary doubling of the author, who has in mind not the kind of academic quarrel where purely allegorical figures are assigned stereotypical roles, but a very real, agonizing, and largely insoluble conflict divided among various characters so that it can be seen from every possible angle. Cervantes purged himself of the absolute faith in literature that seems to be Don Quixote's madness, to which he radically opposed his own reasonable faith, a faith compatible with a lucid vision of reality. But this first doubling is not sufficient because Don Quixote's madness, absolute as it is, does not prevent nature and society from claiming their due and affirming their rights to both his mind and his body. The existence of Sancho, formed from the elements of a reality Don Quixote categorically refuses to recognize, answers to the requirements of this new opposition, an opposition no longer played out between the madness of Don Quixote and Cervantes' sanity, but now between the mind and the body, between the absolute rejection of the body and the naïve acceptance of its needs. Charged by Cervantes with the responsibilities of art, Don Quixote shifts the baser responsibilities of his nature to Sancho. Thanks to the squire's enormous belly, the Don himself is exempt from the need to have a stomach and spared the shame of yielding to its demands; he is allowed to be thin and pure, miraculously freed from natural necessities, almost disembodied. At least so he imagines; naturally, he is mistaken. He has split himself and transferred in vain to Sancho's person all his embarrassing flesh, for the *need* still assails him, proving in the most urgent way that he has a body and that it is wasted effort to deny it. In these moments when the need breaks his enchantment,[2] Don Quixote's heroic resistance, his obstinate efforts to preserve his unity, are perfectly useless. Forced to satisfy the corpulent Sancho, whom he thought he had safely left behind, he himself is doubled.

In this way, Don Quixote reinvents the old folklore theme of the double, which, if it loses some of its obviously demonic character, gains in exchange a quality that might be deceptively reassuring. For the demonic in this apparently innocent case lies precisely in the fact that we do not know who or where the devil is. Is Don Quixote the tempter of Cervantes, the demon he tries to exorcise by writing his book? Is the Don, as he himself fancies, the victim of an enchantment worked by his author? Must he be seen as the devil who effectively seduces Sancho with false promises?[3] Or, on the contrary, as the victim of the demonic squire who always leads him astray, ruining his enterprise? In the system of successive doublings that governs the composition of the novel, all these questions can be examined, but none are definitely answered by the author himself. And from a strictly quixotic point of view they must remain unanswered, the devil here being the agent of division itself, the principal obstacle to unity that the novel wishes to present without distortion. Nowhere can this be more clearly seen than in *The Castle*, where the devil splits everything in two, creating a crowd of doubles among whom K. futilely tries to establish a hierarchy, though he has no recognizable identity himself. Is K. really destroyed by the assistants he takes for low-level demons; or, as their name indicates, do they really assist him? Is Barnabas, who attracts him as much as the assistants repel him, and yet resembles them, truly his aid, or, as K. suspects at the end, the treacherous instrument of his destruction? K. never learns anything on this point, which is so crucial to his very existence (and pivotal for interpretations of the novel). Since he cannot renounce self-knowledge, however, he can only pursue relentlessly the strange quixotic dialogue with his doubles in which, as Kafka says elsewhere in order to define his thought,[4] "reasoning goes hand in hand with sorcery." But reason never triumphs over enchantment, nor does magic fathom the depths of logic.

Notes

1. As a last resort, many authors seek the explanation of these contradictions in Cervantes' unconscious. Certainly, from this point of view, no one has gone to such lengths as Miguel de Unamuno, who, in *The Life of Don Quixote and Sancho Panza*, squarely accuses Cervantes of being mean-spirited and constitutionally incapable of understanding the saintliness of Don Quixote. This accusation is made in all sincerity, and it is logical besides if we look only for the moral and spiritual reflection of the author in his character. This, however, amounts to demanding that Cervantes choose between the two extremes of saintliness and absurdity, when precisely what he demonstrates is that a formal choice between extremes is only a trap or last resort.

2. The wonderful passage in which Don Quixote is brought back to his house in a cage, believing he is enchanted, and finally succumbs to a pressing need that Sancho cannot satisfy for him, does not merit the modest reservations it generally incurs. Its triviality is not an ordinary comic technique but part of quixotism's larger plan, which is above all to throw into question all the moral and spiritual hierarchies that are described as just and unimpeachable by books.

3. With the authority that his exceptional affinities with quixotism gave him in this matter, Kafka settled on the hypothesis that conceives of Don Quixote as Sancho's demon. His commentary provides an indispensable insight into the way he perceived his own Don Quixote, namely K. and all his avatars.

> Without making any boast of it, Sancho Panza succeeded in the course of the years, by feeding him a great number of romances of chivalry and adventure in the evening and night hours, in so diverting from himself his demon, whom he later called Don Quixote, that this demon thereupon set out, uninhibited, on the maddest exploits, which, however, for the lack of a preordained object, which should have been Sancho Panza himself, harmed nobody. A free man, Sancho Panza philosophically followed Don Quixote on his crusades, perhaps out of a sense of responsibility, and had of them a great and edifying entertainment to the end of his days.
>
> ("The Truth about Sancho Panza," by Franz Kafka, translated by Willa and Edwin Muir, in *The Complete Stories*, ed. by Nahum N. Glatzer, Schocken Books, New York, 1971.)

4. "His reasoning goes hand in hand with sorcery. One can escape from reasoning by taking refuge in magic and from sorcery by taking refuge in logic; but one can also eliminate them both at once in such a way that they become a third thing, living magic, or destruction of the world that does not destruct but constructs" (from *Wedding Preparations in the Country*, Cahiers in-octavo). This aphorism, which follows the fragments on the biblical Abraham, defines the quixotic word (la verbe donquichotesque), which is invocation and critique, conjuration and radical probing, both one and the other with their risks and perils.

[Don Quixote in the Lettered World]

Michel Foucault*

With all their twists and turns, Don Quixote's adventures form the boundary: they mark the end of the old interplay between resemblance and signs and contain the beginnings of new relations. Don Quixote is not a man given to extravagance, but rather a diligent pilgrim breaking his journey before all the marks of similitude. He is the hero of the Same. He never manages to escape from the familiar plain stretching out on all sides of the Analogue, any more than he does from his own small province. He travels endlessly over that plain, without ever crossing the clearly defined frontiers of difference, or reaching the heart of identity. Moreover, he is himself like a sign, a long, thin graphism, a letter that has just escaped from the open pages of a book. His whole being is nothing but language, text, printed pages, stories that have already been written down. He is

*Reprinted with permission from *The Order of Things: An Archaeology of the Human Sciences* (New York: Random House, 1973), 46–50.

made up of interwoven words; he is writing itself, wandering through the world among the resemblances of things. Yet not entirely so: for in his reality as an impoverished hidalgo he can become a knight only by listening from afar to the age-old epic that gives its form to Law. The book is not so much his existence as his duty. He is constantly obliged to consult it in order to know what to do or say, and what signs he should give himself and others in order to show that he really is of the same nature as the text from which he springs. The chivalric romances have provided once and for all a written prescription for his adventures. And every episode, every decision, every exploit will be yet another sign that Don Quixote is a true likeness of all the signs that he has traced from his book. But the fact that he wishes to be like them means that he must put them to the test, that the (legible) signs no longer resemble (visible) people. All those written texts, all those extravagant romances are, quite literally, unparalleled: no one in the world ever did resemble them; their timeless language remains suspended, unfulfilled by any similitude; they could all be burned in their entirety and the form of the world would not be changed. If he is to resemble the texts of which he is the witness, the representation, the real analogue, Don Quixote must also furnish proof and provide the indubitable sign that they are telling the truth, that they really are the language of the world. It is incumbent upon him to fulfil the promise of the books. It is his task to recreate the epic, though by a reverse process: the epic recounted (or claimed to recount) real exploits, offering them to our memory; Don Quixote, on the other hand, must endow with reality the signs-without-content of the narrative. His adventures will be a deciphering of the world: a diligent search over the entire surface of the earth for the forms that will prove that what the books say is true. Each exploit must be a proof: it consists, not in a real triumph — which is why victory is not really important — but in an attempt to transform reality into a sign. Into a sign that the signs of language really are in conformity with things themselves. Don Quixote reads the world in order to prove his books. And the only proofs he gives himself are the glittering reflections of resemblances.

His whole journey is a quest for similitudes: the slightest analogies are pressed into service as dormant signs that must be reawakened and made to speak once more. Flocks, serving girls, and inns become once more the language of books to the imperceptible degree to which they resemble castles, ladies, and armies — a perpetually untenable resemblance which transforms the sought-for proof into derision and leaves the words of the books forever hollow. But non-similitude itself has its model, and one that it imitates in the most servile way: it is to be found in the transformations performed by magicians. So all the indices of non-resemblance, all the signs that prove that the written texts are not telling the truth, resemble the action of sorcery, which introduces difference into the indubitable existence of similitude by means of deceit. And since this magic has been foreseen and described in the books, the illusory difference that it introduces can never be anything but an enchanted similitude, and, therefore, yet another sign that the signs in the books really do resemble the truth.

Don Quixote is a negative of the Renaissance world; writing has ceased to be the prose of the world; resemblances and signs have dissolved their former alliance; similitudes have become deceptive and verge upon the visionary or madness; things still remain stubbornly within their ironic identity: they are no longer anything but what they are; words wander off on their own, without content, without resemblance to fill their emptiness; they are no longer the marks of things; they lie sleeping between the pages of books and covered in dust. Magic, which permitted the decipherment of the world by revealing the secret resemblances beneath its signs, is no longer of any use except as an explanation, in terms of madness, of why analogies are always proved false. The erudition that once read nature and books alike as parts of a single text has been relegated to the same category as its own chimeras: lodged in the yellowed pages of books, the signs of language no longer have any value apart from the slender fiction which they represent. The written word and things no longer resemble one another. And between them, Don Quixote wanders off on his own.

Yet language has not become entirely impotent. It now possesses new powers, and powers peculiar to it alone. In the second part of the novel, Don Quixote meets characters who have read the first part of his story and recognize him, the real man, as the hero of the book. Cervantes's text turns back upon itself, thrusts itself back into its own density, and becomes the object of its own narrative. The first part of the hero's adventures plays in the second part the role originally assumed by the chivalric romances. Don Quixote must remain faithful to the book that he has now become in reality; he must protect it from errors, from counterfeits, from apocryphal sequels; he must fill in the details that have been left out; he must preserve its truth. But Don Quixote himself has not read this book, and does not have to read it, since he is the book in flesh and blood. Having first read so many books that he became a sign, a sign wandering through a world that did not recognize him, he has now, despite himself and without his knowledge, become a book that contains his truth, that records exactly all that he has done and said and seen and thought, and that at last makes him recognizable, so closely does he resemble all those signs whose ineffaceable imprint he has left behind him. Between the first and second parts of the novel, in the narrow gap between those two volumes, and by their power alone, Don Quixote has achieved his reality — a reality he owes to language alone, and which resides entirely inside the words. Don Quixote's truth is not in the relation of the words to the world but in that slender and constant relation woven between themselves by verbal signs. The hollow fiction of epic exploits has become the representative power of language. Words have swallowed up their own nature as signs.

Don Quixote is the first modern work of literature, because in it we see the cruel reason of identities and differences make endless sport of signs and similitudes; because in it language breaks off its old kinship with things and enters into that lonely sovereignty from which it will reappear, in its separated state, only as literature; because it marks the point where resemblance enters an age which is, from the point of view of resemblance, one of madness and imagination. Once similitude and signs are sundered from each other, two experiences can be established and two characters appear face to face. The madman, understood not as one who is sick but as an established and maintained deviant, as an indispensable cultural function, has become, in Western experience, the man of primitive resemblances. This character, as he is depicted in the novels or plays of the Baroque age, and as he was gradually institutionalized right up to the advent of nineteenth-century psychiatry, is the man who is *alienated in analogy*. He is the disordered player of the Same and the Other. He takes things for what they are not, and people one for another; he cuts his friends and recognizes complete strangers; he thinks he is unmasking when, in fact, he is putting on a mask. He inverts all values and all proportions, because he is constantly under the impression that he is deciphering signs: for him, the crown makes the king. In the cultural perception of the madman that prevailed up to the end of the eighteenth century, he is Different only in so far as he is unaware of Difference; he sees nothing but resemblances and signs of resemblance everywhere; for him all signs resemble one another, and all resemblances have the value of signs. At the other end of the cultural area, but brought close by symmetry, the poet is he who, beneath the named, constantly expected differences, rediscovers the buried kinships between things, their scattered resemblances. Beneath the established signs, and in spite of them, he hears another, deeper, discourse, which recalls the time when words glittered in the universal resemblance of things; in the language of the poet, the Sovereignty of the Same, so difficult to express, eclipses, the distinction existing between signs.

This accounts, no doubt, for the confrontation of poetry and madness in modern Western culture. But it is no longer the old Platonic theme of inspired madness. It is the mark of a new experience of language and things. At the fringes of a knowledge that separates beings, signs, and similitudes, and as though to limit its power, the madman fulfils the function of *homosemanticism*: he groups all signs together and leads them with a resemblance that never ceases to proliferate. The poet fulfils the opposite function: his is the *allegorical* role; beneath the language of signs and beneath the interplay of their precisely delineated distinctions, he strains his ears to catch that "other language," the language, without words or discourse, of resemblance. The poet brings similitude to the signs that speak it, whereas the madman loads all signs with a resemblance that ultimately erases them. They share, then, on the outer edge of our culture and at the point nearest to its essential divisions, that "frontier" situation — a marginal position and a profoundly archaic silhouette — where their words unceasingly renew the power of their strangeness and the strength of their contestation. Between them there has opened up a field of knowledge in which, because of an essential rupture in the Western world, what has become important is no longer resemblances but identities and differences.

Novelas ejemplares (1613)

Cervantes, El Pinciano, and the
Novelas ejemplares

William C. Atkinson*

["He is nearing the power to get the philosopher's stone."] The reader will remember the alchemist in the *Coloquio de los perros* who was confident that another two months would see him producing silver and gold from the very stones. The incident has a peculiar suggestiveness in terms of Cervantes' own literary career. No creative writer has ever been more critical-conscious of the literary problems involved in creation, or has taken his reader more generously into his confidence throughout. From his first hesitant apprenticeship to the thankless craft of letters until his deathbed, ["with his foot in the stirrups for the next world"], we follow his wrestlings, not with popular approval, not with material success, but with the elusive philosopher's stone that will transmute crude experience into the silver and gold of literature. The *Galatea* has its shortcomings in plot and treatment? Let the reader but await the second part, that second part that the author was still promising when he died. The *Comedias y entremeses* are not, after all, the best in the world? *El engaño a los ojos* will make amends. Looking back from the second part of the *Quijote*, the author recognizes that his artistry in the first was still uncertain: the critics did well to query the introduction of irrelevant tales. If popularity were his only concern, Cervantes might well have rested now on his oars and continued in the same vein. But the alchemist, unsatisfied, continued to experiment, refining ever further the base metal of experience. And at last, Eureka! he has found the philosopher's stone. His own severest critic, in *Persiles y Sigismunda* he offers confidently ["the best work ever written in the language"].

The foundations of modern Cervantine criticism were laid with the demonstration by Castro that all the works of the canon, if highly divergent in artistic merit, present together an intellectual core of serious and profoundly consistent intent: ["The truth of Don Quijote is one with that of the *Galatea* and of *Persiles*"]. There is, we think, one reserve of substance to be entered here, but it is not the least important consequence of the winning of our present profound respect for Cervantes the thinker

*Reprinted with permission from *Hispanic Review* 16 (1948):189–208.

that the ground is prepared thereby for a more fruitful return to the
consideration of Cervantes the artist. Castro registers a proper surprise
that Menéndez Pelayo, who ranged with such easy mastery over the whole
of Spanish literature, should have touched so very occasionally, and so very
superficially, on its greatest glory. Yet the explanation Menéndez Pelayo
had himself supplied. Lacking knowledge of what the artist is seeking to
do, the critic must of necessity be at a loss. ["Cervantes is great because he
is a great novelist, which is to say he is a great poet, a great craftsman of
imaginative works, and this is all that is needed for his glory to fill the
world."] He is a genius, and one attraction of genius to the critic is that it
may absolve him from the attempt at rational explanation. ["Aesthetic
illumination is so quick that the majority of the artists could not tell us
why they chose one way rather than another."] But just what is a great
novel, what constitutes a greatness in the novel, and what if any is the
connexion between the novel and poetry? On these questions Menéndez
Pelayo is silent.

Cervantes' intuition of the greatness of his achievement matters less
perhaps than his clear perception of its novelty. ["I am the first one who
has written stories in the Spanish language"] would be but a minor claim
if it meant only that he was the first to do so in Spain what was already
being done elsewhere. But Cervantes did not write the *Novelas ejemplares*
as he did not write the first novel in the modern sense, without being
aware that he was breaking new ground, and his constant discussing of
literary precept and practice in the course of his imaginative writings is
not merely an invitation to the reader to consider the novelty of the
experiment and to meditate with the author on its problems: it is a
stressing above all of that basic problem that no one had ever yet seriously
confronted, the relation between art and experience in prose fiction.

The field of practice was unhelpful. At one extreme lay the romance
of chivalry, capable once of expressing a remote idealism but long since
divorced from such roots as it ever had in experience. If its escapist value
remained, it was none the less an offence to the intelligence of any reader
who attributed to literature a serious function and bearing on life. At the
other lay the picaresque tale, experience at its crudest and unrelieved.
Such writing might be conceded an informative, never a formative, value;
it knew neither philosophic content nor artistry. It is an elementary
mistake, yet much of Cervantine criticism is vitiated by it, to equate our
author's strictures on the unreality of the chivalresque romance to a
demand for "realism." The mistake is in truth a commonplace in the
criticism of imaginative prose generally, and a salutary indication of the
heresies that flow from regarding the choice of medium — prose or verse —
as a determinant of the kind of literature expressed therein. For one critic
who can appraise the real significance of the *Tragicomedia de Calixto y
Melibea* there are twenty who, insisting on calling it the *Celestina*,
proclaim it a masterpiece of realism. Cervantes was not deceived: ["A

book, in my opinion divine, if it would conceal more the human aspect."]
The excess of realism in the *Tragicomedia* was at once a blot on its artistry
and an impediment to the apprehension of its meaning as a commentary
on life.

Bridging these two extremes, bringing into harmonious conjunction
the twin facets of man's nature in a manner to satisfy both the intellect
and the aesthetic sense, there was nothing. Italy indeed knew other
varieties of prose fiction, the amorous imbroglio, the tale of perilous
adventure by land and sea. Both had more than a hand in permeating the
Spanish *comedia* with that suspense of interest and suspension of probability which were to the *mosquetero* the guarantee of his legitimate two
hours' enjoyment. They served a passing turn in Cervantes' own apprenticeship to the craft of writing: they taught him nothing at all of how to
write literature. Lope could have turned any of the five tales in the
Italianate vein that figure among the *Novelas ejemplares* into a typical
cloak and sword play in an afternoon, and, in adding to his own total,
subtracted nothing that mattered from Cervantes. Whatever their qualities, not one has any bearing on the business or the meaning of life. There
was still the pastoral novel, come too from Italy but thoroughly acclima-
tized now in Spain. It might seem to span the gap, for shepherds at least
were real and contemporary as knights-errant and enchanters were not,
and the accepted theme of their discourse was at once timeless and of a
particular pertinence to Renaissance man in his quest to know himself.
The kind, further, consorted well with poetry, and Cervantes had still
some distance to travel before he was to accept the verdict that ["a lot
could be expected from my prose, but nothing from my verse"]. The
pastoral novel was at all events the nearest model that current writing had
to offer Cervantes for what he sought to achieve; and so, writing the
Galatea and calling it an eclogue, he launched himself on the sea of
letters.

The impediment we have hinted at to full acceptance of Castro's
statement that the "truth" — by which term we understand him to mean
the philosophic implications — of the *Quijote* is at one with that of the
Galatea and the *Persiles* does not lie in any lack of serious philosophic
intent in the *Galatea*. The prologue to this makes specific reference to the
["philosophical ideas"] therein interwoven, in anticipation of the charge
that these are no shepherds but ["very discreet courtiers"]. The difficulty
lies, first, in these very ["philosophical ideas"]. The *Galatea* is one long
disquisition on the nature of true love, and shows our author conversant
with Leon Hebreo's *Dialoghi di amore*. This work was translated into
Spanish, it may be recalled, in 1568, the year in which Cervantes, ["in the
name of the whole school"] of López de Hoyos, was trying his 'prentice
hand at poetry on the occasion of the death of Isabel de Valois, and again
in 1582, when the *Galatea*, that was completed by the end of 1583, may
well have been in process of gestation. The point is of some interest for its

bearing on Cervantes' alleged indebtedness to Italian writers on aesthetic and literary theory. ["If you are on the subject of love"], he will write later, in the prologue to the *Quijote*, ["and have two ounce's worth of Italian, you will come across Leon Hebreo, who will give you full measure"]. Cervantes doubtless had that two ounces of Tuscan, in spite of the macaronic Italian of the *Licenciado vidriera*; the tone of the prologue would still have demanded the presumption thereof had he not. But he did not need it on this occasion, nor probably on others.

But this neo-Platonism is not the "truth" of the *Quijote*, the "double truth" that enables the novel to hold the mirror up to life in the round; it is an academic disquisition carried on in the stratosphere. The characters of the *Galatea* form, not a society, but a debating society, concerned not with life but with one ingredient of the ideal life. It is consequently improper to allege, with Castro, ["the perfect harmony that exists in the opposition of Don Quijote / Sancho on one side, and the *Galatea* and Cervantes' self-criticism on the other"]. The two facets of truth represented by Don Quixote and Sancho appear, interact, and merge in the same work, and it is in virtue of that interaction that the *Quijote* is a great work and something new in letters. In the *Galatea* Cervantes had still not been vouchsafed his vision of the duality of existence. At the least he did not know how to represent it in literature: his prologue ends with a significant confession of technical failure. The *Quijote*, the *Novelas ejemplares*, the *Persiles* are all something new, new in technique, new in their bearing on life; the *Galatea* is old, in an already hackneyed tradition. Between it and the others a deep dividing line is fixed, and the explanation of Cervantes' harping thereafter on the promised second part, if it is to make critical sense, must take that dividing line, and Cervantes' deep awareness of it, into account.

The revelation that came to Cervantes at some date after he had written the *Galatea* concerned, in essence, the relation that literature should bear to life, and, in form, the problem of shaping experience into a work of art. That revelation enabled him to turn the romance of chivalry inside out and fashion of it the *Quijote*, to take the short story then current and fashion of it the *Novelas ejemplares*, to resuscitate the Byzantine novel and fashion of it the *Persiles*. Criticism has boggled long over his intention, and his achievement, in the *Persiles*, and there are obvious qualifications to be made concerning the *Novelas ejemplares*. What matters here is Cervantes' conviction that he had discovered how to breathe new life into outworn forms, and that belief he also extended now to the pastoral novel. The second part of the *Galatea* he promises at the end of the first is not therefore the same as that promised in the *Quijote* and thereafter to the end of his life. In 1585 he could only have written another of the same; later he was confident he could write something very different. Cervantes tells us as much, in the scrutiny of Don Quixote's library, if we would only take him at his word: ["It (*La Galatea*) is

somewhat cleverly imagined. It proposes something and concludes nothing. It is necessary to wait for its promised second part. Perhaps amended
it will fully achieve the mercy now denied it; until this happens, keep it
hidden in your inn"]. In other words: "The framework of the kind is—or
can be made—serviceable enough, but the tale fails to achieve that
relevance to life which should have been the author's objective. The
continuation may make amends in this, and we must await it before
pronouncing final sentence. Meanwhile the first part in itself has no claim
to be spared; keep it under lock and key."

The nature of the dividing line, and the date of the revelation, are to
our mind clear. It is customary to assume that Cervantes, while a youth
soldiering in Italy, drank deep of current Italian writings on literary
theory. Toffanin would have him read the same books as Tasso, hear the
same discussions, even frequent, perhaps, the same company. Castro,
while holding it probable that he had read the Italian preceptists,
recognizes that there is no need to assume this: el Pinciano follows them
step by step. Menéndez Pelayo gave el Pinciano credit for much greater
originality and independence of judgment than Castro would allow, and
in fact rated him far above the Italians: alike in its understanding of
Aristotle and Horace and in its philosophic approach to literature his work
absolved, he held, from any need to turn to Italy. And the date of the
Philosophía antigua poética is 1596. The assumption that this was in fact
Cervantes' immediate source-book—and striking analogies have been
pointed out—not only solves the problem of the *Galatea*. It explains the
constant preoccupation with aesthetics and literary theory that pervades
the *Quijote*, and that argues a more recent and more vivid impact on his
mind than may be explained by the recollection of works read in Italy
thirty years earlier. It does much likewise to explain the *Persiles*, modelled
on that *Historia etiópica* of Heliodorus which el Pinciano repeatedly
extols, bracketing it with the *Odyssey* and the *Aeneid*.[1]

Does it explain also the great disparity in the *Novelas ejemplares*?
Seven of the tales in the collection, as every critic has noted, are divided by
an aesthetic abyss from the other five. These latter—those omitted by
Rodríguez Marín in his *Clásicos castellanos* edition—have no claim to be
either new or exemplary. Conceived in the Italianate tradition of amorous
intrigue, incredible coincidence, and total innocence of philosophic intention, they constitute an artistic anachronism in the company of the other
seven. It will be observed that, were the order of the *Ilustre fregona* and
the *Dos doncellas* reversed, the sequence of the collection would show a
regular alteration of new and exemplary with old and stereotyped; and it
is easier to accept an incidental disturbance of the order of these two in the
process of printing than an absence of design on the part of the author in
so ordering the others. There exist, that is to say, at least *prima facie*
grounds for supposing that, in order to put together a volume for
publication, Cervantes had turned out among his papers manuscripts of

much earlier date. From a reference in the *Quijote* we can carry *Rinconete* back from 1613 to 1604. The insertion of the *Curioso impertinente* and the *Cautivo* in the *Quijote* is proof that Cervantes was not averse from refurbishing earlier compositions for publication when opportunity offered. Evidence that these two may well be much earlier, in fact pre-1596, is furnished by the Cura's criticism of the former in terms precisely of el Pinciano. Four of these five Italianate tales provide no clue to the date of their composition. The internal chronology of the fifth, the *Española inglesa*, is flagrantly self-contradictory. But if its composition may not convincingly be placed after 1604 merely on the grounds, as Icaza and Fitzmaurice-Kelly have it, that Cervantes would not have dared to speak well of Elizabeth and Essex while England and Spain were still at war – cf. Zapata in his *Miscelánea* of c. 1595: ["The new invention is the armed ships which the excellent Englishman Drake used against us in the channel"] – , there would appear to be faint possibility of carrying it back to the neighbourhood of 1596 unless one were bold to postulate that the Essex of the first paragraph may originally have read Drake and that Cervantes brought the detail up to date in revising his manuscript for publication, as we know he revised the *Celoso extremeño*. Enough that the tale, if post-1596, is essentially, in conception and in execution, a throwback, and is properly to be excluded, along with the other four, from any consideration of what Cervantes may have owed to the *Philosophía antigua poética*.[2]

It is from the remaining seven that we can best discover the specific nature of Cervantes' literary problem. Experience had taught him much of life, and he wished to convey its lessons artistically in the form of prose fiction. None of the extant forms in the kind satisfied him in its relationship either to art or to experience. Had literary theory any light to throw on the matter? It was doubtless in an unhopeful frame of mind that he took up el Pinciano, for, while he could himself reach intuitively to Aristotle's principle that each literary kind purveys its own peculiar pleasure – and must accordingly possess its own criteria – , Aristotle's kinds did not include the one in question. There would still remain principles of universal artistic validity, and possibly, in el Pinciano, some recognition that literature had not stood still since Aristotle's day.

He found, to begin with, the firm assertion that poetry was a generic term for all imaginative literature, and that it was not essential that such literature should be written in verse. Nor, he read, was there any fundamental difference between heroic narrative based on fact and that which was pure invention. The novel, that is to say, could be regarded as a variant of the epic. ["About Heliodorus, there is no doubt that he is a poet, and one of the finest epic poets that have written up to now"]. The reference may be taken as the genesis of the *Persiles*, just as the modified praise given to the *Amadís*, with its ["many good parts"], has an obvious relevance to that of the *Quijote*. So too Cervantes' oft-reiterated pride in his inventiveness — ["I am the one who excels in invention"] — goes back to el Pinciano's deprecation of the re-handling of traditional themes: ["The poet should not bind himself to common tales, but imagine and create new ones, for in it (invention) consists its excellence"].

But these are still externals. The marrow of el Pinciano's teaching for Cervantes lay in the theory of imitation and in his discussion of the end of poetry. In that theory he found the mean he desired between the *Amadís* and the *Lazarillo*. The artist must imitate nature, not copy her. Nature is not art, and a transcription of reality, a slice of life, will not of itself be a work of art. Neither will a flight from reality. The beginning of art is verisimilitude: better the impossible probable than the improbable possible (it was on this ground that the priest condemned the *Curioso impertinente*). And the end of art? Some say pleasure, some say edification. Each may in fact be made to subserve the other: ["If the poet imitates with delight in order to teach the doctrine, this (the doctrine) will be the true end (purpose); but if he imitates with doctrine in order to delight, to delight will be the main intent"]. El Pinciano would himself opt for both: ["Let's take it for certain and without a doubt that the most artistic fable will be the one which most gives pleasure and teaches with the greatest simplicity"]. But the means to either, or any, end is form, and since achievement depends on form, it follows that the means in literature matters more than the end. It is a greater offence to el Pinciano that a work of art should err in its form than in its content. Form in poetry begins with imitation, verisimilitude; but there is more to it than that. There is a symmetry and harmony of its parts, a beginning, a middle and an end, a tying and a loosening of the knot, and these elements of form may justify on occasion a departure even from verisimilitude, its essence. ["As long as the action delights, a fable is not to be condemned, nor its author be considered less, because at times the imperfection is not in the artist but in the art form."] In el Pinciano, finally, Cervantes found formulated the cardinal theory of the complexity of truth and of the greater excellence of poetic over historic truth. ["The poet is only obliged to the truth to the degree that verisimilitude seems to require it."]

Such then was the baggage of precept with which, some time after 1596, Cervantes addressed himself, after his false start with the *Galatea*, to the writing of prose fiction. And the first concrete question he must have posed to himself concerned doubtless the value for literary purposes of his own past experience. That experience was historic truth, reality, indubitably interesting, but formless. Art, he now knew, was not reality but the imitation thereof: as free as fancy dictated so long as it kept within the bounds of verisimilitude, and much concerned with form. The only value of experience in this connexion was as a check on fancy, a guarantee that probability would not be outraged. Recollection might supplement the creative imagination, as in the supplying of background detail, but no character, no scene drawn from life was artistically superior or even estimable merely because of its rooting in fact. There is "experience" in this sense in the *Amante liberal*, with the captivity in Africa and the final ["contentment, which is one of the greatest that can be enjoyed in this life, to arrive, after a long captivity, safe and sound to your own country"], as there is intense realism in the description of the storm, but the tale, wholly un-exemplary, is also artistically absurd, and the long account of the storm only annoys by its irrelevance. There is "experience" similarly in the *Cautivo*, but Fernando's comment on the dolorous tale shows the company wholly untouched by its woes and rigours. The seven truly exemplary tales have sloughed this naive approach. Cervantes was never a gipsy, nor one of a thieves' fraternity, nor a student — sane or cracked — at Salamanca, nor a quasi-septuagenarian unhinged by jealousy, nor an errant son taken to the roads, nor an abandoned victim of a designing female, nor a hospital watch-dog. All these are legitimate offspring of his imagination, as much as if he had never known Italy, or Lepanto, or Algiers, or been a grain-collector for the Armada. True, he might not then have etched in with the same detail the cities of Italy in the *Licenciado vidriera*; but would that tale be the worse artistically without those particulars, or the better if he had been able to embroider correspondingly his mention of Antwerp, Ghent and Brussels?

But if el Pinciano had scant use for experience as the stuff of creative literature, there was another sense in which it could be fundamental. A poem, we have seen, might be content simply to give pleasure, and be justified thereby; and it is notable that Cervantes, resuscitating for insertion in the *Quijote* the two early tales aforementioned, defends them both on this ground. ["As for the manner of its telling"], says the priest of the *Curioso impertinente*, ["that does not displease me." . . . "I assure you, Captain"], says Fernando of the *Cautivo*, ["the way in which you have told your strange adventure has been as remarkable as the strangeness and novelty of the events themselves . . . and we have enjoyed listening so much that even if it took until tomorrow morning to tell it, we should be glad to hear it all over again"]. The *Curioso impertinente* was "improbable"; the *Cautivo*, realism itself, made no impact on its hearers because it was unrelated to their experience. Yet both were made tolerable by the telling. It is possible that we have here the explanation of that obscure tercet in the *Viaje del Parnaso*: ["I have opened with my novels a way / by which the Castilian tongue can / show foolishness with propriety"]. ["Stories"], el Pinciano had written, ["without imitation or verisimilitude are not fables but nonsense"]. Cervantes was well aware that five of his tales had nothing of the exemplary about them, he may well have received the criticism on this score that the prologue to the collection clearly anticipates, and he resorts in the *Viaje* to this purely literary defence. Cipión in the *Coloquio de los perros* expresses the matter more precisely: ["Some stories enclose and contain their cleverness within themselves; others, in the manner in which they are told"]. But Cervantes had long since come down decisively in favour of the poem whose subject-matter had an intrinsic interest for the reader. And the key to that interest lay in investing literature with a bearing on life, not the material facts of life, which differ from individual to individual, but the meaning of life, its problems and pitfalls, and our capacity to cope with them. It was in this sense that Cervantes was the better equipped as a writer for his wealth of experience, which he could now see, thanks to el Pinciano, as a matter not of what he had seen and done but of what he had learnt. We may note the difference between experience as reflected in the *Cautivo* and in the *Coloquio de los perros*. Both are cast autobiographically; one deals solely with the facts, the other solely with the lessons of life.

Cervantes now accepts, even demands, that literature shall have a doctrinal content and purpose; but his "doctrine" is to be interpreted in relation to el Pinciano and Aristotle, not—as some would have it—to the Counter-Reformation. He has no interest in dogmatic truth, but only in stimulating the reader to a concern for truth, in making him reflect on the nature of life and of man. For himself he believes in an inner harmony, of the individual within himself, and in a larger harmony, of men with one another and with Nature, and this is often, but not invariably, his theme. Before that ultimate goal can be reached mankind must realise what are the barriers that separate us from it: the beginning of knowledge is self-knowledge. Herein lies the exemplariness of the *Novelas ejemplares*. Only one, the *Celoso extremeño*, carries a moral in terms of the larger harmony. The others are studies of life, mirrors wherein man may study himself in the play of human relations, enriched with reflexions born of the author's own experience. ["There are two delights in Poetics: one comes from the imitation, the other can arise from the lessons it offers"]. The two, it is true, were not on an equal footing: the poem could dispense with doctrinal purpose, it could not dispense with imitation and still be a work of art. Cervantes' achievement in the *Quijote* lies in its felicitous fusion of the two, so that a fable endlessly absorbing in itself, removed from realism but faultless in its verisimilitude, is suffused at the same time with the light of high philosophic truth. In spite of the novelty of the achievement, however, it is fair to remember that el Pinciano's affiliation of the novel to the epic has made our author free of a substantial body of precept and example, and that his masterpiece is in fact conceived on the epic, heroic plane.

But el Pinciano had nothing to say of the short story, and Cervantes' claim to be a pioneer in this field rests on his attempt to work out for himself an aesthetic for the kind. How is doctrinal purpose to be interwoven with the fable on this new, smaller, non-heroic scale? We may begin by noting that Cervantes rejects all three categories of the fable according to el Pinciano: ["the ones that are pure fiction; the ones which shape a single truth out of one lie and one invention; and the ones that make a thousand fictions out of one truth"]. The second of these, the apologue, the only one of the three strictly applicable to the new dimensions, is severely censured by el Pinciano himself for its subordination of artistry to moral ends; and the moral attached by Cervantes to the *Española inglesa* shows how ill at ease Cervantes would have found himself with the form. Here at least was negative guidance. The values, moreover, that Cervantes wished to inculcate were not those of the moralist's copy-book. Life had taught him to esteem, not the virtues, but one compendious and even unorthodox virtue, inasmuch as it hinted most disturbingly at the relativity of all the others. Its name was discretion, and it is the leitmotif of all his serious writing. Discretion was the science, or the art, or simply the doctrine, of the relativity of all criteria of human conduct, and is not to be learnt from the copy-book: it is to be learnt by living. And the novelist can only help others to learn it by depicting his characters as they severally learn to live.

Now it is a truism that the active life is more fruitful of experience, and so of the lessons of experience, than the passive. Cervantes had learnt his lessons the hard way, in Italy, in Algiers, in Andalusia, and no sentiment rings more sincerely in his pages than that ["long journeys make men wise"]. Even in his non-exemplary tales—those we have held as probably ante-dating his reading of el Pinciano—journeying is repeatedly of the essence of the framework: so the *Cautivo*, the *Amante liberal*, the *Española inglesa*, the *Dos doncellas*. The *Quijote* is one long peregrination over the roads of Spain. And the first of his exemplary tales proper, the *Gitanilla*, is again framed against the vicissitudes that befall the wanderer. There is however a difficulty inherent in the scale of the short story; and Cervantes felt the need of some method of infusing into it more of experience than the incidents themselves could normally bear, if the end was not to be defeated by the very brevity of the form. His solution lies in investing a given character or characters with a wealth of past or vicarious experience. And so Preciosa is presented to us—very apologetically, for she is only fifteen and Cervantes is much preoccupied with his verisimilitude—as a monument of discretion, who reads her Andrés, and the reader, many a lesson on the conduct of life. ["It doesn't bother me so much that you are jealous as that you are indiscreet."] Twice we see other characters go to extremes in their, or the author's, concern to show discretion: Andrés as he tries to fathom Clemente's intentions in the gipsy encampment, and the corregidor as he sounds Andrés in gaol. There is no moral as such in the tale: the profit is to be garnered along the way. What meanwhile of its artistry, the form of the fable? A journey in life is over at journey's end. A journey in literature must end in a dénouement. And it is in his dénouements that we note Cervantes' first failure to master the problems of this new art-form. In the *Gitanilla*, it is true, the reader is prepared from the beginning: ["In truth she deserved to be the daughter of a great gentleman."] But the ending is still that of any novelette. El Pinciano we have seen tolerant of inverisimilitude in the dénouement ["so long as the action is pleasurable"], and the first practitioner of the art may claim indulgence if sheltered behind his mentor's suggestion that a given kind might have its own intrinsic imperfections.

The benefit of travel, of seeing new things, rests in the main on the challenge these convey to our conventional assumptions. That challenge, almost always implicit in Cervantes, is made explicit in the *Gitanilla* through the initiation of Andrés into the gipsy community and the consequent exposition of a way of life and a social structure new to the reader, ["that order so well established in reason and fundamentals of politics"] that knew nothing, and cared less, of ["Church or sea or courtly service"]. So too in the *Rinconete y Cortadillo* we witness the initiation of the two newcomers into the fellowship of thieves. But there the resemblance ends: doctrinally, in that there is no suggestion of commendation for the latter but only the pulling aside of a curtain, enlarging our knowledge of life and inviting reflexion on the ease with which piety and rascality may make their bed together; artistically, in that this is not in fact a story, rounded off — however arbitrarily — in deference to a concern for form, a fable with its knot and its unknotting, but a sketch, static and pictorial as the other was episodic and narrative. Of Preciosa's personal appearance we are told exactly nothing save that she was of surpassing beauty; in Monipodio we have one of Cervantes' most finished portraits, its successive touches paralleled by the careful building-up of the background for his dramatic entry. And Cervantes duly recognizes that, not being a story in the ordinary sense, it cannot have a dénouement. Still experimenting to find out how much of life the short story could hold, he had allowed himself to dwell too fondly on his canvas until he over-ran his dimensions. In an ampler narrative kind such indulgences are not necessarily destructive of the fable: hence Cervantes' ending, in which he promises to return to the theme and complete the fable with a full ["life and miracles"]. But it could not then be a short story; as a novel, for which kind Cervantes now had the prescription as a prose-epic, it was cast in the wrong mould, not the heroic but the anti-heroic, perilously near to the sterile formula of the picaresque; and Cervantes never did return to it. The experiment had not come off.

Alike in the *Gitanilla* and the *Rinconete* there was much pungent social criticism for such as could read beneath the surface. Cervantes' bent in this direction was pronounced. But in an age which did not stand up well to social criticism, and under a regime which actively discouraged the appreciation, however objective, of other ways of life, he must often have reflected, with his friend, Bartolomé Leonardo de Argensola, that ["he who freely speaks the truth is inevitably cast down"]. A large part of discretion, therefore, for one who would instill this virtue in his writings, consisted in the ability to do it discreetly. Discretion, as Cervantes understood it, is not merely a more charitable but a more exact term for what some would call hypocrisy. Every artist must take account of the difficulties and the limitations of his medium, and to the writer, concerned with communication, his public and the atmosphere of his age are integral parts of that medium. Verisimilitude itself depends on the wedding of the fable to the reader's understanding. One conventional figure there was, in another kind, who enjoyed a traditional licence to speak his mind openly, and Cervantes envied him his freedom. ["The fool is the most discreet character in the play"], says Don Quixote. But the *comedia* was not Cervantes' kind, and the [fool] could not be carried over as such to the short story. He was, it was true, but the literary descendant of the court jester, and for a moment we surprise Cervantes in the *Gitanilla* wondering whether any possibility to his purpose was to be found here. He decides against: the jester of old has become the [scoundrel], and discretion is no longer his hallmark. ["If they wanted me for my discretion, they still might have taken me"], says Preciosa; ["but in some palaces the scoundrels do better than the discreet people"], and she declined a presentation to Their Majesties.

There remained another privileged individual, the mentally unhinged. There were, Cervantes knew, many kinds and degrees of mental derangement, and much sound sense in the gibe about the madhouse: ["not all those are [mad] who are there, nor are all [the mad people] there"], and he early seized on the literary potentialities implicit therein. The whole fable of the *Quijote* hinges on the derangement in one particular of Don Quixote and the entire compatibility with this of his extreme sanity and discretion in every other; and now, in the *Licenciado vidriera*, he set himself to the query whether the same device could be made to serve in the short story. Again, as in the *Rinconete*, he begins by launching his protagonist on the open road, across Spain, Italy and Flanders. Eight years in Salamanca had given Rodaja profound knowledge of law and humane letters; he was endowed with a good memory and a good understanding. He still lacked knowledge of life, discretion, and ["long journey"] was the formula. Again we are given, incidentally, an exposition of other specific ways of life, those this time of the soldier and the sailor. What is of more note is the fact that here, more than in any other of these exemplary tales, it is clear that Cervantes was tempted for a moment to question Aristotle on the superiority in art of the probable over the real and to draw on the memory of his own years in Italy. The experience was decisive. The journeyings of Andrés and Preciosa, of Rinconete and Cortadillo, are full of significance. Those of Rodaja in Italy give us a wine-list and a page from the guide-book, and are correspondingly innocent of any real bearing on life. The *Quijote*, it may be recalled in this connexion, only begins to take on significance, alike artistic and philosophical, when Don Quixote returns from his first sally and provides himself with a squire. Until then he had had no one to talk to. The play of mind on mind is a great sharpener of experience, and the importance Cervantes gives to good talk in the *Quijote* must be accounted one of his major contributions to the modern novel. Rodaja too was a solitary on his grand tour, and whatever vital impression this left on his mind, it leaves none on the reader. It was a mistake Cervantes was not to repeat. He will never draw on reality again in the same way, and he will never again send a protagonist out on life unaccompanied. Back in Salamanca, and the victim of the potion, Rodaja now has Everyman as his interlocutor and is suffered to speak his mind freely on this and that and what-not. The result is esteemed as an edifying commentary on the Spain of its day, though few pause to note that many of the Licenciado's repartees do not rise above mediocre puns and very few plumb beneath the surface of homely wisdom. Cervantes was no satirist. Later, in the *Viage del Parnaso*, he will disown the sect:

> My humble pen never flew
> Over the region of satire, scurrility
> Which leads to hateful gains and disgrace.

But conceding that the work is solid with comment on life, conceding even a certain penetration to one or two of these comments, *e.g.* on the husband deserted by his wife, or on the genus [scribe], its artistic value as a short story is nil. Play of minds there is none; plot there is none, and so dénouement there can be none. When Cervantes can think of no more butts for Rodaja's wit he gives him back his sanity, and the tale ends. The experiment had pointed nonetheless a further lesson. Henceforth Cervantes knew in practice, what el Pinciano had taught him in theory, not merely that the real was no substitute for the probable in art, but that form in art is more important than content, the fable than its teaching. Here was a second sense in which discretion was called for in the speaking of truth.

In the following tale, the *Celoso extremeño*, Cervantes accordingly gives thought to the fable, and, being more concerned here than in any of the others to underline a particular aspect of the discretion and the harmony that life and Nature demand, he is more concerned equally that the doctrine shall derive of itself from the narrative and not clog its artistry. Is it by accident, or by an instinctive reversion from the faulty technique of the *Licenciado vidriera*, that Carrizales is introduced to us as a man on whom ["many journeys"] had conferred no discretion whatever but only a ruined patrimony and a bitter memory of ["the poor self-governance which characterized his whole life"]? And when, old, sobered, and again wealthy, he plans to settle down and be discreet, he still does not possess the knowledge of life to avoid running his head straight into a wall. The previous tales had sought to inform on life positively, by depicting those who knew it. Here Cervantes reverses the procedure, informing negatively by depicting the tragedy of one who knew it not. If the epic could be in prose, why not tragedy? And, going back to el Pinciano, Cervantes gives us the slow movement of stark, inevitable nemesis. The

Celoso extremeño is by far the best short story Cervantes ever wrote, and just because he has concentrated on the fable first it is the only one which achieves a satisfying ending.

The *Celoso extremeño* is also, as it happens, the *locus classicus* for the theorists of Cervantine hypocrisy, and since Cervantes' aesthetic problem in the short story is so entwined about the balance of [delight] and [instruction], the question calls for brief comment. The 1613 version, as is well known, tones down the brief account given in the Porras Ms. of c. 1606 of what happened at a vital moment between Leonora — there called Isabela — and Loaysa. Castro suggests that the Archbishop of Seville, for whom the Porras Ms. was prepared, may have taken offence at the earlier text, and contends in any case that comparison with the [interludes] of the *Viejo celoso* allows of no other conclusion than that Cervantes was a "wily hypocrite," in which respect ["he has the typical traces of the eminent thinker of the Counter-Reformation"]. ["One must write *exemplary* novels."] To which it may be objected firstly that to represent an Archbishop who could swallow the *Tía fingida*, also contained in the Porras Ms., as straining at the gnat of one sentence in the *Celoso extremeño* — ["Isabela was not as tearful in Loyasa's arms as one might think"] — is to argue a very improbable Archbishop, secondly that the *Viejo celoso* was published not before but two years after the *Novelas ejemplares*, when Cervantes was still less of an age ["to make fun of the life to come"], and thirdly that Castro knows better than anyone else that his implied interpretation here of the term "ejemplar" is wholly untenable. The explanation of the apparent discrepancy he had himself supplied earlier in noting that in the *Viejo celoso* the theme is treated ["comically, as is appropriate for the interlude"]. The difference is not one of doctrine, or of sincerity, but of artistry. What is proper in comedy may be improper in tragedy, and the greatest artistic impropriety in tragedy is to detract irrelevantly from the inevitability of impending doom. Carrizales paid the final penalty not for Leonora's indiscretion but for his own, and it was artistic gain to limit hers to the minimum necessary to set the tragic train in motion. ["I don't blame you, oh ill-advised child!"] he says on his deathbed, and the story ends with a re-assertion by the author of Leonora's innocence. ["We now know"] writes Castro, ["that Cervantes has never presented a case of adultery that at least he does not forgive"]. How then does Cervantes write of Carrizales' discovery of the offence to his honour, knowing, as Carrizales did not, how much of this was deceptive appearance: ["He would take the vengeance that that great evil required, if only he had arms with which to carry it out. . . . With this necessary and honorable decision he returned to his room"]? We read no condonation here.

With the *Ilustre fregona* we are back in the atmosphere of the *Gitanilla*: adventures on the road, a romantic attachment to a lowly maiden of rare loveliness, a denouement depending on a series of coincidences that el Pinciano, for all his tolerance on this point, might well have hesitated to hold justified. Again the fable is inadequate to the doctrinal purpose — the lifting of another curtain from another stratum of life —, and the aesthetic pleasure comes not from the fable but from such incidental episodes as the ["Hand over the tail, Austurian"]. Costanza too is cast for a model of discretion, outstanding in a city ["which is famous for having the most discreet women in Spain"]. Her beauty was the bait to the reader, her discretion the earnest of the edification awaiting him. But whereas in the *Gitanilla* the action all revolved around Preciosa, there has intervened now the *Rinconete*, and Cervantes, in spite of his conscious failure on that occasion, is still attracted down the same fatal byways, enamoured of the infinite variety of life's kaleidoscope, until the structure of the fable is compromised beyond repair and the characters are finally dispatched in a manner reminiscent of the *comedia* at its most irresponsible. Not one but three weddings are arranged off-hand, two involving brides of whom not merely the reader but their respective bridegrooms have never heard before. And even this is nothing to the inverisimilitude of the revelation concerning Costanza's parentage. The conclusion must have been as plain to Cervantes as it is to us: the technique of the short story was something totally different from that of the novel, and called in particular for a self-discipline, an economy of resources, and a concern for the form of the fable that did not come easily to him.

The form of the *Casamiento engañoso* would suggest that Cervantes was here seeking deliberately to impose on himself the needful discipline. To set characters on the road, to embark on the description of a way of life, is to invite the temptations of the bypaths, or indulgence in the purely pictorial, and farewell to artistic fable. Here the narrative is literally a narrative, the action is the past tense, and the protagonist is the narrator. His listener is the automatic check, ready to pull him up if he threatens to leave the lines; and the device appears to work for not until Campuzano reaches the end of his tale does Peralta interrupt. And as there are no discrepancies, so there are no *longueurs*. The *Licenciado vidriera* had shown Cervantes the fallacy, as a technique for the short story, of his cherished conviction about ["long journeys"], but he was still then loath to lay it down. Even the *Celoso extremeño* must still peregrinate over Europe and the Indies before the fable can begin. Carriazo and Avendaño must still foot it from Burgos to Toledo, over many pages, before the *Ilustre fregona* can get under way, just as Rinconete and Cortadillo had had to journey from Alcudia to Seville, but at last Cervantes has shaken off the misconception. The *Casamiento engañoso* begins and ends in Valladolid, and the interest lies not in action, not in movement, not even in psychology. The possibility that in this last lay the true field of the short story seems never to have occurred to Cervantes, to whom it may well have appeared that only the larger canvas after which we have seen him instinctively hanker could do justice to his illuminating misconception of character in solution, as a process of constant becoming, the fruit of interaction. The *Casamiento engaño* is a simple fable, artistically satisfying, of the ["biter bitten"]. And its exemplary value? No moral derives from the telling. Instead — and it is a felicitous discovery — the device of narrator and listener allows the tale to end with a brief colloquy between the two as to whether the experience has in fact any doctrinal significance. The would-be deceiver has been taken in. His wife has abandoned him, taking with her all his valuables. Poetic justice? Granted; but the trinkets and jewels were none of them genuine. She too had been taken in. [" 'If that's how it is,' said the Licenciate, 'the biter is bitten.' 'And so bitten,' answered the ensign, 'that we can just go back and shuffle the cards again.' "] The Leonora of the *Celoso extremeño*, presented merely as a foil to her husband's tragic error, was the first woman in the *Novelas ejemplares* not to be presented as a peerless beauty. Cervantes for once had dropped the romantic convention in these matters to write a tragedy. Doña Estefanía is the second: ["She was not extremely beautiful, but she was attractive"]. Here the convention has gone in favour of comedy. Cervantes is writing for grown-ups who can take the vicissitudes of life with a shrug of the shoulders; if they cannot, his tale may help them to, and that is exemplariness enough. For a second and last time Cervantes has written a short story which is a short story. Has he learnt his technique, or did he stumble upon it all unknowing? And, if fully conscious of his discovery, did the technique once mastered really interest him?

These are the questions posed by the *Coloquio de los perros*. That Cervantes' aim was not merely to solve the aesthetic problem involved in forging a new kind is now evident; he was concerned also to know whether the new kind was amenable to his demands. We have seen doctrinal preoccupation lead to aesthetic failure in the *Licenciado vidriera*. And still Cervantes ponders whether some other device might not succeed, where that of madness had failed, in allowing him to range far and wide over the whole field of human experience. In the Lucianesque dialogue there lay to his hand another form which, eliminating action completely, reduced the narrative to present comment on past experience. The *Casamiento engañoso* had marked a first development in this direction, and the *Coloquio de los perros* appears naturally in the collection as a pendant thereto. By investing dogs with the power of speech, a liberty for which also there was sound precedent, and one which el Pinciano on that score alone would doubtless have admitted to the category of the impossible probable, he added the freedom to range now over the whole of life in search of a standpoint of such demonstrable objectivity as should make the truth acceptable. And Berganza is in fact quoting el Pinciano almost literally when, much corrected by Cipión, he looks forward to Cipión's own narrative to come as one ["that will teach and delight at the same time"]. ["I have it!"] says Cervantes in effect: ["I don't need two months to finish the philosopher's stone"].

El Pinciano, it is true, had reversed the order, putting *deleite* first.

["The most artistic fable will be that which delights and teaches the most. . . . Poetry, wishing to delight looks to delight. . . . The final cause is delight"]. The divergence may be a detail; but we have now been taught to respect even the details of Cervantes' so studied art, and this one we venture to believe vital to his adventures with the short story. For having at last found a form which satisfied him in the scope it gave for doctrinal content, only one aspect of the matter escaped his notice: it was no longer a short story. ["The soul of poetry is the fable."] in the *Coloquio de los perros* we may not find fault with the fable, for fable there is none. The work is a fascinating commentary on life and its teachings, it is a masterpiece of acute observation and fine writing, it gives us, among so much else, the *membra disjecta* of a most suggestive treatise of Cervantes' own on the literary art, it is the one writing of Cervantes that, after the *Quijote*, we could least bear not to have: but it is not a short story. Here too we cannot hope now to learn why the second part was never written. So much of life is covered in the first that Cervantes may have doubted his ability to produce another of equal interest and — as he had been bold to hint — of even superior craftsmanship. Or he may have reflected, as this present essay has sought to do, on the whole course of his farings with this new and so difficult kind and resolved to renounce it.

Our analysis, in following the order of presentation of these seven tales, has not necessarily assumed this to be that of composition. There can be no proof positive that this was so, though neither, to our knowledge, is there convincing evidence to the contrary. But in default of such proof or disproof we are entitled to assume at least that the sequence is not fortuitous. We believe we have demonstrated the elements of a progressive development in Cervantes' approach to the aesthetic problem he had taken up, and we believe he would have admitted to finding the kind refractory to his instinctive bent in regard both to form and, even more, to content. His philosophic mind required freedom to move at its ease, and his essential trouble with the short story was that he addressed himself, not to finding out just what it was capable of as an art form, but to the attempt to make of it another and too subservient vehicle for his own conception of the connexion between life and letters. In the attempt he found the aesthetic demands of the fable constantly getting in his way, and he ended, with the arbitrariness of genius, by thrusting the fable aside. Whereupon, inevitably, the experiment came to an end.

Notes

1. *Vid.* William C. Atkinson, "The Enigma of the *Persiles*," in *Bulletin of Spanish Studies*, October, 1947.

2. Since this article was written Mack Singleton has demonstrated the feasibility of assigning the tale to 1596: "The Date of *La española inglesa*," *Hispania*, August, 1947.

Viaje del Parnaso (1614)

Cervantes' Journey to Parnassus Elias Rivers*

It is surprising to find that Cervantes' most overtly autobiographical work has been quite inadequately studied.[1] (It may have been a "pot-boiler," but so was the *Quijote*.) The fact that the *Viaje del Parnaso* is a mock-epic written in *terza rima* perhaps discourages modern readers from approaching it seriously. But the burlesque element is also essential to the *Quijote*, that is, to the maturity of Cervantes' literary career. Do we then accept his burlesque in prose, and not in verse? Yet his most popular poem was, and is, his sonnet on Philip II's tomb in the Cathedral of Seville, a gigantic construction of papiermâché representing the Escorial, designed and decorated by the leading architects and artists of the city. Thousands went to gaze gaping at this impressive, but very temporary, monument. In his sonnet Cervantes gives us the over-emphatic exclamations and the empty gestures of two histrionic sightseers, one an oath-snorting soldier and the other a sycophantic tough guy from the local slums. Nothing could be more radically burlesque than to treat in this oblique way the death of an imperial monarch.[2] Also written in verse is one of Cervantes' most amusing dramatic interludes, the *Rufián viudo*: blank verse heightens the slang and the purely comic grief of the pimp for his late mistress, whose earnings he sorely misses. Burlesque poetry is in fact essential to the mature Cervantes: he uses it to frame the first part of the *Quijote*, and he constantly plays with Carolingian ballads during his mad hero's exploits, including the famous mock-heroic underground vision in the cave of Montesinos.

As for the autobiographical aspect, we may feel that we know Cervantes personally because he sometimes lets us catch glimpses of himself as the inventor of his stories, the master puppeteer who manipulates narrators, narrations and their interruptions as he edits the translation of an Arab's chronicle. Less evasive is the author that we see dramatizing himself in his famous prologues, as he presents his works to the reading public.[3] His modest irony is most ingratiating as he depicts himself, with paper in front of him, his pen behind his ear, elbow on the

*Reprinted with permission from *MLN* 85 (1970):243–48.

desk, chin in hand, trying to write a prologue to Part I (1605) of the *Quijote*. He begins his prologue to the *Novelas ejemplares* (1613) as a sequel to the preceding one, though eight years have gone by in between: "I would like, if it were possible, dear reader, to get by without writing this prologue, because I had so much trouble with the previous one." He also uses his prologues to advertise other works that he is writing and will soon publish, or to defend his whole literary career, sometimes rather bitterly. The imagination of the novelist seems often to run wild in his prologues, invading his dedications and even, in one case, a censor's official [approval].[4] Cervantes' own illness and approaching death are topics of great pathos as presented in the dedication and prologue of the posthumous *Persiles*. Yes, we feel that we know Cervantes personally when he presents himself dramatically to us in this way, just as we feel that we know Montaigne from his *Essays*.

In a work of more deliberate literary art like the *Viaje del Parnaso*, Cervantes does not of course present himself in so intimate a style. No doubt the prologue to Part I of the *Quijote* is also to some degree fictionalized; but a friend may in fact actually have come into Cervantes' study and helped him write the prologue. In the *Viaje*, on the other hand, we knew that Cervantes' trip through the Mediterranean to Mt. Parnassus was wholly imaginary (Croce has called it [an "ideal voyage"]; it was as imaginary as his invitation to teach at a Spanish college in the court of the Emperor of China (see dedication to Part II of the *Quijote*). The *Viaje del Parnaso* is a literary "dream-journey," containing within itself a "dream-vision" of an even more imaginary, allegorical world. Yet the narrator-protagonist is called Miguel de Cervantes, and the central theme of the poem is in fact Cervantes' own public reputation as a poet and critic. Masks and mythological fictions serve to put some distance between the author and his subject; burlesque and irony frequently increase this distance. But the whole business is clearly of the greatest personal importance to the writer Cervantes himself. Laughter can not always disguise an underlying bitterness with which our aged and indigent author views himself in the context of Madrid society, surrounded by the greater fame and wealth of inferior writers. The *Viaje del Parnaso* is, I submit, an attempt on the part of the author to establish, by means of self-deprecating irony and broadly satirical burlesque, a secure "public image" for himself as an author and critic of poetry. He can not successfully separate, in his own mind, the question of the "intrinsic" value of good poetry, from the question of the economic rewards and social status of the poet. Surely, from an ideal point of view, the latter should depend upon the former. But, in the real world of the Spain that he knew, there was in fact no discernible correlation. Above all, Cervantes had a firm conviction, especially after the international success of Part I of the *Quijote* (a success from which he did not profit financially, since he had sold his rights), a firm conviction that he was a better writer than most of his competitors in Spain; and yet he was having trouble feeding and clothing himself, and he knew that commercial successes like Lope de Vega frequently sneered at him. These are the personal problems that underlie the burlesque mythology and battles of the *Viaje del Parnaso*.

Cervantes begins his poem by describing his literary model, the *Viaggio in Parnaso* (1582) by Cesare Caporali di Perugia (1531–1601). He begins by saying, in effect, "Caporali made a trip to Parnassus on a mule and was well received by Apollo; he returned pennyless but famous. I would like to do the same. The distance is great, but my desire for fame is even greater. So, mounted on destiny, behind free choice in the saddle, I set out, being a very light load, since I am a poet, with no suitcase." Here there is a brief digression on the mad flights of moneyless poets, quixotic individualists who ignore wealth and honor. But Cervantes has sense enough to put bread and cheese in his saddlebags. His farewell to Madrid ends with a reference to hunger reminiscent of the *Lazarillo* (p. 17): ["Farewell, subtle hunger of an impoverished gentleman,/So as not to find myself dead at your gates,/Today I take leave of my home and myself"]. There is no doubt that two years previously, when the Conde of Lemos, Cervantes' eventual patron, was named Viceroy of Naples, our poet would very gladly have gone into exile with him, if he had been invited to, as the Argensola brothers were. But now, in the face of economic necessity, he is ready to leave, not only Madrid, but even himself, behind, in his imaginary journey to Parnassus; there he will help the god Apollo in his war against the invasion of bad poets, anti-poets who, like the "Blue Meanies" of the *Yellow Submarine*, threaten to engulf the world.

Apollo has drawn up a list of good Spanish poets which Cervantes is to use for recruiting soldiers, ["very few well, and most poorly, dressed"] (p. 36). When they finally arrive at Apollo's *locus amoenus*, a garden where Art competes with Nature, Cervantes feels hungry (p. 51), but no one else seems to, least of all the god of poetry himself. Worse yet, there is a rustic seat for everyone else, but none for our poet, who realizes as in a paranoid nightmare that even on Mount Parnassus Fortune is persecuting him. It is in protest against such gross injustice that he now recites to Apollo a proud bibliography of his publications, past and future, with comments on their critical reception. But Apollo can still find no seat of honor for him, and so, Cervantes says (p. 57):

> [I bowed my head to the great leader;
> I remained on foot, since there is no good chair
> which is not fashioned out of wealth or favor.
> Someone objected, seeing me far
> from the glory he thought I was due
> and full of virtue and the planet of light.]

In the presence now of true Poetry, Cervantes finds to his surprise that she is a very richly dressed lady, well learned in all the arts and sciences, the queen of the intellectual world. He seems to be particularly irritated by those scrupulous clerics who pretend to conceal the fact that they are poets, yet hypocritically desire literary fame; he says quite frankly (p. 64): ["I openly desired/praise for the good work I had done"]. But honest praise is one thing; vainglory, based upon flattery and lies, is a repugnant ally in one's battle against the injustice of cruel Fortune. Her poisonous inflations explode at the end of the dream (Capítulo VI) which Cervantes has on the night before the great Battle of the Books. After the battle it is the question of prizes which raises once more the topic of social recognition and of mutual envy among poets. The honor of good Poetry herself has been theoretically vindicated, but in her farewell speech to her heroic defenders she can only promise them a distant hope of wealth in another world. After an envious glimpse of the festivities in Naples, where other luckier poets enjoy rich patronage, Cervantes finds himself once more walking the streets of Madrid, where he has to conform with the hypocrisy of social courtesy even as he fears a stab in the back at every turn, and is called "senile" in his judgments by aspiring young poets. The poem itself ends on this bitter note. In the prose epilogue, written later, Cervantes seems to have recovered a more tolerant sense of humor; the ridiculous guild of poets is now governed by the hilarious rules and regulations of a bureaucratic Apollo, who stipulates the reduction of theater admission prices for comic poets. Apollo's final ordinance is that poets should not beg from their wealthy patrons, for if God provides for the beasts of the fields, He will surely feed poets, no matter how beastly.

The *Viaje del Parnaso*, as we have said, is mock epic, in the tradition of late Classical Antiquity and of Renaissance Italy. Homeric mythology and heroism are subjected to the ridicule of being parodied in terms of modern everyday life. There are also traces of the Spanish picaresque novel here: a first-person narrative in which the humble protagonist is often hungry while his superiors speak of "higher things." Poetry becomes a material substance to be hurled at one's enemies in a free-for-all competition. The worst poetry, cheap commercial plays, is produced in quantity to be sold at a financial profit.

What was the source of Cervantes' malaise? It was clearly both literary and social. He was perhaps somewhat nostalgic for a semimythic golden age of Erasmian humanism which, as his teacher López de Hoyos may have told him, had flourished in Spain under Charles V. The breakdown of this earlier Renaissance synthesis, with no firm Aristotelian or neo-classical tradition in Spain to offset it, caused a deep preoccupation which is evident in many of Cervantes' discussions of literature, for in theory at least he was a classicist. But classical standards had been openly challenged by Lope de Vega and many other Spaniards.[5] To what standards could one then appeal?

In Italy and France, not only had classical literary standards of some sort been maintained, but an aristocratically oriented society provided patronage for significant intellectual and artistic creations produced by members of a nascent middle class. This system, which was to evolve and survive in Europe generally until the eve of the Industrial Revolution, had already begun to break down in the strangely anti-aristocratic and anti-intellectual mass society of Spain. Cervantes not only was aware of this peculiarly Spanish attitude, but was himself subtly affected by it. In 1615 a member of the French Embassy in Madrid expressed his amazement that a man of Cervantes' literary merits had no government pension or aristocratic patronage (see the Márquez Torres [approval] for Part II of the *Quijote*, studied in the article cited in note 4). Cervantes knew that in Naples he would not only have had the Viceroy's financial support, but would have found in the more sophisticated academies of that city an appreciation, for his works as well as his literary theories, which he could not find in the cultural anarchy of Madrid.

It was with depressing thoughts such as these in his mind that Cervantes wrote his characteristically ambivalent mock-epic poem, using heavy irony and satirical humor to defend his own integrity. On the one hand Cervantes did believe, theoretically, in a rationally controlled, well thought-out literary art, dependent upon the timeless principles drawn by Horace and Aristotle from ancient models. But what he saw on the Spanish cultural scene constantly undermined his faith in such order and reason, whether in literature or in society; the morally serious and learned artist tended to be ridiculed in the back of his mind by another sort of wildly playful artist, exemplified by the *pícaro* Ginés de Pasamonte, the galley slave who was writing the unfinished story of his own life, who ingeniously stole Sancho's donkey, and who, as Maese Pedro, manipulated so exciting a puppet show that Don Quijote was made to confuse once again the subtle illusions of art with the physical violence of life.[6] Could poetry really be kept at a classically controlled distance in order solemnly to teach us morality and truth? Or was poetry really a playfully tricky illusion which only a quixotic madman could take seriously? The *Viaje del Parnaso* humorously suggests this fundamental ambiguity in Cervantes' own mind; as a poem it is often very amusing, but no careful reader can be unaware of a certain underlying seriousness which is sometimes quite grim.

Notes

1. Benedetto Croce's study of 1899 is still fundamental for the historical background ("Due illustrazioni al *Viaje del Parnaso* del Cervantes: I. Il Caporali, il Cervantes e Giulio Cesare Cortese; II. Viaggio ideale del Cervantes a Napoli nel 1612," first published in the *Homenaje a Menéndez y Pelayo*, I [Madrid, 1899], pp. 161–193, and subsequently in Croce's collected *Saggi sulla letteratura italiana del seicento*, Bari, 1911, 1924 . . .). There are several helpful editions: J. V. Gibson's bilingual one (London, 1883), and those of R. Rojas (Buenos Aires, 1916), Schevill-Bonilla (Madrid, 1922), J. T. Medina (Santiago de Chile, 1925), F. Rodriguez Marín (Madrid, 1935), and A. del Campo (Madrid, 1948). Of limited value is G.

Correa's "La dimensión mitológica del *Viaje del Parnaso*, de Cervantes," *Comparative Literature*, XII (1960), 113–124.

2. Fundamental for historical data is F. Rodriguez Marín's "Una joyita de Cervantes: Al túmulo de Felipe II," first published in 1905 and subsequently in his edition of the *Viaje del Parnaso* (1935) and in his *Estudios cervantinos* (Madrid, 1947). An excellent interpretive essay is that of F. Ayala, "El túmulo," *Cuadernos Americanos*, Año XXII, Vol. CXXIX (julio-agosto, 1963), pp. 254–263, and *Realidad y ensueño* (Madrid, 1963), pp. 42–56.

3. See A. Porqueras Mayo, *El prólogo como género literario*, Madrid, 1957, for an important treatment of this mode.

4. See my note "On the Prefatory Pages of *Don Quixote*, Part II," *MLN*, LXXV (1960), 214–221.

5. See my essay on "Lope and Cervantes Once More," *Kentucky Romance Quarterly*, XIV (1967), 112–119.

6. Apropos of the literary significance of this episode, see George Haley, "The Narrator in *Don Quijote*: Maese Pedro's Puppet Show," *MLN*, LXXX (1965), 145–165, and Ruth Snodgrass El Saffar, *Distance and Control in Don Quijote: A Study of Narrative Technique*, (Chapel Hill: University of North Carolina Studies in Romance Languages and Literature, 1975).

Comedias y entremeses (1615)

Cervantine Variations on the Theme of the Theater within the Theater

Jean Canavaggio*

In many ways a precursor of Lope de Vega and the "new theater," Cervantes is reputed to have introduced on the Spanish scene the technique of the theater within the theater. Rightly so, it seems: we can surely find several examples of "actio intercalaris"[1] in certain dramatists of the Renaissance, in particular in Lope de Rueda, but the intercalated action of the plays of Rueda are always totally distinct from the work they frame; and, generally, these unsure attempts, these sporadic endeavors do not have anything in common with the treatment of this theme by Cervantes.[2]

Three of the ten plays which the author of the *Quixote* has left us effectively register the theater within the theater: *Los Baños de Argel, La Entretenida, Pedro de Urdemalas*—to which we must add the most famous of his interludes: *El Retablo de las Maravillas*.[3] Far from a mechanical exploitation of a simple theatrical device, these plays suggest, on the contrary, many correspondences with the mirror games—interpolated stories; the novel within the novel; Master Peter's puppet show—from which *Don Quixote* acquires a part of its complexity and its richness.

Such a predilection does not simply make for complications. It justifies, to our mind, a singular approach to the texts, one that goes beyond all research for sources or influences. This approach seems to permit us better to discern the exact importance of this motif, before we try to extricate its meaning and its intrinsic scope.

Envisioned as a dramatic technique, the inclusion of the theater within the theater obeys, at the beginning, a double imperative. On one hand it assumes the autonomy, or at least the provisionary autonomy, of the framed play. On the other hand, autonomy does not mean independence: as opposed to the intercalated action, the framed action is addressed to the actors and to the spectators of the main action at the same time; the solidarity of the two actions thus draws a perspective with a dual background.

Los Baños de Argel offers us a characteristic illustration of that

*Reprinted with permission from *Revue des Sciences Humaines* 37 (1972):53–68. Translated for this volume by Julie Campagna.

architecture which somehow associates thematic opposition with formal connection. We know that we have here one of the plays which was inspired by Cervantes' stay in Algiers, one in which the romanesque plot is supported by a more or less transposed real life experience. Among the tableaux which make up the historic decor of the play, one of the most spectacular is that which opens the last act. On the occasion of the Easter festival, the Spanish captives are assembled in the convict prison of the king to attend an improvised theatrical production: a pastoral colloquy of Lope de Rueda is going to be presented by some benevolent actors.[4] The difference between framed play and main play is then all the more marked in that — an unusual situation — the two works are not written by the same person.[5] But at the same time, the common condition of the audience and the actors unites the two actions from the start: put on in a very rudimentary fashion, Rueda's colloquy is nothing more than a spectacle of fortune, having become, as one of the spectators says: ". . . a captive drama,/poor, hungry, and unfortunate,/naked and disoriented."[6] It is integrated without difficulty into the universe of the Spanish theater.

Thus we find the double aspect, to which we have just referred, respected within the play. Considered from the outside, this spectacle exudes the misery of the prison; but analyzed from within, as from the position of the exile it evokes, it is an exact contradiction of itself. There is thus no rupture. A discontinuity is immediately established, however, between the pastoral convention and the reality of the prison, a discontinuity which accentuates the reality of the play and underscores its value as witness to a historical reality which precedes all dramatic stylization.

We verify here, beyond a doubt, the most immediately perceptible effect of the process of the theater within the theater: while expressing in its quintessence the part of the convention which is inherent in all dramatic fiction, the actors in the framed segment dig a ditch between the main play and the action they are representing. Abolishing for the moment the distance which separates us from the main action, they contribute in this way to reinforcing its credibility.

This use of the process is surely not unique to *Los Baños de Argel*; we observed that in *La Entretenida*, a similar technique allowed Cervantes to produce a comparable effect. This comedy of intrigue whose theme is the amorous rivalry of young gentlemen of Madrid exploits at will the contempt which this rivalry arouses. The framed segment which is introduced here is inserted in the course of the third act, in the form of an interlude played by servants before their masters.[7] It deals then with an extrinsic action, different from the main action, in the sense that, this time, actors and audience are from different social classes. A frontier which is at the same time social and aesthetic thus separates the world of servant-actors from that of master-spectators. Confronted suddenly with the inevitable conventions of an interlude whose autonomy has been underlined,[8] the universe of the "comedia" seems — in that moment — freed from those conventions which are its own.

The confrontation is even clearer in *Pedro de Urdemalas*. Here the motif of the theater within the theater is not developed, though it is suggested at the end of the last act.[9] But that small touch is nonetheless highly significant. The play has been justly defined as a mosaic of miscellaneous episodes, which owes its coherence solely to the continual and very decisive intervention of the protagonist.[10] Cervantes knew how to crystallize the substance of an imaginary life around this infinitely variable character taken from folklore. Capable of adapting himself to the most unforeseen of situations, quick to fire up intrigue after intrigue, master of the art of pulling the puppet strings of those whom he meets on the way, Pedro de Urdemalas proves that he is, by instinct, a skillful director and a born actor. Here's where fate is going to hold him to his word. With consummate art, our hero has succeeded in stealing two chickens from a naive peasant, making him believe that their price was going to be used to free two prisoners. Chance spectators at a farce of which they soon become the benevolent collaborators, two professional actors lead Pedro to discover his real vocation. Seduced by his natural gifts, the troupe's director takes him on immediately. To be exact, he has agreed to offer the production of a "comedia" to the king and queen. Their Royal Highnesses are becoming impatient: Pedro's test will be all the more valuable for it; and, while we witness the final preparations of the spectacle intended for the illustrious audience and while the real scene becomes the preparation for the imaginary stage, the authentic play comes to an end at the moment when the announced production begins.[11]

The formal relationship which by definition unites the main play and the framed segment, winds up thus reduced to its most simple expression. In *Los Baños de Argel*, actors and spectators belonged to the same world, since they lived together the drama of the captivity; in *La Entretenida*, the dialectic of the master-servant relationship established a different, but indisputable link between the two layers of fiction; in *Pedro de Urdemalas*, the complementarity of the two actions is assumed only by he who is their common inspiration in a like fashion. The division between the two worlds thus confronted is dug deeper each time: the pastoral colloquy of Lope de Rueda and the domestic interlude of *La Entretenida* were certainly only spectacles of fortune; at least the magic of the word conferred a presence on them. The play announced by Pedro is only a fantasm which evaporates at the moment when one believes it is about to be born: thus, on the rebound, the enhanced credibility of the action presented before our eyes. By shedding the old man in order to take on the name of an authentic stage professional,[12] Pedro clearly indicates that from now on he'll be only the sum of the masks which he'll take on one after another in accordance with his new trade. But this ridiculous result — this "chimera" as he himself says — is the exact antithesis of the prestigious fate of the heroine, Belica. A young gypsy of humble birth, Belica has just, within a matter of minutes, seduced the king and provoked the queen's jealousy, and has discovered that she was in fact the niece of the royal couple: an adventure of pure fantasy, to be sure, but one which takes on a whole other resonance, once Pedro compares her to his own story, and learns the lesson of this confrontation: "Your presumption and mine/have come to their conclusion:/mine only in fiction,/yours in reality."[13] By opposing his imaginary destiny to the destiny of Belica, Pedro, by an effect of contrast, confers on the romanesque the mark of the credible.

Whatever the envisioned work may be, we have here a recurring effect of the procedure which, while determining a whole series of concurrences between *Los Baños de Argel*, *La Entretenida*, and *Pedro de Urdemalas*, seem to bring to light the coherence of the Cervantine drama.

Nevertheless, it would be a grave mistake to make do with an arbitrary scheme out of a desire to subordinate everything to a concern for coherence. He who uses the term theater within the theater seems to support a contradiction between two levels of fiction. But this contradiction is only a point of departure, a first given. The main action and the framed action come quickly to interfere in favor of the confrontation which at first opposed them. A thematic or symbolic complimentarity is created which is infinitely richer than the formal connection which initially guaranteed the dependence of the intercalated action. Subtle exchanges take place which bit by bit transform a simple technical device into a multi-echo motif, capable of transforming the most diverse meanings. Cervantes' theater is not unaware of these nuances; on the contrary, it offers us an astonishingly varied range of them, and this very variety merits our attention.

Is the assertion applicable to *Los Baños de Argel?* The almost immediate contradiction which is established between the bucolic convention and the world of the prison would seem to prove just the opposite. But this connection is going to be modified considerably by the actual production of the colloquy. Indeed, the production takes an entirely unexpected turn with the intervention of a character, the sacristan, whose episodic appearances have had the function, up until now, of periodically relaxing the dramatic tension and of enlivening the action. Just when the spectacle is about to begin, a brief exchange of rejoinders between two prisoners, Osorio and Vivanco, makes it seem that the sacristan is not going to fail in his mission:

> — Who is singing?
> — The sacristan,
> who is skillful in everything.[14]

Invested with an ambiguous function, midway between the two actions, our hero is going to turn this to his account in order to show all he is capable of. To be sure, the brief musical prelude which was his responsibility is barely completed before he is back to open the colloquy with a tirade during which he piles up burlesque confidences with an undeniable verbal virtuosity[15] — an ambiguous preamble, which one isn't sure makes up the "loa" of the work or is, on the contrary, the fruit of an untimely initiative on the part of the narrator. Here is the reaction of one of the spectators: "Is this part of the play/or is this character a clown?"[16] These uncertainties reflect exactly a growing confusion between the two actions.

This confusion does not last, however. It comes to an end with the appearance on stage of the real protagonist of the colloquy, the shepherd Guillermo. But the interventions of the sacristan do not cease, whether he interrupts the actor by his farcical leaps and bounds or when he surreptitiously inserts himself in the pastoral fiction.[17] In this very way, if he undoes, in his own fashion, the conventional character of the bucolic theme, the fact remains that this undoing is itself the source of an impromptu in which all the characters participate, whether voluntarily or not. It is reflected in the impatient remarks of the actor interrupted in the playing of his role which answer the impertinences of the sacristan; in the indulgent and amused comments of the other spectators which answer the curses of the prestigious host who has been deprived of the pleasure on which he was counting. An ephemeral spectacle — since it is soon interrupted by tragic news: the massacre of Christian captives by Turks, who, fooled by a mirage, believed they saw a Spanish float rise up in front of Algiers[18] — but nonetheless a spectacle sufficiently coherent to suggest, between the pastoral world and the realistic evocation of the miseries of the prison, more complex connections than those we had originally thought we discerned.

La Entretenida offers us a still more expressive illustration of this growing interference of the two levels of fiction. We saw that the traditional interpretation willingly places the accent on the autonomy of the interlude within the *comedia*, but that interpretation does not seem to us to take enough account of the circumstances surrounding the interlude's production. Certainly, the initiative of the spectacle reverts to the servants: Torrente, Cardenio, Cristina, and Dorotea; but with the step taken by Cristina, who has come to seek the permission of her masters, is associated her master's sister, Marcela, whose authority and credit allow her to carry out the decision.[19] On their part, D. Antonio and D. Francisco do not limit themselves to yielding to the wish of the two girls. They offer to take part in the spectacle. In this way an intervention is sketched — discreet, but indisputable — of masters in action put on and animated by the servants.[20]

These still fleeting connections become precise in the course of the two scenes which are inserted between the preparations of the production and the interlude itself. The previous appearances of Torrente and Ocaña let us know that the two were disputing the favors of Cristina. This rivalry, which played a marginal role in the development of the play itself, will momentarily occupy center stage in the form of a "questione d'amore" treated in the burlesque style. By accepting the handkerchief Ocaña offers her and by giving hers to Torrente, Cristina maliciously sets her suits back-to-back.[21] This episode thus takes on a deliberately theatrical character — which underlines, furthermore, Ocaña's appeal to the verdict of the public.[22] Far from creating a solution of continuity, the movement from the play to the framed piece within it is effected gradually.

The transition is a progressive one, then, but it nonetheless makes the return of the masters on stage perceptible. This time having become mere spectators, they establish, by their very presence, the necessary distance between framed and main plays. Even better, while Cristina and her companions play the first scenes of their masterpiece before our eyes, the acclaim of the public seems intended to accentuate this distance.[23]

With that said, does this totally classic device exactly produce the intended effect? Far from it. If, indeed, this scenic space seems to be organizing itself in the direction of an opposition between the two actions, this opposition is going to find itself contradicted by the content itself of the interlude: the protagonists of the new spectacle not only keep their names and original conditions; their remarks and their retorts have as their sole aim the eccentricities and idiosyncrasies of their masters, and, at the expense of a minimal stylization, they directly transpose the "real" world. So, just when the frontier which separates the play from the interlude seems established, a close relationship between decor, theme and atmosphere is established which upsets our certainties and denounces the fragile character of the balance thus obtained.

This ambiguity only lasts a while, however, at least if we consider it in the light of the second scene of the interlude. This time it's a question of a dance, whose purely scenic character re-establishes the separation between the two levels of fiction.[24] This separation becomes even more pronounced at the moment when Torrente and Ocaña, scandalized by the lewd character of certain persons, condemn the growing intimacy of the dancers and the musicians. The curses of the two suitors and the objections that these curses raise on the part of the accused demonstrate that the "real" — let us understand by "real" the secondary loves of Cristina — can erupt in the midst of the fiction. Is the real going to go so far as to abolish the fiction? Everything points to believing so, from the moment when, with the tone rising, Torrente and Ocaña come to blows. This unforeseen brawl which throws the two rivals into conflict comes to a bloody conclusion: Ocaña's fist having knocked off Torrente's nose, the latter replies by running his adversary through.[25]

This unexpected distortion not only creates a brutal change of tonality but also brings about, it seems, a reduction of the framed action, invested, then invaded, and finally annexed by the main action. Moreover, an entire series of incidents tends to confirm this impression: cries from the public, the fainting of Marcela, the coming and going of the assassin, the appearance of justice at the end.[26] However, at the heart of this wisely orchestrated concert, the attentive spectator cannot help perceiving some dissonant chords: at the horrified surprise of Marcela, the indifference of Cristina makes a curious echo; at the pressing questions of the bailiff, one notes the equally curious echo of alternating recriminations between the dying man and his murderer. The sudden reappearance of Torrente's nose, and the miraculous resurrection of Ocaña wind up confirming what we were beginning to suspect: this tragedy is only a farce, or more exactly, the last event of the interlude. Taking on their masters, Cristina and her accomplices promoted them to the role of involuntary collaborators. Therefore the interference of the two actions is operating in a way directly opposed to that which we had imagined; it is the world of the interlude which, for a time, has annexed the world of the play, and this to the extent that a fiction contemplated and consented to by lucid spectators has been substituted for a fiction lived and endured by a public which is the victim of comic illusion.

What makes such an annexation possible is, obviously, the fact that the fiction of the interlude directly transposes the "reality" of the play. The apparently bloody brawl of Torrente and Ocaña takes its likeness from the sworn enmity of Cristina's two suitors; and the lesson which Ocaña gleens from the adventure,[27] just as Torrente's speech to the public,[28] gives ample proof that the separation of the two worlds is again not as clear as one might believe: ["deceptions"] and ["truths"] continue to maintain delicately nuanced relationships, beyond even the unexpected result of a skillfully constructed domestic farce.

From this deepening of an ever-more complex rapport, *Pedro de Urdemalas* offers us the most suggestive example, this time not on the side of an unexpected comic ending, but with an ending whose true meaning comes at the interface of the play which is to take place and the one which has already been performed. At first the confrontation of the two actions probably tends to assure the credibility of a fantasy intrigue. But it is more surprising to see, simultaneously, the profoundly romanesque character of the adventure of Belica made prominent. Just when the young girl has discovered her true birthright, and the imminent festivities are going to crown the general gaiety, the voices of some musicians of the troupe proclaim a romance whose theme is none other than the ephemeral loves of the King: "Let the gypsy girls dance,/the King watches them;/the queen, out of jealousy,/orders them jailed."[29] "Lyric mirror of the action,"[30] this brief romance suddenly decides the immediate stylization of a story which, until then, affected the rhythm of the real-life romance. At the king's exclamation: "But listen: I seem to/be hearing my own story sung,/and it's a sign that memory of me/will last for many centuries."[31] — is echoed the even more significant invitation that the Queen, now assured by the bonds of blood that tie her to her rival, extends to her husband to compel him to go to the spectacle: "Let's go listen to the play/with pleasure, since Heaven/did not ordain that my jealousy/would make of it a tragedy."[32]

Thus, the announced play is no longer just the counter-proof destined to assure the veracity of the action represented: it is the direct prolonging and denouement of it.

In favor of a "turning of life into literature" ("Literarisierung des Lebens") intrinsic to the work,[33] the fiction of the imminent spectacle is planned around an imaginary adventure whose similarity is no longer any more than a pretense.

Interference of the two actions in *Los Baños de Argel*, episodic confusion in *La Entretenida*, permutation of plots in *Pedro de Urdemalas*: such an evolution clearly brings about a progressive deepening of the relationship of the real and the imaginary. This should come as no surprise from an author whose entire work tirelessly reflects and surprises the problematic character of this relationship. Let it suffice, in that respect, to think for a moment of the multiple effects Cervantes derives from this throughout the *Quixote*: interpolation, in Part I, of the story of the "Tale of Foolish Curiosity" and the history of "The Captive's Tale;" the splitting at the beginning of Part II of the completed novel and the novel which is being created; the adventure of "Master Peter's Puppet Show" with its accompaniment of illusions and errors. Of this relativism whose roman-esque expression has been the object of remarkable studies, the Cervantine theater offers us a fascinating image which up until now has scarcely held the critics' attention.[34] The image is an original one, however, whose nuances do not yield to the "chiaroscuro" of the fictional narrative. It is also an ambiguous image, whose fluctuations demand elucidation. When all is said and done, how does one interpret these variations? Are they merely the scenic translation of the contradictions, the doubts, even the skepticism of Cervantes? Wouldn't they refer, rather, to an order of the world whose meaning, still implicit, demands clarification?

In just limiting ourselves to *La Entretenida*, we could be tempted, for an instant, to rally around the first hypothesis. However, it is not enough that the game of tricks and truths which takes place here illustrates only a negative relativism. Certainly, the interference and the confusion of the two plots of fiction seem to prolong themselves up until the end of the play, since we still perceive there the echo of the events of the interlude.[35] But this reference expresses, in fact, a more secret connection, to which the ultimate fate reserved for Torrente bears witness. Indeed, this hurried intermediary is not only the leader of the game of the interlude; he is also — "in the city" — the advisor and the accomplice of Cardenio. Carde-nio, wishing to seduce Marcela, has passed himself off as her cousin, the rich "indiano" Don Silvestre de Alméndarez. The unforeseen arrival of the true Don Silvestre allows Cardenio and his evil genius to be confused. Thus, to the momentary success of the artificial Torrente responds his final downfall; to the fiction of the accepted, sustained and finally revealed interlude, responds the fable of the play, a sustained but finally unmasked fiction.

This simple nuance fixes definitively the frontier between the two universes. If the subterfuge of the interlude has been able to abuse, for a moment, everyone who was contemplating it, it goes without saying that alone, the characters of *La Entretenida* fall into the trap laid for them by Cardenio and Torrente; the public of the play knows constantly what to stick to concerning the two friends. A paradox, one will say: to an inscribed action which immediately wins over the complete adherence of the public is opposed a main action which implies a constant alienation effect between protagonists and spectators. In fact, this very alienation is essential to the play. In a large part, in effect, *La Entretenida* is a travestied denunciation of the many conventions of the "comedy of errors," of all the methods and recipes which the overripe Lope de Vega had been exploiting for nearly twenty years: conventions of intrigue — quid-pro-quos, false obstacles, prefabricated endings; conventions of theme — by means of the burlesque treatment of the traditional "cuestiones d'amore" — ; conventions of character: the stereotyped young gallant, the evanescent lady, the impertinent and abusive fool; conventions of form and of style.[36] The confrontation of the two schemes of fiction contributes, in its own way, to this questioning of the commonplaces of an entire school of drama. Strong in its action, in its rhythm, in its illusory power, the framed interlude acts as a foil in underlining, by means of contrast, the artifices of the play, a disembodied mechanism whose cogs Cervantes apparently takes pleasure in dismantling. One could not imagine a more rigorous censure of the kind of theater whose success the author of *Don Quixote* willingly recognized, but which never received his complete acceptance.[37]

Thus, these apparent uncertainties concerning the conditions of apprehending the real, recover, once and for all, the lucid critique of an aesthetic judged unacceptable. Could it be then that Cervantes only wanted to pass down to us the message of a man of letters, the disillusioned testimony of a playwright simultaneously disappointed in his ambitions and reticent before the compromising of conscience of the school of Lope? One can imagine it for *La Entretenida*, whose first meaning seems to us strictly modeled on the parodic design of the author.[38] But *Pedro de Urdemalas* is enough to prove that the characters of the Cervantine theater would not know how to be reduced to abstract entities. While *La Entretenida* limited itself to confronting, then to mixing and finally to opposing again two parallel fictions, *Pedro de Urdemalas* suggests to us a problematic rich in different ways in the rapport between the real and the imaginary. Elusive, since it vanishes at the moment when we thought we were attaining it, inevitable nonetheless, since it is at the time of the denouement that it reveals that the destiny of the hero has been accomplished, the projected action communicates to the represented action both its presence and its absence. Embodied by Pedro, the motif of the theater as life is projected onto the destiny of the other characters, and sketches, by way of counterpoint, the opposing motif of life as theater.

One easily recognizes here the classic theme of the theater of the world. If Calderón, at the end of the Golden Age, was to give this theme the breadth one knows he did, Cervantes, before him, had already perceived its interest: a famous page in *Don Quixote* bears witness to the fact.[39] Again it is advisable to make it clear the limits which he assigns to it here. An "always circumstantial actor in the comedy of the world,"[40] Pedro maneuvers at will everyone he meets, thus proclaiming the ridiculous nature of their existence. But it is at the exact moment when he is going to fulfill himself completely in his role that he disappears and seems to dissolve: henceforth, his truth is that of the myth, and, in accordance with the image which folklore suggests to us of him, he affirms himself beyond the reach of any empirical approach. From then on, the other characters reintegrate on the rebound this existence which seemed denied to them: all the while testifying that life is only an illusion, they assume fully the appearance of life. Thus they create in the viewer the conditions for a methodic doubt regarding the meaning of human existence, while sparing him or her the vertigo of a hyperbolic doubt on the very nature of this existence: we are no longer beings of fiction, but beings in question.

Now, it is to this interrogation that *Los Baños de Argel* is going to bring the definitive answer: more precisely, the *coup de théâtre* which, in the middle of the last act, brutally interrupts the interlude and the pranks of the sacristan. In one sense, the massacre perpetrated by the Turks, just like the martyrdom of the young Francisquito, put to death for having refused to abjure his faith, are just so many bloody episodes[41] which by reinstituting the sinister truth of the barbarous slavery place an end to the constant interferences of the real and the imaginary. But, at the same time, it is curious to note that this massacre is due to a mirage; and it is no less revealing to see the agony of Francisquito played on stage in the manner of an edifying spectacle whose theatricality Cervantes intentionally underlines.[42] Thus the formula by which one of the captives learns the lesson of this lamentable adventure takes on a new coloring: "our plays about prisoners/always end in tragedy."[43] This surely indicates in the first place that the interruption of the pastoral colloquy does not imply a pure and simple falling back into the everyday world. Despite a violent change of register and of tonality, the rights of poetry remain intact. It undoubtedly manifests, therefore, that, comic or tragic, this poetry is none other than that of the comedy of life which we play at the theater of the world. But, especially, it suggests that this theater has a meaning: that it is not, despite appearances, a story "full of sound and fury, signifying nothing."[44] The painful example of the martyrdom of Francisquito shows, on the contrary, just how fertile the tragic illusion that provoked it can be: in exchange for the temporary confusions of the real and the imaginary, characteristic of a universe where man's senses are constantly abused, is substituted, by the grace of God, the indissolvable relationship in which the here and now and the world beyond are blended; in exchange for the game of mirrors of earthly life, one gets the certainties of salvation in eternal life.

It is thus to the captives of *Los Baños de Argel* that Cervantes returns, having dissolved the confusions of a provisional skepticism, to lay the foundations of an edifice whose balance seemed shaky up until then. The solution is in perfect accord, in its coherence, with the religious ideology of the Golden Age, and is one which Calderón, fifty years later, will develop on an entirely different scale.[45] The solution is nonetheless Cervantine, in the sense that it opposes the fleeting incertainties of an empiric truth to definitive certitudes, a fundamental theme of *Don Quixote*.[46] A verification, nevertheless, is called for, for while this ideology never directly informs the novelistic universe of Cervantes, his theater, on the other hand, manifests on many occasions an undeniable will to edify in a patriotic or religious sense. *La numancia, Los tratos de Argel, El gallardo español, El rufián dichoso*, are all proofs of this.[47] Does this desire to edify express itself equally in each of the three works which concern us here? On the one hand, *Los Baños de Argel* belongs indisputably among his collection of exemplary plays.[48] On the other hand, *Pedro de Urdemalas* is related to Cervantes' masterworks by its deliberate refusal of any *a priori* thesis. Between the two, *La Entretenida* reduces the Cervantine ethic to the dimensions of an aesthetic, but does not totally escape the snare of a rather narrow didacticism. Thus, the more the didactic intention is clearly affirmed, the more elementary is the expression which (through the slope of the theater within the theater), the ambiguities of the real and the imaginary redress. Wavering between the devices of provisionary relativism and the explicit adherence to a consecrated dogma, the Cervantine theater gives in sometimes to the seductions of the comic illusion, and other times to the temptation to the edifying message.

That Cervantes — at least in his plays — did not manage to overcome the opposition is probably one of the least ambiguous signs of his inability to impose a theater distinct from that of Lope. But this semi-failure is still not, however, his last word as a man of the theater: *El Retablo de las Maravillas* is there to convince us of that. If up until now we haven't said anything about the last of the four Cervantine plays which inscribe theater within the theater, it is not because this play belongs to a different genre — the interlude. It is because the dramatic formula which it illustrates represents, to our eyes, the only means by which Cervantes succeeded in breaking the circle.

The Cervantine interludes have been called "free theater," since in them Cervantes seems not to have concerned himself with either political or religious edification, nor with aesthetic problems.[49] The description is correct in the sense that, the interlude having been originally a light entertainment, its characters are simply types established by tradition. Nonetheless, Cervantes' interludes are the exact opposite of elementary farces. The genius of the author lies in his having known how to bestow a human truth upon the best among them, in such a way that the characters finally escape their original condition as simple marionettes. The freedom of the interlude comes to be, from that moment, the freedom of a work which eludes every anxious exegesis which seeks only a narrow illustration of a pre-established idea. *El Retablo de las Maravillas* offers us an admirable example of this freedom: we would like to try here to show how this freedom is affirmed by means of a method of scene evaluation which we are beginning to try out.

Returned to its original premise, the interlude is simply made up of a wager. If Cervantes takes up his bet, he confers upon the peasant illusion a justification which is as convincing as it is subtle: Chanfalla has taken care to announce that only those who have been "conceived in wedlock" can see his production, and those who are not descended from "some race of converts."[51] From then on, our charlatans have a good chance of making the public see everything which is passing through their heads. In other words, the value system upon which the Spanish society of the time rests determines among those who make it up, a reciprocal mistrust which reigns in the doubt that each spectator is tempted to feel in the presence of the stage.[52] At this price only does the magic of the word of Chirinos and Chanfalla find an echo in the reactions of the villagers, to the degree of provoking an actual collective hallucination.

Founded on the rock of the prejudices of the entire era, the fragile edifice constructed by Cervantes takes on new proportions. The theater within the theater is no longer here a scenic device suited to making an episode, an event, or an unforeseen denouement appear. It constitutes the material, the actual substance of the interlude. As such, it decides its progression, all the while sketching a space where the action will unfold. The mute sheet of the tableau, the descriptions of the two buffoons, the reactions of the mass of spectators, the asides of the Governor, who, in a low voice, is amazed and despairs at seeing nothing of that which each one claims to behold, all these create a composite universe where the materiality of the stage, the illusion created, the illusion undergone, the secret deception of the privileged spectator, correspond to so many distinct but interdependent levels. There is therefore no more interference or upheaval of perspectives: the traditional distinction between the main play and the framed play disappears to make way for a sort of prism whose support proves to be, at the same time, an illusion and a reality of seventeenth-century Spain.

To be sure, this "Pirandellism before the fact"[53] transposes while making more profound a typically Cervantine relativism. But we who are the spectators remain sheltered from mental vertigo: our immediate complicity with the leaders of the game protects us from the beginning to the end of the spectacle. Thus we benefit from a clarity comparable to that which was used to raise in us the edifying outcome of *Los Baños de Argel*. But whereas in *Los Baños* this sudden awareness was the result of a pre-established didactic plan, here it is engraved at the very heart of the interlude and it clarifies its denouement. We know that the denouement is taken charge of by a *furrier*, who, at the end, erupts upon the stage. An efficient agent of our alienation effect — it is he who breaks the charm — he symbolizes, in this respect, our own clairvoyance; but, at the same time, the relentless hallucination of the villagers attempts to integrate him into the spectacle; and, if he exposes their illusion, he shares just the same their prejudices of blood and race.[54] In this sense, he introduces a supplementary dimension into the game of mirrors which is offered to our eyes. Thus, at the very moment when, faithful to the tradition of the interlude, Cervantes empties the stage with cudgel blows, at the moment when the paper castle born of the collective illusion comes tumbling down, the mechanism of this illusion and its possible resurgence is traced in filigree. It is enough that the message which the *Retablo* offers us transcends the historic conditions of its appearance: beyond the volution of customs and beliefs, the abiding parable of human credulousness vanishes, triumphant.[55]

At the impass which the Cervantine play had reached, *El Retablo de las Maravillas* substitutes a miraculous outcome. It is miraculous because the sterile alternative between theater of shadows and edifying spectacle is thus surpassed. It is miraculous also in the sense that it respects and verifies the constants of an aesthetic and the foundation of an ethic. Finally, it is miraculous by the very fact that the truth of the theater within the theater is unveiled while abolishing itself: a fleeting solution, but an admirable one, and one which fully summarizes the vocation at the same time aborted and accomplished of Cervantes the playwright.

Notes

1. See the comic interludes of *La Comedia Eufemia* (scenes 2 and 7) and those of *La Comedia Medora* (scene 11).

2. A prefiguration of the method appears in an unpublished work of 1595, *Los Naufragios de Leopoldo*, attributed by the manuscript to "Morales." The main characters of this play are found to be, for a few moments, the spectators of an interlude, then of a comedy, which are represented in succession in the wings; the rumors of the production, of the bribes, of retorts even, reach all the way up to the stage, creating for the moment a doubling of perspectives. See the introduction of E. Julia Martínez in her edition of *La Comedia de El Caballero de Olmedo*, *Revista de Bibliografía Nacional* II (Madrid: CSIC, 1944), 63–69, and our edition of Morales, *Comedia de los amores y locuras del Conde loco* (Paris: Centre de Recherches hispaniques, 1969), 79–84.

3. Cervantes published in 1615 — a year before his death — his *Ocho comedias y ocho*

entremeses nunca representados. Unfortunately we do not have an exact chronology of his dramatic work. *Los Baños de Argel* seems to have been conceived at the time of his dramatic debut (1585–95?), then to have been touched up and completed twenty years later. *La Entretenida* and *Pedro de Urdemalas* date seemingly from the years 1608–1612. *El Retablo de las Maravillas* finally, is certainly not before 1600. For a discussion on the present state of the question, see the introduction of F. Yndurain in *Obras dramáticas de Cervantes*, B.A.E., CLXVI, Madrid, 1962, pp. VII and subsequent pages. (We have borrowed our references from this edition.)

4. *Los Baños de Argel*, op. cit., pp. 162a–169b.

5. For a possible identification of this colloquy, see Schevill-Bonilla, editor of Cervantes's *Comedias y Entremeses*, Madrid, t.I, 1915, p. 380.

6. *Baños*, p. 164b.

7. *Ibid.*, pp. 402a–408b.

8. See Cotarelo Valledos, *El teatro de Cervantes*, Madrid, 1915, p. 443 ("an interlude which . . . separates itself entirely from the main action"); F. Maldonado de Guevara, ed., Cervantes, "Entremés de *La Entremida*", *Anales cervantinos*, VII, 1958, pp. 318 and subsequent; F. Yndurain, Intr., cit., p. XLIII.

9. *Ibid.*, pp. 468b–473b.

10. See Robert Marrast, *Miguel de Cervantès dramaturge*, Paris, L'Arche, 1957, p. 91 and following.

11. *Pedro de Urdemalas*, p. 473b.

12. Nicolás de los Ríos, who died in Madrid March 29, 1610, see Schevil-Bonilla, *op. cit.*, t. III, p. 258.

13. *Ibid.*, p. 473b.

14. *Baños*, p. 164a.

15. *Ibid.*, p. 165b.

16. *Ibid.*, loc. cit.

17. *Ibid.*, p. 166a–b.

18. *Ibid.*, p. 168a–b.

19. *Entretenida*, p. 397b.

20. *Ibid.*, p. 398a.

21. *Ibid.*, p. 401b. On the sources of this episode see Montesinos, "Una cuestión de amor en comedias antiguas españolas," *RFE*, XIII, 1926, pp. 280–83; Crawford, "Again the 'Cuestión de amor' in the early Spanish Drama," *HR* I, 1933, pp. 319–22; J. Casalduero, "Parodia de una cuestión de amor y quejas de las fregonas," *Estudios sobre el teatro español*, (Madrid, Gredos), 1962, pp. 73–81.

22. ["Let the truth regarding this matter/be decided in the peanut gallery"] (*Ibid.*, p. 401b).

23. *Ibid.*, pp. 4021–403b.

24. *Ibid.*, pp. 404a–405a.

25. *Ibid.*, p. 405a.

26. *Ibid.*, p. 405b.

27. "All that is now deception / later will be truth." (*Ibid.*, p. 407b).

28. *Ibid.*, p. 408b.

29. *Pedro de Urdemalas*, p. 470b.

30. We are borrowing this happy definition from N. Salomon, *Recherches sur le thème paysan dans la "comedia" au temps de Lope de Vega*, Bordeaux, 1965, p. 557.

31. *Pedro de Urdemalas*, loc. cit.

32. *Ibid.*, p. 472b.

33. We know that it is the title of a study of Leo Spitzer on *La Dorotea*, which appeared in Bonn in 1932. Consult José F. Montesinos, *Estudios sobre Lope*, Mexico, 1951, p. 85, and M. Bataillon, *"La Celestina" selon Fernando de Rojas*, Paris, 1961, p. 238.

34. On Cervantine relativism and its romanesque expression see in particular Américo Castro, *El pensamiento de Cervantes*, Madrid, 1925, pp. 30 and following; Leo Spitzer, "Perspectivismo Lingüístico en el *Quijote*," which appeared in *Lingüística e historia literaria*, Madrid, Gredos, 1955; R.-L. Predmore, *El mundo del Quijote*, Madrid, Insula, 1958; J.-B. Avalle-Arce, *Deslindes cervantinos* Madrid, Edhigar, 1961; Alban K. Forcione, *Cervantes, Aristotle, and the Persiles*, Princeton University Press, 1970) — On the dramatic and scenic translation of this relativism, some brief but suggestive remarks, in R. Marrast, *Cervantès dramaturge*, pp. 112–113, F. Yndurain, "Cervantes y el teatro," which appeared in *Relección de clásicos*, Madrid, 1969, pp. 108–11, finally J.-M. Pelorson, *Cervantès* Paris, Seghers, 1970, p. 68.

35. As Torrente declares to Cristina: "You should have remembered / beguiling harpy, / the handkerchief and the interlude." (*Entretenida*, p. 418b).

36. See the suggestions of J.-B. Avalle-Arce, in "On *La Entretenida* of Cervantes," *MLN*, LXXXIV, 1959, pp. 418–21, as well as J. Casalduero, *Sentido y forma del teatro de Cervantes*, Madrid, Gredos, 1966, p. 166.

37. Just as in witnessing, in particular, the statements of the Priest and the Canon, in Chapter 47 of *Don Quijote*, Part I. For an essay on this observation, see F. Yndurain, *op. cit.*, pp. 89–99.

38. Of course, this travestied sketch does not exhaust, far from it, the ultimate sense of the work; and this, to the extent that the quid-pro-quos which make the action jump back are fed by the ambiguous behavior of Marcela and her brother, a behavior which suggests the underlying presence of a more or less conscious incestuous desire. (On this point, see A. Castro, *El pensamiento de Cervantes*, p. 50, n. 3). It remains that this ambiguous theme is, in some way, proclaimed by the scenic expression which it redresses, and that the introduction of the theater within the theater appears as one of the forms of this proclamation.

39. Cf. *Don Quijote*, II, 11: "Regarding the strange adventure that happened to the valerous don Quijote with the coach or cart of the Theater of Death." On the preceeding and ultimate fortune of the theme, see E.-R. Curtius, *La littérature européenne et le Moyen-Age latin* (French translation), Paris, 1956, pp. 170 and following; Antonio Vilanova, "El tema del Gran Teatro del Mundo," *Boletín de la real academia de buenas Letras de Barcelona*, XXIII, 1950, pp. 153–99; and Jean Jacquot, "Le Théâtre du Monde, de Shakespeare a Calderón," *RLC*, XXXI, 1957, pp. 341–72. — On the interference of this theme with the method of theater within the theater, cf., Anne Righter, *Shakespeare and the Idea of the Play*, London, 1962.

40. The formula is that of R. Marrast, *op.cit.*, p. 99.

41. *Baños*, pp. 168a–169b, and 173b–174a.

42. *Ibid.*, p. 173a: "A curtain is pulled to reveal Francisquito in a state that moves one to great pity."

43. *Ibid.*, p. 169b.

44. Shakespeare, *Macbeth*, V, 5. — It is as much to say that Cervantes refuses the temptation of a J.-L. Borges, attentive to perceive, through the bias of a scenic method, "our possible condition as imaginary beings." (see A.-M. Barrenechea, "El infinito en la obra de Borges," *NRFH*, X, 1956, pp. 13 and on). More generally, his attitude is situated at the antipodes of a certain romantic vertigo of theater within the theater, where W. Jankélévitch reveals the product and the underlying product "of a consciousness of self which is incapable of finding its first simplicity and naïvity." (*L'ironie ou la bonne conscience*, Paris, 1950, p. 135).

45. In this sense, the theater of Cervantes develops here and now that which will become one of the major themes of the so-called "baroque" era. Cf. Jean Roussett, *La Littérature de l'âge baroque en France*, Paris, 1953, pp. 28–31 and 66–74, and Emilio Orozco Díaz, *El teatro y la teatralidad del Barroco*, Barcelona, 1969, pp. 171 and following.

46. V. Avalle-Arce "Conocimiento y vida en Cervantes," in *Deslindes cervantinos*, pp. 15–80.

47. On this point see the analysis of Casalduero, *Sentido y forma del teatro de Cervantes*.

48. cf. Casalduero, pp 77–103, and Marrast, pp 62–71.

49. Marrast, p. 114.

50. *Retablo de las Maravillas*, ed.cit., p. 531a.

51. *Ibid.*, p. 532b.

52. Regarding this, besides the classic works of A. Castro, one will be rewarded by reading the pages which Noël Salomon dedicated to the repercussions of the concern with purity of blood in the peasant world and the "comedia" of rustic inspiration. (*Recherches sur le thème paysan*, pp. 819 and on).

53. Marrast, *op.cit.*, p. 133.

54. *Retablo*, p. 540b.

55. On this subject see the enlightening exegis of E. Asensio which appears in *Itinerario del Entremés*, Madrid, Gredos, 1965, p. 109.

Writing for Reading: Cervantes's Aesthetics of Reception in the *Entremeses*

Nicholas Spadaccini*

Miguel de Cervantes Saavedra (1547–1616) wrote largely during the latter part of his life. After the appearance of his pastoral prose fiction, *La Galatea* (1585) and a brief engagement as a practicing playwright in the last part of the sixteenth century, he is heard from again officially in 1605 when *Don Quijote* I is published in Madrid. All of his other works appear in print between 1613–1617: *Novelas ejemplares* (1613): *Viaje del parnaso* (1614); *Don Quijote, II* (1615); *Ocho comedias y ocho entremeses* (1615); and *Los trabajos de Persiles y Sigismunda* (1617).

Since most of Cervantes's known works were not only published but were also, probably, composed or reworked toward the very end of his life, it could be argued that an analysis carried out on a single text or on texts belonging only to the same genre might, in some instances, be less productive than a transversal analysis which cuts synchronically across generic lines. Such an analysis is apt to single out orders of relations resting on what Jacques Dubois calls "the laws of the collective unconscious which leave their traces on the work and allow us to perceive the most socialized

*This essay was written specifically for this volume and is published here for the first time by permission of the author.

aspect of the message." It also allows one to focus broadly on questions of poetics and discourses.[1]

In Cervantes's "popular" one-act comic pieces (called *Entremeses*, or Interludes), one finds an intensification of the dialogic relationship with the *comedia nueva* ("new theater") that had been initiated formally in *Don Quijote I*, and which extended to a number of *comedias* as well, especially *La entretenida*, *El rufián dichoso*, and *Pedro de Urdemalas*. That is, by the early 1600's Cervantes's attention is directed against the theory and practice of the new theater as defined largely by its major proponent and ideologue, Lope de Vega. The significance of that dialogue rests on the fact that while Lope had rejected Aristotelian poetics on grounds that it implied a closed canon, Lope's own *arte nuevo* was also a strategy for the exclusion of certain discourses; it was a different kind of closed canon.[2]

Cervantes's subtle views of the Spanish theatre of the early 1600's are outlined in his Prologue to *Ocho comedias y ocho entremeses* (1615).[3] He begins by commenting on his lack of commercial success as a playwright while reminding the reader that he had brought a number of innovations to the Spanish stage: "I was the first to bring the imaginings and hidden thoughts of the soul on stage, taking moral figures into the theater, to the widespread and delighted applause of the audience" (p. 92). He points out that the psychological and moral dimensions of his characters were both innovative and pleasing to the public. He is vague about the number of *comedias* he composed (he mentions, casually, twenty or thirty), yet he talks unashamedly of his total eclipse as a functioning playwright when, having left the theater for a number of years, the Spanish stage came to be dominated by Lope de Vega: "I had other things concerning me. I stopped writing and making plays, and then the 'monster of nature,' 'the great Lope de Vega,' came on the scene, establishing his dramatic *monarchy*. He enslaved and placed under his *jurisdiction* all the actors around" (p. 93, emphasis mine).

If one were to take literally Cervantes's own account, by the time he resumed writing plays, the new, self-crowned king of the *comedia* (Lope) had reduced his subjects (the actors) to order and his non-followers to silence.

Cervantes's dialogue with Lope goes beyond playful irony in as much as it deals with questions of aesthetic production and reception and leads to a distinction between the public and private spheres of art. Seen from this perspective, Cervantes's absence from the theater is but a temporary pause. It is a silence that is translated into a strategy: to direct his writing for the theater away from the public sphere of performance and representation on stage to the private sphere of reading. This is how Cervantes explains it, ironically, in the Prologue: "It has been some years since *I returned to my old idle ways*, and, thinking that the period still lasted in which my praises were being sung, I went back to writing plays. But I found no birds in last year's nests, that is, *I found no director willing to take my work*, even though they knew it was there. So I *locked* the plays away in a chest and consecrated and *condemned them to perpetual silence*" (p. 93, emphasis mine).

Cervantes's initial decision to condemn his plays to perpetual silence can thus be seen as an ironic affirmation of freedom; it is nothing less than an unwillingness to conform to the poetics of a genre — the *comedia nueva* — that exists in the minds of playwrights and audiences and which is codified by Lope de Vega in his *Arte nuevo*. Cervantes's reluctance to write plays for an undiscriminating "mass" audience ("el vulgo")[4] that has been coopted ideologically by one of the vehicles of official culture (Lope's *comedia nueva*) compels him to redirect his own theater toward the private sphere of reading. It is in that context, I believe, that Cervantes goes on to renounce the mediations of producers and actors and directs himself to an ideal discerning reader. It is the latter who is asked to judge his *comedias* and *entremeses*, on both artistic and moral grounds: "You will see it, *my reader*, and if you should find that [the plays] have any good in them, when you run into my evil-tongued director, tell him to straighten up, since I offend no one, and to realize that [my plays] have no open or outlandish idiocies. *The verse is exactly what the plays require, which has to be, of the three styles, the lowest. The language of the interludes is appropriate to the figures therein introduced*" (p. 94, emphasis mine).

Since the Prologue ends by categorizing plays along classical precepts of separation of styles, it will be argued here that it expresses conflict between Cervantes's purported adherence to those rules and his attempt to redefine that low, "popular" genre (*entremés*) along more open, non-canonical lines. That redefinition takes place through a process of textualization which precludes closure.[5]

In approaching Cervantes's *Entremeses*, therefore, two important facts must be kept in mind: 1) they were not produced on stage during Cervantes's time and, 2) their publication in Madrid came just six years after Lope de Vega had issued his now famous *Arte nuevo*. Significantly, Lope's manifesto had rejected the basic premises of Aristotelian poetics ("I locked the unities under six keys") for his "new" plays, while reaffirming traditional precepts for the "old" plays, i.e., the interludes. Lope speaks of "the custom of calling *the old plays / Interludes*, in which dramatic art is still in force / since they have a single action among common people. / An interlude about kings has never been seen" (v5., emphasis mine).

Lope's paradoxical position of being innovative in defining the new plays and traditional in viewing the interludes was not lost on Cervantes who, in his own *Entremeses*, rebukes Lope while testing the limits of Aristotelian poetics. That is, while conforming to the unities of time, place and action, the focus of the *Entremeses'* aesthetic reception is shifted from that of the ideologically homogeneous theater-going public of the early

1600s to the transdiscursive world of the reader of his own time and of the future. Such a shift away from the domain of public opinion carries with it the possibility of a redefinition and expansion of the concept of verisimilitude,[7] one that would have less to do with what was given in a tradition and more with the lived experience of readers.

By contrast Lope, as playwright, was to make compromises which were meant to assure his plays a favorable reception: he was to subjugate art to the realities of the marketplace ("fame and reward"). His idea was to give the new theater-going public (the common man) what it wanted: lots of action; a variety of verses and stanzas; and, above all, the dramatic structuration of concepts with which spectators could identify: love, honor, monarchy. In his *Arte nuevo* Lope defends the primacy of pleasing and entertaining over what was right artistically, in the traditional Aristotelian sense: "I stand by what I wrote, therefore, and I know / that even if it might have been better done another way, / [the plays] would not have given the pleasure that they gave, / for sometimes that which goes against what is right, / for that very reason gives delight" (vs. 372–76). Fundamentally, Lope's public can identify with a system of values that stress collective ideals: the defense of the monarchy; the further solidification of an entrenched estate system; the safeguard of honor as the *raison d'être* of individual and social life; and the constant reaffirmation of love as a universal justification.[8] The theater-going public of the *comedia* thus possessed a code, i.e., a horizon or system of expectations,[9] which Lope and other playwrights took into account so that their plays could be understood and received favorably. One of the key characteristics of that public is an absolute homogeneity along ideological lines. That is, from the lowest social classes to the merchants, artisans, bureaucrats, etc., the public identifies with the values of the dominant class, the nobility.

Largely through the efforts of Lope, therefore, the *Comedia nueva* becomes a major well-defined genre by the early 1600's. The *entremés*, on the other hand, continues to be a dependent genre,[10] drawing not only on a variety of literary and folkloric sources but assimilating as well into its structure various other popular forms of entertainment, especially lowly ballads (*jácaras*), music and popular dances (for example, *la zarabanda*). Moreover the *entremés* is constantly being redefined *vis à vis* the *comedia*, i.e., the dominant genre with which it is associated by the viewing public. Such is the case at least until the eighteenth century when virtually everything that was perceived to fall within the broad category of popular culture — *entreméses*, sermons, bullfights, *auto-sacramentales*, and the *comedia* itself — was condemned by neoclassicists on aesthetic and / or moral grounds.[11]

In a pioneering study of the *entremés* from Lope de Vega to Quiñones de Benavente, Eugenio Asensio summarizes some of the basic differences between *comedia* and *entremés*. He argues that the former brings all conflicts to an ultimate resolution while the latter perpetuates disorder and chaos; that the *comedia* moves the spectator to identify with the aspirations of the hero while the *entremés* allows the viewer to feel superior to the characters; that in the *comedia* the comic is embodied by the servant (*gracioso*) who functions in contrast to a master who embodies noble emotions, while in the *entremés* the comic ambient undermines the seriousness of characters and situations; finally, that in the *comedia* the poetic word predominates while the language of the *entremés* requires gesticulation.[12]

Asensio's definitions underscore two key problems: 1) since the entremés is viewed exclusively in terms of classical poetics (i.e., as a low genre), it is not surprising that it should be appreciated exclusively for its entertainment value ("a toy for a quarter of an hour"); and 2) since it is reduced to a determinate and invariable norm, a sufficient distinction is not made between Cervantes's conception and use of the *entremés* and that which many of Cervantes's contemporaries had of the same comic genre. The issue, of course, is that Cervantes circumvents the "normative," bypassing the horizon of expectations of the theater-going public and addressing his plays directly to readers. Thus in a subtle comment in his *Viaje al Parnaso* (1614), Cervantes differentiates between the private act of reading and the public reception that takes place in a theater; between the solitary figure who probes the printed text in the privacy of his thoughts and the theater-going individual who is swept by collective expectations. He says of his plays, "but my idea is to publish them, *so that one can perceive slowly that which passes quickly*, or what is veiled, or what is not understood, when presented on stage" (emphasis mine).[13]

It is important to recall here that, under normal circumstances, *entremeses* were produced between the acts of *comedias*. Given the polyphonic nature of the performance and the collective expectations of the viewing public, it is not unreasonable to conclude that a spectator witnessing the performance of an *entremés* in the public space of a theater is more likely to be led toward a predictable reception (and to be conditioned by generic considerations) than a reader who is probing the printed text. Unlike the spectator who is distracted by songs, music, and lascivious dances which often end the performance of an *entremés* in a theater, the reader is deprived of those multiple sensorial experiences. He must be content to imagine a joyful ending to the play while remaining conscious of the fact that basic conflicts are left unresolved.

The private reception through reading allows Cervantes to circumvent the possibility of a closed canon. That is, while closure is achieved in an *entremés* within the framework of a staged performance, within the private sphere of reading there occurs a textualization which virtually excludes that possibility. In the case of Cervantes's *Entremeses*, the private reading of those comic pieces allows for a reception that is potentially demystifying and subversive. In a society dominated by the ideology of the spirit, by a virtual negation of earthly pleasures, by countless prohibitions (especially of a sexual nature), and by a massive propaganda campaign which makes use of theater, sermons, chapbooks, festivals and other vehicles of "popular" culture to preserve the socio-political status quo, Cervantes's *Entremeses* circumvent the public sphere of representation and, by so doing, negate an otherwise predictable trivialization of the material. Through pranks, jokes and other kinds of antidotes to the conventions of language and thought, and through a series of what Pierre Macherey calls "voids and absences,"[15] those "popular" comic pieces bypass the horizon of expectation of the theater-going common-man and afford the perceptive reader the possibility of laughing at the deceiving idealisms of official culture.

Cervantes's own interludes might be examined from the standpoint of aesthetic production *and* reception; they might be seen both as the imposition of an artistic and social will that embarks upon the reinterpretation of a closed canon at a particular juncture in Spanish history *and* as theatrical pieces that become inscribed within changing horizons of expectations, in different cultural contexts and over time. In the latter sense one would have to agree with Jauss's argument that "a literary event . . . can continue to have an effect only if future generations still respond to it or rediscover it."[16] With several of Cervantes's interludes it is clear that the latter requirement has been met. Such is especially the case with *El retablo de las maravillas*, a masterful comic-serious play which on a universal level deals with human folly, prejudice and false consciousness, as well as with the inability of most people to see themselves as they are. In the pages that follow I will concentrate on *El retablo* and shall refer briefly to a number of other plays as I illustrate how Cervantes subverts the classical ordering of genres and goes on to redefine the existing canon.

The *Retablo* sets up a dialogical relationship with those early seventeenth-century *comedias* that show the peasant's sense of honor as being embodied in wealth and in the racial (and racist) notion of blood purity. That is, in the *Retablo* the rural theme is treated in a burlesque fashion, while the butt of the joke is the same representative of the minority group of rich farmers which is given a privileged status in the *comedia*. To cite an example, I shall refer briefly to a well-known piece by Lope—*Peribáñez o el Comendador de Ocaña* (1610?)—which seems to be slightly earlier than the *Retablo* and toward which Cervantes probably directed his critical gaze.[17]

Peribáñez shows the conflict between a nobleman and a peasant, his vassal (and also refers to the struggle between the landed peasants and the petty rural nobility of the country gentlemen). The outcome is already foreshadowed in the second scene. When the Comendador de Ocaña begins to court Peribáñez's wife Casilda, the peasant anticipates the consequences awaiting a lecherous lord who fails to be socially responsive toward the vassal: "It is enough that the *Comendador* pursues my wife; / it is enough that he takes away my honor / when he should be honoring me. /

I am his vassal, he is my lord, / I live under his defense and protection; / if he plans to take away my honor, / I will take away his life."[18] The peasant seems to conceive of two kinds of honor: one that is feudal, linked to class hierarchy (and therefore extrinsic); the other intrinsic and linked to the idea of blood purity. One of the *comendador's* servants refers to this second kind of honor, at the same time relating it to Peribáñez' wealth and to the moral power he can wield through the esteem of his peers: "Peribáñez is a peasant from Ocaña, / an Old Christian and rich, a man / held in great esteem by his peers, / and if he wanted to cause a stir now, / in this town all those who go out to the fields with a hoe / will follow his name / because he is, although a peasant, a man of honor" (vs. 824–30).

Peribáñez is not linked to the *comendador* as a servant but as a vassal. Since this kind of relationship was only possible within the seignorial tradition, the implication is that "the wealthy peasant is capable of noble emotions."[19] At least this idea is emphasized in the play's outcome. Peribáñez justifies his killing of the *comendador* before the king, Henry the Just, by referring first to the purity of his bloodline ("I am a man, though of peasant cast, / of pure blood, never / of Hebrew or Moorish stained"), and later to his recently acquired prestige and title of captain: "Finally, the *comendador* / gave me a valiant squadron of a hundred peasants. / With the title of captain / I went out with them from Ocaña." In this tragicomedy, the peasant thus defines himself in terms of his wealth, his purity of blood, and through his rise in military power.

While honored and distinguished in Lope's *comedia*, in Cervantes's interludes the rich farmer becomes the object of laughter. Heroes such as Peribáñez, who are able to assert their dignity and honor, enter the realm of farce, turning into manipulated "spectators" or marionettes. A socio-historical reading of the *Retablo* clarifies the text's dialogical dimensions: Cervantes's invective against some rustic townspeople is a satire against the majority group of wealthy peasants "whose legal and political goal" (through exploiting the day laborers and struggling with the petty rural nobility) was "to enter the ranks of the aristocracy."[20] In other words around 1612, in an interlude written without hope of "fame or reward" and intended for a reading public, Cervantes turns into mockery the pretensions of some wealthy villagers who assert the importance of a bloodline that is, after all, "inoperative . . . that does not lead to the prestige of effective power, such as that exercised, through rents and revenues, by a bourgeoisie-like nobility that, even though it disdains commerce and does not renounce its feudal prerogatives, accepts the treatment of land like an investment capital."[21]

The image of the rich peasant in the *Retablo* contrasts not only with that put forth from about 1608 to 1615 by the playwrights of the "establishment," but also with the model presented by those economists who were writing about the agricultural crisis. If the former convert the *villano* into a theatrical hero who can assert his dignity and honor within an *estamental* society, the latter make him into a socio-political paradigm who can solve the country's economic crisis.

Cervantes's interludes subject these images to a process of demystification. The character-spectators of the *Retablo* (the lawyer Gomecillos; the *regidor* Juan Castrado and his daughter, Juana Castrada; the judge Benito Repollo, his daughter Teresa Repolla and nephew Repollo; the notary Pedro Capacho) are ridiculous in their peasant pretentiousness, in their alienating desire for legitimacy, and in the illusions of power they have acquired through the wealth that gives them access to the city council. The irony is particularly cutting in the case of the judge and the *regidor*, since they represent "a rustic domain that is still independent, but already threatened in its independence."[22]

The grotesque assertion of lineage by the wealthy peasants of the *Retablo* dominates the structure of the interlude. This obsession for legitimacy has obvious socio-economic and ethico-moral ramifications. On the one hand it implies a desire for incorporation into a privileged status; on the other it subverts the humanist concept of virtue — a concept deeply rooted in Cervantes's thought — that "everyone is the child of one's own works."

In *El retablo*, two swindlers (Chanfalla and his wife Chirinos) and an accomplice (the child "musician" Rabelín) head for a town with the idea of cheating the country bumpkins. To succeed with the swindle they count on the ignorance, vanity and socio-radical presumption of the wealthy administrator-peasants of the village. The "author" Chanfalla presents himself before the public, credulous and blinded by its mania for legitimacy, as a descendent of wizards and sorcerers: "I, my good sirs, am Montiel, one who brings with him a theater of marvels (*Retablo de las maravillas*)" (p. 219). Through this parodic reference to the standard enchanter and manipulator of magic objects (Montiel) are established the origin of the tableau and the conditions necessary to see it: "[The tableau] was made and put together by the wise Tontonelo with such parallels, lines and stars, with such points, characters and observations, that no one can see what is shown on it if they have any Jewish blood or if they were conceived out of wedlock" (p. 220).

This atmosphere of magic and superstition serves as backdrop for the illusory representation staged by Chanfalla and Chirinos through their verbal magic. That is, the wonders of Tontonelo's puppet show depend on the power of language which, in turn is anchored in the uneasiness of a particular class and the foolishness of a particular group. It is well known that, from a social point of view, the lack of a pure bloodline and illegitimate birth are obstacles that keep one from rising in the hierarchy of an *estamental* society or even from gaining access to any kind of work. In *El retablo* the presence of these so-called "common diseases" will, according to Chanfalla's irony, blind the public that attends Montiel's magic tableau: "and he who might be contaminated by these two so common afflictions can forget about seeing the unheard of and never-before seen things on my stage" (p. 220).

Bastardy and impurity of bloodline refer to two types of legitimacy (of birth and lineage) and operate on two levels at once: "that of the socialization of the individual, that is to say, one's position in the social and socio-economic system of one's own experience, and that of one's psychic existence, which is conditioned by one's position in the filio-parental triangle."[23] In this scheme, the wealthy, integrated and virile peasant of the rural dramas of Lope and some of his contemporaries, becomes a character-victim, a "spectator" manipulated by the mystifying practice of the swindlers and their young accomplice. In other words, the figure of the wealthy peasant is inverted and thereby demystified. The wealthy peasant-administrators of the *Retablo* are impotent, despite a wealth that even allows them the luxury of sponsoring the performance of a play in their house. This impotence is revealed not only in moral and physiological terms, but also socially and economically. They are shown to be totally paralyzed when faced with any kind of creative activity. Besides representing a class that does not turn its capital into commercial activities, the peasants of the *Retablo* are neither the "children of their parents" ("hijos de sus padres") nor "children of somebody" ("hijos de algo"), nor "children of their own works" ("hijo de sus obras").

The peasant "spectators" of Montiel's (Chanfalla's) magic tableau are blinded by their own uneasiness about legitimacy as well as by the mystifiers' dazzling words (of Chanfalla and Chirinos) and disorienting "sounds" (of Rabelín). Only that way can they "see" the "wise" Tontonelo's puppets that parade in front of them through the conjurations of the wizard (Montiel). In the midst of this public uneasiness "appear" successively on the stage Samson (the blind and symbolically "castrated" Jew of the Old Testament); the bull of Salamanca (with its ravishing horns); a horde of rats (gnawing and phallic) who descend directly from those raised in Noah's Ark; the water from the River Jordan (an enriching and rejuvenating water); two dozen raging lions and swarming bears (heraldic figures who are at the same time representations of virility); and finally the elegant damsel Herodias (a figure from the New Testament who here replaces her daughter, the leading figure of "castrating" dances).[24]

The villagers' belief in the illusions of the tableau becomes so exaggerated that Benito Repollo's nephew breaks into the linguistic space to "dance" with Herodias. The substitution of the mother Herodias for her daughter Salome, according to Maurice Molho, acquires significance from the fact that the dancer is "a woman defined . . . only by the distinctive feature of her maternity, a phallic mother who is the seducer and castrator of her son, and who, upon entering the dance, meets the forbidden spectacle face to face."[25]

The only character who fails to enter this illusory world of the theater within a theater (in the space created by the mystifiers' skills and the villagers' anxiety) is a *furrier* (an official charged with providing for soldiers) who arrives at the village to arrange billeting for "thirty men at arms" (p. 233). When the *regidor* Juan Castrado tries to bribe him with Herodias' castrating dance, we see an act of demystification. The *furrier* says "are these people crazy? What devil of a damsel is this, and what dance, and what Tontonelo?" (p. 235). The *furrier* does not know about the two necessary criteria for seeing what is happening in the tableau. He cannot give credence to what he does not see objectively. But his humanity (materiality) cannot affect the illusions of the obsessed villagers who go on believing (with the partial exception of the cowardly and grotesque Governor and poet, the lawyer Gomecillos) in the reality of the fictious tableau and in the validity of the concepts of legitimacy, the supposed prerequisites for being able to see it.

The outcome, it is clear, does not lead to any resolution of the conflicts. The villagers reproach the *furrier*, twisting the language of the Gospel of Matthew: "He is one of them." He, in his turn, calling them peasants and Jews, raises his sword and attacks them. Except for the child Rabelín, who is beaten up by the effeminate Benito Repollo, the mystifying swindlers have succeeded in completely controlling their enchanted public. Chanfalla says, "The event has been extraordinary. The virtue of the tableau remains intact, and tomorrow we will show it to the whole town. We ourselves can sing the triumph of this battle saying, 'long live Chirinos and Chanfalla!' " (p. 236).

This work of "low" style — undoubtedly the most successful of Cervantes's interludes — deals with an important theme which, from the historical perspective of 1612, we can identify with the crisis of the minority group of *labradores ricos*. The grotesque image of the impotent *labrador* is Cervantes's answer to the myth of the integrated peasant created in the rural dramas of Lope de Vega; it is the inverted figure of those wealthy peasants of the *comedia* who claim dignity and honor for themselves and even succeed in entering the ranks of the aristocracy (cfr. Peribáñez and the children of Juan Labrador, the main character of Lope de Vega's *El Villano en su rincón*). Cervantes's lesson is a satire on lineage, one that implicitly reaffirms the humanist notion that true honor comes not from blood purity or from one's last name and coat of arms, but from one's ability and deeds: everyone is the child of one's own works.

Even though Cervantes in *El retablo* sets up a dialogical relationship both with the myths, beliefs, and escapisms of the idealist literature of the sixteenth century (the topos of the *locus amoenus*, the *Beatus Ille* theme, the Arcadia motif, etc.) and with the propagandistic incorporation of those themes into the new theatre of the early seventeenth century, its success lies in its elevation of the theme of legitimacy to a universal dimension. *El retablo* suggests that those who are gripped by prejudice cannot distinguish reality from appearance, that is, that they are predisposed to see that which objectively does not exist. Racism is a blindness that induces people to live as if enchanted, outside of the natural order of things. Eugenio Asensio seems to refer to this same duality and richness of interpretive possibilities when he says that *El retablo* "is a parable of the infinite credulity of people who believe what they want to believe. It is a strategy for criticizing the morbid mania for purity, that lying creator of the false values that poisoned Spanish society. And it is a satire of the peasant contemplated not as a rising force who aspires to full dignity, but as a comic object good for producing raucous laughter in the spectator: within the apparent free play of the imagination a social antagonism lies hidden. Such is the wealth of possible perspectives."[26] The rural village drama of the *Retablo* is also, finally, a human drama. Behind the joking and laughter (laughter also directed toward the rural dramas of Lope) lies an important and vital message.

Cervantes's mockery of the peasant-village administrators whose *raison d'être* was based on blood purity was anticipated in *Los alcaldes de Daganzo* (1610?). In that interlude, as in *El retablo de las maravillas* (1612), the satire reaches its culmination through a dialogical language which, besides demystifying the notion of the village-refuge of the shepherd-courtiers and the poets who "fled" the worldly noise of the court, points to an Arcadia that is full of conflict and opposes it to the rural world invented by the *comedia nueva* toward the end of the first decade of the seventeenth century.

Cervantes indeed subverts the classical ordering of genres and proceeds to redefine the existing canon. That redefinition takes place through the textualization of materials drawn from literature and folklore—the latter often through mediations—as well as from personal reflections about art and social life in the Spain of his time. It is precisely Cervantes's textualization of those materials, effected in a dialogic relationship with the *comedia nueva*, while directed toward an ideal reader, that adds a serious dimension to the hitherto comic genre "entremés". To return to Jauss's aesthetics of reception, one might argue that the reader's expectations regarding the *entremeses* are shaped not only by the rules that govern that genre but by other readings as well, including Cervantes's daring, experimental works like the *Novelas ejemplares* (1613) and *Don Quijote* (1605, 1615).

It goes without saying that the interlude has its own system of signs which, in turn, imposes a linguistic code. Cervantes himself acknowledges as much at the end of the cited Prologue as he reminds the reader that the language of his interludes "is appropriate to the characters introduced in it." That language is often colloquial and, as with Sancho's speech in *Don Quijote*, it relies a great deal on proverbs and popular sayings. There are also times when the codified language of Cervantes's interludes belongs to a specific social group or subculture, as for example the sayagués of the rural types of *Los alcaldes de Daganzo* or the slang of ruffians and the underworld in *El rufián viudo*.

It is evident that the linguistic code of the interlude betrays the popular origins of the stock types that enter its world. Hence, from the mid-sixteenth century *Pasos* of Lope de Rueda (with its "simpleton", "old man", "sacristan", "barber", "student", "woman hustler" etc.) to the interludes in vogue during Cervantes's lifetime, the comic figures belonged to a limited number of stereotypes: the foolish cuckolded husband who is often old and impotent; the clever young wife who seeks physical pleasures outside of marriage; the young lover — generally a barber or a sacristan — who completes the mischievous triangle.[27]

What is significant for the purpose of our topic is Cervantes's break with key elements of the genre's poetics. Cervantes redefines the audience of his interludes, thus redirecting the reader's horizon of expectations. That movement away from the undiscerning common man toward the discriminate reader or "my reader" implies as well a rearticulation of the conventional and recuperative uses to which folklore had been subjected by the vehicles of official culture: the *comedia nueva* and the non-Cervantian *entremés*, i.e., the type of *inter-lude* that rarely breaks out of the traditional carnavalesque circle.[28]

Notes

1. Jacques Dubois, "Pour une critique litteraire sociologique," in *Le Litteraire et le social*, ed. R. Escarpit, Paris, Flammarion, 1970, pp. 56–75. Critical references to materials that appear in a language other than English are cited in translation. On the question of poetics and discourses I am guided by the insightful work of M. Bahktin, especially his "Discourses and the Novel," in *The Dialogic Imagination*, ed. M. Holquist (Austin, University of Texas Press), 1981.

2. See Lope's long verse defense of his dramatic practice in *Arte nuevo de hacer comedias en este tiempo* (1609), reproduced in H. J. Chaytor's *Dramatic Theory in Spain* (Cambridge, 1925), pp. 14–29.

3. The Prologue can be found in my edition of the *Entremeses*, (Madrid, Cátedra, 1982). Subsequent references both to the Prologue and to the *Entremeses* are to this edition.

4. For a discussion of Spanish Baroque theater as socio-political propaganda, see José Antonio Maravall, *Teatro y literatura en la sociedad Barroca* (Madrid, Seminario y Ediciones), 1972. See also Maravall's now classic study, *La cultura del Barroco. Análisis de una estructura histórica* (Madrid, Ariel, 1976) for a connection between *masa* and *vulgo*. The latter is defined as "the mass of common people who are carried away by passion, without reason, and without an objective and intellectually elaborated norm" (p. 200).

5. Cfr. Umberto Eco, *Opera aperta* (Milan, Bompiani, 1962).

6. Cfr. Bruce W. Wardropper, "El entremés como comedia antigua", in *La comedia española del Siglo de Oro* (Barcelona, Ariel, 1978), p. 25.

7. A theoretical discussion of the changing concept of verisimilitude is found in the classic essay of Gerard Genette, "Vraisemblable et motivation," in *Communications*, No. 11 (1968), 1–21: "One would only reject the naive first meaning [of the term "verisimilar"], that which would imply a relation [of the text] with reality. The second meaning is that of Plato and Aristotle: the verisimilar is the agreement of a particular text with that general and diffuse other text which one calls public opinion. Among the French of the Classical period one finds already a third meaning: comedy has its own verisimilitude, different from that of

tragedy. There are as many verisimilitudes as there are genres, and the two concepts tend to be confused [the appearance of this meaning of the word is an important step in the discovery of language: one goes here from the level of the spoken to that of speaking]" (p. 3). Cervantes's propensity for questioning norms and redefining them is well known. Cfr. Alban K. Forcione, *Cervantes, Aristotle, and the "Persiles"* (Princeton, 1970); and, E. C. Riley, *Cervantes's Theory of the Novel* (Oxford, 1962). See also the latter's "Teoría literaria" in *Suma Cervantina*, ed. J. B. Avalle-Arce and E. C. Riley (London, Tamesis, 1972), esp. pp. 294–95.

8. See José María Díez Borque, *Sociología de la comedia española* (Madrid, Cátedra, 1976); and, *Sociedad y teatro en la España de Lope de Vega* (Madrid, Antoni Bosch, 1978).

9. For a theoretical discussion of this notion, see Hans Robert Jauss, *Towards an Aesthetics of Reception* (Minneapolis, University of Minnesota Press, 1982). For an application of Jauss's notion to the Spanish *comedia*, see Maria Grazia Profeti, "Código ideológico-social, medios y modos de la risa en la comedia del siglo XVII", in *Risa y sociedad en el teatro español del Siglo de Oro* (Paris, C. N. R. S., 1980), p. 13–23.

10. William S. Jack, *The Early Entremés in Spain: The Rise of a Dramatic Form* (Philadelphia, 1982), pp. 131–32; and Eugenio Asensio, "Entremeses" in *Suma Cervantina*, op. cit., esp. pp. 172–74.

11. Cfr. Ignacio de Luzán, *La Poética. Reglas de la poesía en general y de sus principales especies* (1737; 1789), Ed. Russell Sebold (Barcelona, Labor, 1977), esp. pp. 547–51; Nicolás Fernández de Moratín, *Desengaño al teatro español* (Madrid, 1763), p. 9.

12. Eugenio Asensio, *Itinerario del entremés: desde Lope de Rueda a Quiñones de Benavente* (Madrid, Gredos, 1965), p. 39.

13. *Viaje del Parnaso*, ed. Vicente Gaos (Madrid, Castalia, 1973), p. 183.

14. "I did not write them with this intent [to publish them], nor so that the ears of the theater be turned into the censure of the inns." ("Prólogo" to *Novena parte*, cited by Díez Borque, *Sociedad y teatro*, p. 262).

15. See Pierre Macherey, *Pour une théorie de la production littéraire* (Paris, Maspéro, 1974).

16. Jauss, *Towards an Aesthetics of Reception*, p. 22.

17. On the date of Peribáñez, see S. Griswold Morley and Courtney F. Bruerton, *The Chronology of Lope de Vega's comedias* (New York, 1940); and Courtney Bruerton, "More on the Date of 'Peribáñez y el Comendador de Ocaña' " *Hispanic Review*, XVII (1949):35–46. The date for the *Retablo's* composition is placed at around 1609–1612 (probably 1610). See also, Noël Salomon, "Simples remarques à propos du problème de la date de 'Peribáñez y el Comendador de Ocaña' ", *Bulletin Hispanique*, LXIII (1961):251–58. On the dates of composition of Cervantes's *Entremeses*, see Jean Canavaggio, *Cervantés dramaturge. Un théâtre à naître* (Paris: Presses Universitaires de France, 1977), p. 23, where he also offers a synopsis of the chronologies that have been proposed, from the early 1900s to recent times, by a number of investigators: C. Valledor, R. Schevill, A. Bonilla, M. Buchanan, A. Marín, A. Agostini, and E. Asensio. Most modern critics place the *Retablo's* date of composition at about 1612.

18. Ed. Charles Aubrun and José F. Montesinos (Paris, 1944), vs. 1746–53. Subsequent references to *Peribáñez* are to this edition.

19. Maravall, *Teatro y literatura*, p. 89.

20. Noël Salomon, *Recherches sur le thème paysan dans la 'comedia' au temps de Lope de Vega* (Bordeaux, 1965), pp. 317–18.

21. Maurice Molho, *Cervantes: raíces folklóricas* (Madrid, Gredos, 1976), p. 151.

22. *Ibid.*, p. 149.

23. *Ibid.*, p. 164–65.

24. *Ibid.*, p. 176 ff. in which it is argued that "each of those names operates as a sign in

which there is inscribed the psycho-dramatic function of the character in the crisis of the *Retablo*" (p. 176).

25. *Ibid.*, p. 211.

26. Eugenio Asensio, "Entremeses" in *Suma Cervantina, op. cit.*, pp. 190–91.

27. Jean Canavaggio, "Introducción," *Miguel de Cervantes, Entremeses* (Madrid, Taurus, 1981), esp. 10–23.

28. I wish to thank my colleagues Wlad Godzich and René Jara for a number of helpful suggestions regarding this study.

The Persiles (1617)

[The Christian Romance Structure of Cervantes's *Persiles*]

Alban Forcione*

[E.C.] Riley is undoubtedly right in observing that Cervantes' "literary theory gives no hint of concern with the more recondite species of unity — thematic and symbolic, as opposed to mere formal unity" and "his expressed ideas on the unity of the novel are based on current ideas of epic unity."[1] Such ideas may reveal much about Cervantes' intentions in the *Persiles*, but they tell us little concerning his realization or the intent of the work itself, and they are certainly inadequate criteria of unity if we wish to understand the work. The fact is that the vision which Cervantes embodied in the *Persiles* had a coherence of its own, one which demanded literary techniques of which Cervantes was theoretically unaware and which compelled him to develop or "abuse" the Heliodorean techniques of disposition which he had studied in the *Aethiopica* and the poetic treatises of his time. That is to say, his vision demanded the independent episode, the proliferation of event and episode, and the continuing fragmentation in the development of narrative threads. Regardless of what Cervantes said about his desires to write a prose epic, the unity of texture or theme of the *Persiles* is to be sharply distinguished from the linear unity acclaimed by sixteenth-century theorists in the classical epic.

The *Persiles* is a quest romance in which the heroes must abandon an imperfect society, journey through strange worlds full of menacing forces, and suffer numerous trials and struggles before reaching their destination. Here their sufferings are rewarded with superior wisdom, and they can return to elevate their society to the state of perfection which they themselves embody. The principal narrative line presents a sequence of adventures involving the heroes, each of which in structure and thematic implications repeats the cyclical pattern of the overall quest. Accompanying the major plot are numerous secondary lines of narration, each forming an episode and presenting a quest of a secondary figure. Each

---

*Excerpted and reprinted with permission from *Cervantes' Christian Romance* (Princeton: Princeton University Press, 1972), 29–51.

secondary quest represents a miniature analogue of the quest of the heroes, both in its structure and its thematic implications. The major effect of this structure is an accumulation of power in the statement of theme through ritualistic repetition. Moreover, through fragmentary narration Cervantes succeeds in superimposing the episodes on the main plot, creating a richly complex texture and heightening the effect of timelessness that springs from the recurrence of ritual.

The structure of the *Persiles* is animated by the spirit of orthodox Christianity, as the adventures often have biblical overtones, suggesting an analogy between the heroes, God's chosen in search of the Promised Land, and mankind awaiting the advent of the Redeemer and the establishment of the custodian of his Word, the Holy See in Rome, itself to be followed by the New Jerusalem. Thus one can observe in the *Persiles*, in symbolic concentration, the entirety of history as presented by the Christian mythology. One of the most important factors sustaining this level of analogy is the movement of the heroes from their benighted kingdoms at the northern extremities of the world (Tile, the kingdom of Periandro, is in fact described in the work as the "end of the earth" [p. 465]) to the ["head of the world"], Rome (p. 441).[2]

At another symbolic level the quest of Periandro and Auristela reenacts the basic myth of Christianity: man in his fallen state must wander in the sublunary world of disorder, suffering in the world of human history, and be reborn through expiation and Christ's mercy. Here too the symbolic implications of the protagonists' journey have an important function, as they move from a realm menaced by war, an oppressive king, and the threat of sterility to the city which traditionally images the Kingdom of the Blessed. Here, at what might be described in the traditional terminlogy of allegorical exegesis as the "anagogical" level of the *Persiles*, we discover the importance of the motif of ["the labors"],[3] which the title announces and which becomes a principle of unity, providing a thematic nexus between the many disparate narrative threads which have little coherence in terms of the current neo-Aristotelian criteria. At two points in the work we discover a traditional Christian commonplace: [". . . our souls are ever in constant movement, and they cannot rest except at their center, which is God, for whom they were created"] (p. 275 and p. 458). The *Persiles* represents this apparently endless movement of the soul through the "labors" of the earthly life, as its multitude of characters must wander about the earth tormented and driven onward by desire for a point of repose: ["They all had desires, but for none of them were those desires fulfilled: a condition of human nature, which, although God created it perfect, we, of our own fault, find it lacking. As long as we continue to desire, we will always experience lack"] (p. 176). The point of repose continues to elude them until they emerge from darkness and the sea and reach Rome, that point which images Augustine's center of repose, God and the Heavenly City.[4]

Although the *Persiles*, symbolically interpreted, can be seen as Cervantes' divine comedy, its actions are confined to the real world. It must be remembered that the work was conceived in terms of neoclassical literary theories, stressing the imitation of nature and maintaining that verisimilitude is one of the most important qualities in fiction.[5] There is here no entry into the Heavenly City nor a direct vision of God rewarding the pilgrims. The work ends rather with the restoration of peace and fertility to the northern kingdoms and the diffusion of Catholic enlightenment to their inhabitants. Moreover, the diabolical forces and monsters, the "dragons" of the medieval fantasy, which the heroes must overcome, are only those whose existence the Renaissance mind accepted as possible in the natural order. Nevertheless, through traditional symbols and allusions to Christian and classical mythology, a mythic movement running parallel to the movement of the plot is established. Although the degree to which this movement approaches the surface of this high mimetic work varies, it is continuously present and sustains the total symbolic meaning of the events of the narration.[6]

For example, the goal of the pilgrims is Rome, which had been traditionally regarded not only as the center of the world but also as the simulacrum of the City of God (at one point in the *Persiles* Cervantes writes: ["Rome is earth's heaven"] [p. 192]). The author reinforces the traditional association as the pilgrims ritualistically ascend a hill overlooking Rome, where they kneel in adoration of the goal of their quest ["as if before a sacred thing"].[7] As Frye points out, the hill is one of the archetypal locations for the point of epiphany, at which the "undisplaced apocalyptic world and the cyclical world of nature come into alignment."[8] Like the Bible, the *Persiles* presents several mountain-top epiphanies, and it is logical that in this, the most important of them, Cervantes would attempt to reactualize the climactic moment of the Revelation when John the Divine is carried to a high mountain to observe the New Jerusalem descending from heaven. The archetypal hill and the traditional associations clustering around the city of Rome are not the only means by which Cervantes keeps the level of myth present in this scene. As they contemplate the Eternal City, the pilgrims overhear a poem which renders its relationship to the City of God, which has been introduced earlier into the context of the *Persiles* in Feliciana de la Voz's song describing the celestial paradise, explicit: ["There is no part in you [Rome] which does not serve as example/of sanctity, as if drawn out on grand scale/from the City of God"] (p. 426). As we shall see, most of the poems in the *Persiles* establish a mythic background for the events of the narration and prescribe the direction in which an allegorical commentary on the fictions must proceed.

In what Renaissance literary theorists would regard as the major plot of the work, the *Persiles* consists of a sequence of adventures in which the young heroes must struggle with numerous antagonists, which are usually linked to demonic agencies. These adventures follow a cyclical pattern, as a moment of struggle, bondage, or "near death" alternates with a moment of resurrection or triumphant vision of the final goal of the quest. Thus all adventures repeat in miniature the circular pattern of the entire quest, which encompasses them. Quite appropriately in view of both the overall movement from the lower order of fallen man to the restored paradise which the *Persiles* symbolically represents and the *in-medias-res* structural technique perfected by Heliodorus and recommended by the theorists, Cervantes chooses to begin the *Persiles* at the lowest moment in the fortunes of the hero and the moment when he is most distant from the climactic vision of his goal from the hill and his return to his kingdom. Separated from his beloved Auristela, Periandro lies imprisoned in the depths of a cave on the island of the barbarians, where his heart is to be ripped out and devoured by his captors. In composing this scene, Cervantes was probably recalling the descriptions of such startling practices in sixteenth-century chronicles about the new world and its inhabitants. Moreover, he may have been following contemporary literary theories concerning the legitimate marvelous and specifically Tasso's suggestion that the poet describe the realities of the new world, which, although strange and wonderful, are verified by the historians and accepted as true by the reading public.[9] However, the marvelous detail has an important function within the symbolic rhythm of the *Persiles* and is the first of the various details showing how Cervantes assimilated contemporary history to his underlying theme. Cannibalism is an archetypal demonic motif in literature, and appearing here, it imaginatively links the hero's persecutors not only with the American Indians but also with the powers of hell.[10] The connections between barbarian society and Christian mythology are rendered more concrete in their prophecy, which associates them specifically with the false prophet and Antichrist of the Apocalypse. They are ["convinced by either the devil or some aged shaman whom they take for very wise, that a king will emerge from their number who will conquer and win a large portion of the world"] (p. 57). Subsequent references to the few good barbarians as angels reinforce the link between their demonic society and that of the fallen angels. The cave in which Periandro is imprisoned is described as ["rather a tomb than a prison, filled with the living bodies of those entombed in it".] The isolation of the hero is revealed dramatically in his inability to understand the language of his captors, which is likened to ["a terrible din"]. After Periandro's executioners have hoisted him from the dungeon and wiped the dust from his face, the beautiful youth ["raised his face and beheld the whole of the sky"] and thanks God for delivering him from the darkness of the cave and allowing him to see His light before his death. As if by providential design a storm suddenly delivers the youth from his captors, as the raging sea destroys their raft, drowns them, and bears Periandro to his rescue by the ship of

Prince Arnaldo, in which he ["returned to himself, as if from death to life"] (p. 54).

In the first scene of the romance we observe what we might call, using the terminology of the fugue, a complete statement of the subject and the answer of the major theme, which will be repeated endlessly with variations throughout the work. The motifs of bondage and deliverance, death and rebirth, darkness and light are sounded rapidly. The linkage of these archetypal motifs to a Christian context is obvious in Periandro's prayer; and hence we associate the darkness within which the hero lies with the realm of the demonic and the light of the heavens with the divine. Moreover, the numerous biblical allusions and motifs that appear in the narration of the following scenes allow us to see in the natural cataclysm which destroys the evil forces and delivers the chosen the Red Sea and the great flood of the Scriptures.

The pattern which begins the romance continues as Periandro immediately returns to the island of the barbarians to search for Auristela. There he finds his beloved in a similar situation, standing before her executioner awaiting the death blow. Again the heroes are miraculously delivered, as Periandro's beauty arouses a sodomitic passion in Bradamiro, a quarrel erupts between him and the other barbarians, and a blazing fire ravages the island. Periandro and Auristela wander lost amid the confusion around them. Again the motif of darkness appears at the moment of catastrophe: [". . . night closed in, dark and terrifying, as has been said"] (p. 69). But ["heaven does not forget to come to their aid"], and a young barbarian leads them along a tortuous path through a dark cavern to an illuminated refuge. As a second deliverer appears, Cervantes' description suggests very strongly that God's angels have guided the protagonists to safety, just as the angel and pillar of fire guided the elect through the wilderness before the pursuing armies of the Pharoah.

> ["Praise be to God," said the barbarian in Spanish, "who has brought us to this place, which, though we might be in some peril, it is not the peril of death!"
> At that they saw a great light come streaming toward them, just like a comet . . .
> "Heaven bless you, *human angel*, or whoever you are . . ."
> At that the light arrived, carried by one who seemed a barbarian . . .]
> (p. 70)

The young barbarian explains that an impulse sent from heaven prompted him to save the Christians from the fire and sword of their enemies, and the heroes observe in their escape one of God's miracles.

As in the first deliverance, we observe in the background a cosmic disaster of apocalyptic overtones, as the all-consuming flames (Sodom and Gomorrah, Jericho, the Apocalypse) devour the society of the barbarians and leave the chosen few, safely sheltered in their refuge, to endure a night which is longer than usual, as the smoke from the smouldering embers remains impenetrable to the rays of the rising sun,[11] and to continue in their quest. In the midst of the motifs of "near-death," imprisonment, darkness, fear, and natural disaster, the motif of physical death is sounded, but its tone points toward Christian resurrection and the goal of the ["labors"]. The aged servant of Auristela dies, her ["eyes fixed on heaven, and nearly broken"], declaring: ["I die a Christian in the faith of Jesus Christ, and in the same faith as that of the Holy Roman Catholic Church"] (p. 78).

From this moment of epiphany on, the motif of regeneration begins to dominate.[12] Up to this point the few details concerning the landscape of the island (rocks, crags, caves) have suggested ruggedness and sterility, reflecting the condition of its inhabitants and symbolically linking the island to the forces of evil. On emerging from the refuge on the morning following Cloelia's death, Periandro and Auristela behold in astonishment the fruit-bearing trees of a verdant circular area nourished by several fresh-water streams: [". . . the grass was high because of the continuous water that streamed from the rocks and kept it perpetually green"] (p. 79). The geometrical configuration of hell — the labyrinth — has been replaced by the perfect form — the emblem of eternity; the salt waters of death by the life-giving waters flowing down from the mountains; the demonic cave, by the earthly paradise.[13]

Antonio's wife resumes her history, describing her instruction in the Catholic faith by Antonio and her baptism in the waters of the mountain stream, and repeating the Credo. Her declaration of faith at this early moment in the romance offers a complete statement of the religious principles inspiring the *Persiles*: faith in God, the Son, and the Holy Spirit, obedience to the ["Holy Roman Catholic Church, reigned over by the Holy Spirit and governed by the High Pontiff, vicar and viceroy of God on earth, legitimate successor of Saint Peter, its first shepherd since Jesus Christ, who is the first and universal shepherd of his wife the Church"] (p. 82), faith in the Virgin, and the belief in the sanctity of Christian marriage and its fruits. The goal of the quest of the heroes is Christian instruction in the city of Rome and sacramental marriage following that instruction. Ricla's words here point toward the realization of their goals and foreshadow the words of instruction which Auristela will hear at the conclusion of their journey. Following Ricla's account the remaining captives in the dungeon-cavern, in which Periandro began his adventures among the barbarians, are delivered from its darkness; the small group kneels at the shore, prays to God for guidance, and sets out in the boats of their captors with high hopes of reaching civilization.

In addition to revealing rapidly and directly the Christian themes of the romance, the opening adventures of the *Persiles* demonstrate very clearly the cyclical process which is to recur throughout the work. The heroes must struggle against an adversary and overcome him in order to continue in their quest. In their struggle they must endure a momentary defeat (imprisonment, "near-death," passage through the labyrinth or the purgatorial fires) before their triumph, and their triumph is generally rewarded with a moment of vision of the goal of the quest. Thus Periandro's uplifted gaze and prayer, Cloelia's gaze toward heaven in death, and Ricla's recitation of the Credo are the first of a series of intermediary visionary moments which follow on the upward turn of the recurrent cycle and lead toward the climactic vision of Rome from the hill.

Angus Fletcher has observed that allegorical literature often moves through a series of such epiphanies toward a final one and has employed Eliade's term the "symbol of the center" to describe these moments. The term is, I think, particularly applicable to the *Persiles*, in which all characters are in search of a ["point"] and discover that the only point which ultimately quiets the desire driving them forward in their quests is to be found at the true ["center"] of the universe, God. ". . . we find that central to most such rituals [Fletcher is referring here to the ritualistic character of allegorical composition] there are special moments of particular exuberance, particular intensity, particular vision, and these moments involve what we have called 'symbols of the center.' To recall the main criterion: from the spatial point of view such a symbol, as Eliade has described it, would be a temple or indeed any sacred place to which the hero is drawn and in which he receives his initiation into the vision of his true destiny. . . . It appears that any temporal moment of particular intensity can serve as a symbol of the center, or, putting it another way, just as space is "sacred space" in the Temple, so time is "sacred time" in the Temple, while we can sometimes be shown a moment of sacred time without any of the spatial trappings that go to make up a proper temple. Interpreted somewhat freely, these notions allow a wide variety of things and experiences to possess the qualities of holiness."[14] Thus the shore from which Periandro gazes toward heaven following his emergence from the underground dungeon and Antonio's hidden refuge and circular garden are spatial settings for the "temple experience," and they will be recreated often in the *Persiles*; the hermitage of Renato, the temples of Lisbon, the monastery of Guadalupe, the cave of Soldino, the church of Valencia, and the hill overlooking Rome are the most important. If Periandro's prayer begins the series of triumphant visions, his cave-dungeon introduces a series of negative symbols of the center, which mark the lowest point in the downward turn of the recurrent cycle.[15] Generally oppressive, enclosing space is the dominant characteristic of the many recreations of the place of bondage in the *Persiles*, e.g., the various prisons, the hollow hill, the ship-leviathan, the hollow tree trunk of Feliciana, the chamber of Hipólita, and the small boat of Antonio, but they can often be created in less conven-

tional spatial circumstances, e.g., the islands of ice, the palace of Policarpo, and the dark alleys of Lisbon, which become a labyrinth for Ortel
Banedre.

The *Persiles* moves endlessly back and forth between the positive and
the negative symbol of the center, reenacting ritualistically the Christian
eschatological vision of bondage and restoration in the same way in which
it is reenacted symbolically in the Revelation, where the vision of the city
of Babylon yields to the triumphant vision of the New Jerusalem. Accompanying the respective moments of this cyclical movement between the
upper and lower centers are the motifs of struggle-triumph, bondage-
deliverance, darkness-light, sterility-fertility, death-resurrection, all of
which are resonant with overtones of traditional Christianity. Thus there
is usually a suggestion through allusion, imagery, and symbol that in the
struggle of the heroes divine and demonic forces are in combat and that
the heroes' quest is analogous to that of God's Elect in the Bible.

The continuous reenactment of the same ritual in the *Persiles* produces that effect of timelessness which normally attends ritualistic activity,
that "abolition of time through the imitation of archetypes and the
repetition of paradigmatic gestures," to which Eliade refers in his discussion of the ontological conception of primitive man.[16] This effect is in large
part the result of the endless recurrence of the specific motifs which
accompany the respective moments of the cycle. We have the feeling that
each episode and each adventure, regardless of who is involved, whether
the setting is the stark landscape of the north or the civilized world of
southern Europe,[17] and whether the subject matter assimilated to the
underlying ritual is historical or literary — biblical, classical, or chivalric —
contain all that has gone before and all that will come afterward.[18]

Moreover, by rapid shifts from motifs surrounding one moment of the
cycle to those surrounding the other, and, what is more important, by the
occasional intermingling of motifs from the respective moments, Cervantes succeeds in producing an effect not of *succession* but rather of
simultaneity of moments within the cyclical movement of the ritual itself.
For example, amid the dominant motifs of death, isolation, and darkness,
the single motif of distant stars will sound to maintain the other moment
of the cycle as present; during the festivity celebrating the restoration of
separated lovers and marriage, the motif of death will emerge in a dark
undertone. Such polyphony[19] is thematically important; for it underscores
the interdependence of both moments of the cycle and the preservation of
the moment of bondage and evil in the moment of liberation, i.e., the
value of ["the labors"]. In the words of the sage, Mauricio: [". . . good
fortune does not come without the counterweight of unhappiness, which
has authority and license to enter into the realm of happy events so that we
realize that neither the good is eternal nor the bad lasting"] (p. 116). The
discursive narrator returns to this theme, employing the image which
recurs so often in the work, the spatial point at which all converges: ["It

seems that good and evil are so close to one another that they are like two coinciding lines that, although originating in different places, wind up at the same point"] (p. 464). We observe here, in addition to a metaphorical statement of the necessity of evil in God's providential order, an effective geometrical analogy of the union of opposites in a higher synthesis which underlies the Christian vision of fall and redemption and the ritual which reactualizes this vision repeatedly in the *Persiles*.[20]

It is curious that Cervantes shows a great deal of concern with chronological time in the *Persiles*, often informing his reader of the number of days which pass as his heroes wander from location to location. Such comments are one of various elements which reveal the importance of the author's neo-classical literary theories in the composition of the work, for the references to time of travel, just like the references to real geography, are made in the interest of verisimilitude. (A modern commentator has observed that, in view of the location of the "frozen sea" and the Categat, Cervantes' statements that Periandro's journey between these points lasted a month and covered four hundred leagues are those of a skilled geographer.[21] Despite Cervantes' concern for temporal plausibility, the references to chronological time in the *Persiles* seem to be inappropriate and nonfunctional; that is to say, the work remains fundamentally atemporal and ahistorical.[22] It is the visionary moment rather than the duration of history, the exemplary and essential in man rather than the individual (i.e., "character"), the paradigmatic gesture rather than unique or new human activity, and the symbolic rather than the individuating gaze on the external world which form the fabric of Cervantes' final work. It was in the *Quixote* that Cervantes conceived of the ingenious idea of juxtaposing the archetypal, timeless reality characteristic of the world of literary romance to historical reality. In doing so he founded a new genre of literature, a genre based on all that the *Persiles* rejected — in a word, history.[23] To seek the novelistic in the *Persiles* is just as idle as to censure it for its failure to be novelistic.

Notes

1. Cervantes's Theory of the *Novel* (Oxford, 1962), p. 130.

2. The protagonists seek Catholic instruction, as in the northern kingdoms ["the true Catholic faith is not in as pristine a state as it should be"] (p. 432). ["Sigismunda had vowed to go to Rome to learn there about the Catholic faith, since in those northern religions [where she is from] it was somewhat broken"] (p. 467).

3. Covarrubias' *Tesoro* (1611) offers two meanings of the word. In addition to the most common meaning of the Latin *labor*, English *work* or *task*, the word also had the important secondary meaning of the English *ordeal* or *trial*: [". . . anything which brings with it struggles or need, and affliction to body or soul we call labor ('trabajo')"] (ed. M. de Riguer [Barcelona, 1943], p. 971). Don Quixote claims that he is ["valiant, courteous, generous, well-mannered, open-hearted . . . patient, sufferer of labors ["trabajos"], and of confinement . . ."] (I. 501). It should be pointed out that the symbolic range of the *Persiles*

includes a celebration of Christian ethical values, particularly those of patience, perseverance, and faith in God in adversity. At this "tropological" level of the work the motif of "los trabajos" is of course equally important. For the popularity and significance of the symbol of the pilgrimage in literature of the Counterreformation, see A. Vilanova, "El peregrino andante en el 'Persiles' de Cervantes," *Boletín de la Real Academia de Buenas Letras*, 22 (Barcelona, 1949), 97–159.

4. The classical statement of the vision of the restlessness of the soul and its state of unfulfilled desire in its estrangement from Eternity is of course St. Augustine's *Confessions*: "Is not the life of man upon earth all trial? Who wishes for trouble and difficulties? Thou commandest them to be endured, not to be loved." "In Thy Gift we rest; there we enjoy Thee. Our rest is our place . . . When out of order, they are restless; restored to order, they are at rest." "They be affections, they be loves; the uncleanness of our spirit flowing away downwards with the love of cares, and the holiness of Thine raising us upward by love of unanxious repose" (ed. Everyman's Libr., tr. E. B. Pusey [London, 1926], pp. 228, 313–15). The fundamental Augustinian concepts of desire and the point of repose recur as motifs in a number of variations throughout the *Persiles*. For example, both appear in Arnaldo's words of joy on discovering his beloved Auristela in Golandia: ["You are well-met, north-star by which my chaste thoughts are guided, and fixed star which leads me to the harbor in which my good desires will find rest"] (p. 122). Similarly Auristela sees herself to be ["the axle of the wheel of [Periandro's] fortune, and the sphere of movement of his desires"] (p. 473). Referring to her beloved, the tormented Isabela Castrucho asks: ["Am I not after all the center in which his thoughts find rest? Am I not the target at which his desires aim?"] (p. 410). A humorous interlude with the Spanish man of letters collecting aphorisms is the occasion for the restatement of the motif: [*"Do not desire and you will be the richest man in the world"*] (p. 418). The sober narrator punctuates a downward turn in the fortunes of the protagonists: ["There is so little security in human pleasure that no one can promise himself in them a place of solidity"] (p. 473). Counseling Sinforosa in her love problems, Auristela remarks: [". . . how well I know that our souls are in constant movement, even while they cannot stop loving a particular person"] (p. 170). It goes without saying that such fundamental principles underlying the creation of the *Persiles* were widely expressed in the literature of the Counter Reformation. Tasso describes the end of history and the repose of eternity (*Mondo creato*, VII, 418–26):

> It is right and well that if finally
> the movements of fixed and moving stars will end
> that those of the human mind and soul
> will also join the course of the heavens.
> Then all will have peace in the fixed point
> of the Divinity. Eternal rest
> will be our love and understanding
> which now vary and change in so many ways
> and with so many constant turnings.

5. See my *Cervantes, Aristotle, and the "Persiles,"* Chs. I, VIII.

6. I use "high mimetic" here as Northrop Frye defines the term in his theory of modes (see *Anatomy of Criticism* [Princeton, 1957], pp. 33–34). More will be said of the "varying degree of presence" of the mythic below, and examples will be given.

7. This scene reminds Farinelli ("El último sueño romántico de Cervantes," p. 134) of the scene in Tasso's *Gerusalemme liberata* in which the Christians contemplate the walls of Jerusalem (Canto III). The comparison is in my opinion very relevant; for the city, as the organizing principle for the action of the work, as a symbol of the heavenly kingdom, as a point of order in a world of suffering and deception, and, as goal of a quest and the emblematic representation of the moral values associated with that quest—faith in God,

perseverance, and duty — has the same function in each work (see A. Bartlett Giamatti, *The Earthly Paradise and the Renaissance Epic* [Princeton, 1966], pp. 179–210.

8. *Anatomy of Criticism*, p. 203.

9. As Aristotle had observed that epic and tragedy should be both marvelous and verisimilar, Renaissance literary theorists devoted much attention to techniques and types of subject matter by which the poet could arouse *admiratio* without destroying the reader's faith in the possibility of the actions of the plot. They distinguished a legitimate marvelous from an illegitimate marvelous. The former is based on poetic language, structural elements such as peripeteia, variety in descriptions and subject matter, great historical occurrences, and the Christian supernatural. The latter arises from uncontrolled multiplicity in subject matter and violations of the laws of empirical reality which have no causes in the Christian supernatural. (See Forcione, *Cervantes, Aristotle, and the "Persiles,"* Ch. I.) Throughout the *Persiles* Cervantes employs only the legitimate marvelous. For Tasso's remarks about the new world, see *Del poema eroico*, p. 109.

10. "It is consistent with this that the Eucharist symbolism of the apocalyptic world, the metaphorical identification of vegetable, animal, human, and divine bodies, should have the imagery of cannibalism for its demonic parody. Dante's last vision of human hell is of Ugolino gnawing his tormentor's skull" (Frye, *Anatomy of Criticism*, p. 148). Within the total context of the *Persiles* the barbarians' cannibalism represents the demonic perversion of the Holy Sacrament, which is introduced concretely and celebrated in one of the heroes' adventures in Spain (see below). Similarly the barbarians' grotesque marriage (the bridegroom must pass the test of swallowing a human heart without wincing) and its prophesied offspring, the conqueror of much of the world, are demonic counterweights of the various Christian marriages which the work celebrates and of the true Messiah.

11. ["The sun was slower than usual that day in showing itself to the world, it seems, because the smoke and embers of the island's conflagration made it hard for the sun's rays to reach earth"] (p. 79). Compare: ". . . he opened the shaft of the bottomless pit, and from the shaft rose smoke like the smoke of a great furnace, and the sun and the air were darkened with the smoke from the shaft" (Rev. 9:2).

12. Cervantes' insertion of Cloelia's death at this point is startling, as nothing in the narration has pointed toward it and the author makes no effort to present a plausible cause of death. The incident, which has an emblematic quality, has a double function in the symbolic movement of the work. Antonio, the deliverer of the heroes, is narrating his life story, and he has just described his escape from the sea, the moment of "near-death" and isolation in his expiatory quest (see below). This is hence the moment of his quest paralleling the present moment in the quest of Periandro and Auristela. Cloelia's death punctuates this parallelism of narrative threads and points toward the way of ascent in both quests. Her visionary experience is immediately repeated within Antonio's narration by the barbarian's wife Ricla. More will be said of the effects of such parallelism and repetition of motifs below.

13. See Frye, *Anatomy of Criticism*, pp. 141–50.

14. Angus Fletcher: *Allegory, The Theory of a Symbolic Mode* (Ithaca, N.Y., 1964), pp. 350–51, hereafter cited as "Fletcher." See also Otto F. Bollnow, *Mensch und Raum* (Stuttgart, 1963), p. 141–43; Mircea Eliade, *Das Heilige und das Profane* (Hamburg, 1957), Chs. I–II.

15. "Such a positive value cannot always be ascribed to the symbol of the center. Literature and, unfortunately, history have presented the opposite kind of sacred place, and we commonly call it 'hell.' " In these places we discover "a terrible alienation from the comic world of love, marriage, dance, and merriment" (Fletcher, p. 213–14).

16. Mircea Eliade, *The Myth of the Eternal Return: or, Cosmos and History*, tr. W. Trask, Princeton / Bollingen Paperback no. 258 (Princeton, 1971), p. 35.

17. In my opinion, Cervantists have placed far too much emphasis on the differences

between the first and the second part of the *Persiles*. While the Christian mythology is generally less displaced in the northern adventures than in the southern adventures, the *morisco* episode, the occurrences in the temple of Guadalupe, and the arrival in Rome all demonstrate that it can approach the surface of the action just as in the most "symbolic" of the northern scenes. At the same time we observe in most of the adventures in Policarpo's kingdom a displacement of myth which is essentially the same as that in many of the "realistic" southern scenes. The traditional distinction between a symbolic and a realistic half of the *Persiles*, which survives in Casalduero's observation of a distinction between the imagination and reality, myth and history, in the northern and southern adventures respectively, ignores the fact that the second half of the work continues to reactualize the Christian mythology and employs the symbolic methods of the first half to do so (see *Sentido y forma de "Los trabajos de Persiles y Sigismunda"* [Buenos Aires, 1984], pp. 173 ff.). Walter Boehlich is correct when he points to certain similarities between the northern and southern adventures and suggests that the traditional distinction between them is invalid ("Heliodorus Christianus: Cervantes un der byzantinische Roman," *Freundesgabe für* Ernst Robert Curtius [Bern, 1956], pp. 103–24.

18. ["The *leitmotif* in music and poetry allows things that appeared earlier to resound again in order to make connections available to the senses by way of the feeling. The result is an increase in the content."] ([Berlin, 1917], p. 78). The effect of Cervantes' motifs in the *Persiles* is analogous to that which Bach would achieve in music and that for which Wagner would strive and on which he would base his theory of the *Leitmotif* two centuries later. ["Wagner's conscious intention was to allow the unity of a temporal separation to be heard in the music, the intertwining of the past and future life in the concrete present. In the resonance of the motifs the living depths of the concrete relationship of our existence is present in every fulfilled moment, this mystical unity of time, of our existence, where every present moment is pregnant with the future and all the past is swallowed up in it. In the deepest sense everything is contemporaneous. Bach also created through the medium of music in this extraordinary way."]

19. Here too music offers an effective analogy for describing this type of effect. Nohl writes that of the various artistic media music best achieves the "unification of the plurality of expression in a single harmony that is the deepest meaning of polyphony. What we feel most strongly is this intertwining of what is separate." He writes of Bach's music: "The decisive thing here, however, is that the contrasts between the legal and evangelic view of Death appear not as a dramatic conflict of two powers in which one of them would be overcome. On the contrary, they are juxtaposed until the end. The historical succession is in the deepest sense an intertwining. Its religious essence consists in the tension between one and the other and at the same time the release of that tension—using a Hegelian term 'The Rose in the Cross of Actuality.' " (*Die Asthetische Wirklichkeit*, pp. 173–77; see also *Stil und Weltanschauung* [Jena, 1920], p. 113).

20. See also ". . . happiness and unhappiness tend to go so hand in hand that there is no way to separate them; pain and pleasure walk together in a pair . . ." (p. 162).

21. Ricardo Beltrán y Rózpide, "La pericia geográfica de Cervantes demonstrada con la 'Historia de los Trabajos de Persiles y Sigismunda,' " *Boletín de la Real Sociedad Geográfica*, 64 (1923), 286–87.

22. The peculiar coexistence of geographical exactness and symbolic space in the *Persiles* is analogous. As will be pointed out below, the symbolic nature of the various settings described thoroughly eclipses their reality as measurable or geographical space. Several studies have shown that Cervantes reveals a thorough knowledge of contemporary geography in his work. Indeed all his locations can be found on maps of the age, even such seemingly fantastic places as the Island of Fire and the Island of the Hermits. However, in one notable case the importance of symbolic space causes Cervantes to sacrifice absolute geographical precision and verisimilitude. Rome, as "cabeza del mundo," "Eternal City," and a real city, was well-suited to be the goal of Cervantes' heroes. However, those maps of the time that had

the greatest pretensions to scientific accuracy offered no city or country with such symbolic power for the origins of the quest. Hence Cervantes turns to classical geography, locating Periandro's kingdom on Thule. He underscores its traditional associations as a hallowed kingdom and "the end of the earth" by introducing Virgil's [". . . and may the sailors / worship only your gods: may the distant Thule serve you"] (p. 465). At the same time the author is careful to legitimize the momentary lapse, as shortly after the allusion, a character says: [". . . Thule, which is now commonly called Iceland . . ."] (p. 469). (See my remarks below on the occasional tension between the verisimilar and the symbolic in the *Persiles*.)

23. ["Cervantes moved the accent, which had until then pointed toward the "essence" of the literary figure, and placed it on the tense and problematic vital process of that figure. On the literary figure created by Cervantes are projected, in shifting lights, his actions and those of the characters around him who create together the woven and interlocking texture of human life"] (Américo Castro, *Cervantes y los castecismos españoles* [Barcelona, 1966], p. 21). See also Raymond S. Willis' excellent observations on Cervantes' revolutionary treatment of the dimension of time in the *Quixote* (*The Phantom Chapters of the Quijote* [New York, 1953], pp. 14–15). Considered in the context of literary history, the *Persiles* is certainly a much more *conservative* work than the *Quixote*.

Uncanonical Nativities:
Cervantes's Perversion of Pastoral   Diana Wilson*

"Diga qué misterio tiene el llamarse de la Voz, si ya no es el de su apellido."
— *Persiles*, III.4

"Let your women keep silence in the churches, for it is not permitted unto them to speak."
— I Corinthians 14.34

"What is there to say concerning childbirth?"
— Mallarmé

The critical question of what's in a name, always a fertile one for Cervantes's narratives, remains for the character of Feliciana de la Voz not only unanswered but unasked. As the heroine of the central episode of Cervantes's last romance, *Los trabajos de Persiles y Sigismunda*, this young Extremaduran woman can explain only the social derivation of her odd cognomen: that all who have heard her sing acknowledge her to have "the best voice in the world."[1] But the figurative operations at work in Feliciana's depiction suggest forces well beyond the range of such provincial singing talents. The constituents of her rich and crucial narrative, with its pronounced acoustic and rhetorical qualities, reveal Cervantes, once again, in the art of generic transformation. A nativity story with

*This essay was written specifically for this volume and is published here for the first time by permission of the author.

complicated intertextual relations, Feliciana's tale turns on events that would seem entirely remote from her musical gifts. Its plot explores the structures of female desire, its interdiction by patriarchal law, and its flight into elemental nature as a place for coming to voice. Feliciana herself narrates the interpolated "historia" of her crisis: her illicit sexuality and occulted pregnancy; the freakish delivery of her infant; and her desperate escape into a crude pastoral world where she finds asylum in a sheep-cote. Here she is enclosed and nurtured, within a "pregnant" tree, by an aged shepherd who sees no difference at all "between the parturition of a woman and that of a cow" (299). What is Cervantes doing with the representation of such antipoetic events? And what, in turn, is their relation to the main plot of the *Persiles?* If the episode of Feliciana de la Voz qualifies, as several critics have noted, for the spatial and symbolic center of the *Persiles*,[2] then an exploration of the strategies of representation at that center should illuminate the entire text. Those narrative strategies — interruptions, imitations, incorporations — shed light not only on the transformational structures of desire of the *Persiles*, but also on its relative disprisal within the European literary canon.[3] My own strategy in what follows is to bring into focus certain forces in the text, context, and subtexts of Feliciana's story that have been repressed in canonical interpretations.

Overhearing Feliciana's voice while en route to kill her for dishonoring the family, her father remarks, "Either that voice belongs to some angel among those confirmed in grace, or to my daughter Feliciana de la Voz" (306). Collapsed into this sentence is the very either / or opposition — between an *un*fallen angel and a fallen woman — which Cervantes's text, by granting the voice of an angel to a fallen woman, dismantles. That Cervantes chooses the character of an unwed and sexually discredited mother to sing a twelve-stanza hymn to the Virgin Mother has been rhetorically remarked in a modern critical reading that mirrors and repeats the above paternal logic. The rhetoric of Feliciana's enraged father, in other words, would seem to anticipate future misreadings of his daughter's story: "The novel of Feliciana and Rosanio is an adventure, through the lands of Extremadura, in which the most opposed circumstances are to be found: the voice of an angel in a newly-delivered woman, a hymn to the Virgin by a mother not yet married in the eyes of the Church."[4] Dismissed as "opposed circumstances," these antitheses reflect the tenacity of some ancient and deeply misogynist notions. Canon Law had once decreed, for example, that *no* mother could enter a church to pray until forty days after childbirth. The attitudes behind such prohibitions have intricate linkages with the scholastic infrastructures of thought so widely found in Renaissance texts. This intellectual infrastructure, where it bears upon notions of woman and of sex difference, is radically contested throughout the *Persiles*. Cervantes's deployment of the Virgin / Fallen Woman pairing may still be taken, if only by literalists, as further validation of the separability of "icons and fallen idols" — one of the most stubborn dualities informing the Renaissance notion of woman.[5] The narrative of Feliciana de la Voz, as I read it, radically questions this stale and ossified hierarchy, and, in the process, the very channels through which women, fallen and unfallen, might "come to voice."

This tale of the consequences of "not yet married" motherhood in 16th century Spain, an elaboration of the maternal position unusual for its time and place, exhibits profound disjunctions, not just between Virgin and Fallen Woman but between what may be called natural and unnatural childbirth. The narrative does indeed invite a distinction between character and discourse — between a "calumniated Mother" and her song about the world's most venerated mother. It also invites us to reflect on a third literary maternity, sedimented into it through a sequence of oddly disturbing elements: a pregnant and suicidal girl; her knife-wielding father; her escape into pastoral; a "pregnant" tree; a mother's inability to nurture her infant; its fosterage by pitying caretakers. These elements, to be taken up later in this essay, advertise their derivation from Ovid's myth of Myrrha, transformed into a pregnant myrrh-tree for her "criminal" incest.[6] What is the meaning of the ironic intertextuality of these three nativities, textual and subtextual, at the heart of Cervantes's posthumous work? Forged out of such conflictual materials, the episode of Feliciana de la Vox presents an interpretative challenge of special appeal to critics awakened to the significance of sexual codes in literature. The interweaving of these three mothers — Feliciana, Mary, Myrrha — has to my mind a complex of institutional aims: to expose and conceptually restructure the Golden Age mythology of motherhood; to rescue female desire from the scapegoating mechanisms of patriarchy; and to represent the rise, as it were, of the fallen woman. This last category, Casalduero assures us, is by no means reserved for the sexually transgressive woman: "In the Baroque period, *every* woman is a fallen woman, daughter of Eve, whose tear-filled eyes must elevate themselves towards the paradigm of grace and virtue: the Virgin."[7] As an exemplary model of this Baroque Everywoman, then, Feliciana would represent the privative half of the Mary / Eve opposition, a hierarchy whose separability might be called the *credo* of scholastic sexual theory. Cervantes's strategic use of this polarity enables him to explore, at a centrally figurative space in his last work, the darker sides of the female psyche: the beguiling relations between voice and sexuality, between maternity and desire, between purity and incest.

Let us rehearse the plot of Feliciana's "exemplary" novella before we leap backwards to what I regard as its germinal staging in the opening chapters of the *Persiles*. Feliciana's path interthreads with that of the protagonists five leagues outside of Badajoz, Extremadura, and half-way through their pilgrimage to Rome. Her episode, over three chapters long (III.2–5), involves the main characters as listeners, exegetes, and agents. In the middle of the pilgrims' journey and (shades of Dante?) as they are traversing a dark wood, a horseman suddenly confronts them, a knightly apparition who begs from them a boon: the transport of an infant, for the reward of a gold chain, to the nearby city of Trujillo. "The Knight of the Infant," as the text refers to this character in free indirect discourse (290), hands over the infant and gallops off into the night, returning briefly to inform the party of surrogate parents that the child is still unchristened. Soon after this strange encounter, the pilgrims arrive at a sheep-cote at the same time as a weeping, disheveled young woman stumbles forward to beg asylum. An aged shepherd lines the hollow of a huge oak tree with sheepskins, lifts the traumatized girl into it, nourishes her with milk-sops and wine, and covers over the aperture with more skins. The pilgrims guess the woman to be the mother of their infant and, when a troop of menacing horsemen arrives to inquire after her, keep silent. All the following day the old shepherd attends to the fugitive, convalescing within her tree, while he also arranges for the baby to be tended by his sister in a nearby village. By the third day, the newly-delivered mother emerges from her enclosure ready to tell her story.

Beginning her narrative with a currency metaphor, Feliciana opts to forgo "the credit of a chaste woman" (292) in order to gratify an audience eager to hear her "caso." Their eagerness is understandable: Feliciana will be advancing *their* story as she narrates her own problem, whose fundamental nature — imposed triangulation — is a repetition in a Mediterranean key of the originary drama of the *Persiles*. Like Sigismunda, Feliciana is forced to choose between two noble suitors and by her choice subverts the institutionalized mechanisms of sexual control. Unlike Sigismunda, however, Feliciana gives herself sexually to her lover. Out of this "canonically irregular" liaison, Feliciana becomes pregnant, or as she herself puts it, swerving the language of a popular ballad, "my dress shrank as my infamy grew" (293).[8] Two days before her due delivery date, Feliciana's father decides, peremptorily, to hold a betrothal ceremony for his daughter and the suitor of *his* choice.[9] In a state of shock over this announcement, Feliciana retires to her chamber where, between tears and thoughts of suicide, she suddenly delivers "an infant onto the floor" — an "unheard of event," as there had been no warning labor pains. Looking back, she is now able to describe the crisis in markedly "literary" language: "the betrothed down in the drawing room, awaiting me, and the adulterer — if he can be called such a thing — in a garden outside my house" (294). Feliciana's trustworthy maid gives over the newborn infant to the "adulterer," who runs off with Feliciana's father at his heels. Feliciana herself escapes into the street, running from there into the countryside and, finally, coming to rest in the sheepfold which now serves as the setting for her confessional narrative. She concludes by leaving its ending "to heaven" (295), an intervention which indeed materializes several chapters after her self-disclosing narrative.[10]

Before that, however, there is a radical interruption within her episode, a deep fissure which offers a revealing glimpse of its structuring. Having decided "to turn her back on the country in which her reputation was buried" (298), Feliciana asks to accompany the pilgrims into Italy. En route to Cáceres, their afternoon siesta in a meadow is disrupted by the figure of a young man, impaled by a sword, who darts abruptly through the bushes to collapse dead in their midst. It is clear that "treacherous hands" have killed him, since the sword pierces his body from back to front. Upon a careful search of the corpse, the pilgrims discover the picture of a woman surrounded by four circular lines of Petrarchan verse. This evidence moves Periandro (Persiles) to conjecture that the man's death "must have been born out of amorous circumstances" (301). While the party is reflecting on motives, a posse of the Holy Brotherhood suddenly breaks into the picnic to arrest the pilgrims as highwaymen and murderers.[11] After a complicated whirl on the machines of Spanish justice in Cáceres, the pilgrims are acquitted when a local innkeeper produces a letter written by the dead man. Identifying himself as don Diego de Parraces, this exemplary masochist accuses his kinsman, with honorable belatedness, of his murder: "I think he's planning to kill me; should this happen, and should my body be found, let it be known that they killed me treacherously." For his collusion in the codes of blood vengeance, the murdered man gets what he asks for and no more: his kinsman, as it turns out, is never caught and the crime remains "unpunished" (303).[12]

It is suggestive that all the unresolved questions of this episode are fictional *as* unresolved: an unknown motive, an unquestioning victim, an uncaught murderer. What is don Diego's death — "born" out of an amorous triangle — incorporated into the center of Feliciana's episode? Why must her story of speech contain, as its problematic core, his story of silence? Within Cervantes' controlled disruption of narrative, the meaning of don Diego's victimization invites displacement onto Feliciana: both are persecuted by kinsmen whose sense of "honor and life" (303) demands a blood vengeance. Never once voicing his side of the story, don Diego marches off to sacrifice like the proverbial lamb to the slaughter: "trusting in my innocence," his posthumous letter explains, "I yielded to his malice and accompanied him" (303). Although this dynamic, as we shall see, will be imaged within Feliciana's hymn, her own life-story corrects and criticizes it. Diego de Parraces's revealing metatext, in short, functions to expose the structures and strategies of a text which it appears simply to interrupt. Feliciana is saved from being slaughtered by her kinsmen — described by the narrator as "more like executioners than brother and father" (306) — who catch up with her at the famed shrine of Guadalupe. Having dragged out their victim into the street because of their scruples about murder in a cathedral, the would-be "executioners" are restrained from wreaking vengeance on the "traitor" by villagers, the police and, finally, the "Knight of the Infant" who, masked in black taffeta, gallops into the square in the nick of time. Feliciana's lover then proceeds to ask her kinsmen to be given by consent what he knew how to take "by industry" (307). A wildly paratactic reconciliation scene follows, with tears and swoonings and the vocal intervention of friends, during which the enraged kinsmen are defused. They even manage to gain the reputation, as the text wryly puts it, of "prudent" men. When, again three allusive days later, Feliciana's father holds his grandson, it is to edit his nativity story: "A thousand blessings on the mother who bore you and the father who engendered you!"(309).

It is not Feliciana's father, however, but the Madonna of Guadalupe who has the last word in this episode. For Feliciana's hymn to the Virgin is reproduced for us not when she sings it but when she inscribes it at the episode's closure. She gives the full text as a farewell token to Auristela (Sigismunda), at this point in the pilgrimage still a literal reader of reality.[13] The discourse of this twelve-stanza hymn, which spans the whole of Old Testament history, from Genesis to an imaginative point in time just prior to the Annunciation, has been typologically and archetypally interpreted in several modern readings.[14] To these rich commentaries I would add only two observations, the first in response to the hymn's opening four stanzas (the *only* stanzas which Feliciana sings before she is interrupted by her brother brandishing a dagger) (309). These stanzas focus, through metaphors of architecture, on the building of an edifice which represents Mary. The opening stanza thrice depicts the genesis of Mary as an event occuring "before" Genesis ("Antes . . . y antes . . . y antes"), a conception which stands counter to the patriarchal tradition of Genesis, whose recent and repeated deconstructions reveal that "the repression of the mother is the genesis of Genesis."[15] Equally pertinent to my reading of Feliciana's story is her own direct address, in the hymn's tenth stanza, to Mary as an *interruptor* of sacrifice — as "the arm of God, who detained / Abraham's rigorous knife" (311). She who detained Abraham from sacrificing Isaac, in short, intervenes again, this time at her own shrine, to detain Feliciana's kinsmen from sacrificing her. Their rigorous code, with its univocal understanding of violence and the sacred, is prefigured not only by Abraham in the Old Testament, but also by the sacrificial society of "barbarians" at the beginnings of the *Persiles*, Cervantes's "secular scripture."[16]

If the happy ending of Feliciana's story does not deafen us to the rhetoric of her kinsmen's fury, we shall hear its affiliation — by a resonant formula metaphorizing voice — to the opening words of the Persiles: "VOCES daba . . ." [The barbarian Corsicurbo was *giving forth voices* (lit.) into the narrow mouth of a deep dungeon] (51).[17] In the height of their anger and confusion, Feliciana's kinsmen are described by the text as "dando voces" [giving forth voices, shouting] for their victim (307), an echo of Cervantes's barbarians as they bark out orders, in the work's *in-medias-res* beginnings, for yet another sacrificial victim. The opening words of the *Persiles*, then, forge the equation of voice with sacrifice. And the behavior of Feliciana's kinsmen replicates, in a civilized key, the behavior of the inhabitants of Cervantes's Barbaric Isle: a violent, all-male sacrificial community whose "Law" or ritual idolatry dictates, as it does for Feliciana's family, the circulation of women as a commodity. Feliciana's story attempts to rescript the sexual economy of the Barbaric Isle, Cervantes's emblematic landscape of patriarchal law. And Feliciana's voice, as what follows will argue, functions as Cervantes's analysis, lamentation, and critique of the institution of patriarchy.

Who are Cervantes's "barbarians"? And what are we to make of their antic disposition whose energetic portrayal spans the opening four chapters of the *Persiles*? The logic of their representation is resolutely linked to their business: the continual purchase of women, "at the highest prices, which they pay with chunks of gold ore and extremely precious pearls" (57). The women they purchase are then fetishized as incubators for the community's potential messiah.[18] This male traffic in women, as the narrator is at pains to explain, by no means implied their abuse: "whether purchased or robbed, they are well treated by [the men], who only in this show themselves not to be barbarians" (57). The only notable deprivation for women on the Barbaric Isle would appear to be speech: or as one of them explains, "these my masters do not wish me to dilate my speech in anything other than what is pertinent to their business" (620). The voices of the Barbaric Isle, is it clear, are predicated on the suppression or domination of other voices, not always female ones: in order to survive his self-exile on the Barbaric Isle, the Italian dancing master Rutilio, for instance, must feign the handicap of a deaf-mute (95). The Barbaric Law which Rutilio recounts to the pilgrims has been more fully disclosed by Taurisa, a potential "slave" on the Isle: it appears that the barbarians legislate sexuality on the grounds of an "impertinent prophecy" that one of their men will father a world conqueror on an imported woman. Since "they do not know who this awaited king may be" (57), they expect his sire to reveal his identity through a ritual: through the manly act of swallowing, with no show of repugnance, the pulverized hearts of sacrificial victims. Sacrifice is thus a way of eliminating the *invisibility* of this paternal honor.[19]

At the heart of the Barbaric Isle's social contract, then, guaranteeing its continuity and sustaining its "vanity" (58), is the legislated traffic in women. The economic particulars of Cervantes's curious "overture" to the *Persiles* will scarcely be lost on readers even faintly familiar with Levi-Strauss's analysis of elementary kinship structures, shown to be founded and grounded upon the circulation of women.[20] Cervantes's Barbaric Isle, the tuning fork of his final work, is an insular patriarchy mediated by chunks of gold, a society which confounds the commercial with the genealogical transaction. It is a society, moreover, which holds as "inviolable and certain" the power of its sacred origins and its manifest destiny: the continuity, at any price, of the Barbaric Law. Traditional readings of the *Persiles* have tended to gloss over the symbolic exchange of power and goods that *is* the Barbaric Isle. The paradigm of male primacy that supports the barbaric "institution" has lately been nudged, however, in Eduardo González's intricate reading of the episode, indebted to Gilles Deleuze's *Logique de Sense*. If the latent design of male priority that sustains patriarchies is indeed, as González parenthetically suggests, "*(man was here before woman)*,"[21] then I would submit, in turn, that Cervantes's Barbaric Isle narrative is a devastating parody of that paradigm.

Built into that narrative are features that will iterate throughout the *Persiles*, one of the most salient being the representation of voice as problematic. The discursive power of the barbarians, who are ever anxious to limit or negate the voices of others, is represented as confused: a society of bow-and-arrow gesticulators, they communicate by "sign language" or by a "clamor" which is "articulately understood by nobody" (53, 51). Their understanding of desire is univocal: "This woman is mine because I want her" (67). It is this articulation of desire, expressed by one of the barbarians "in a loud voice," which signals the beginning of the end of the Barbaric Isle. Because one barbarian's "coming to voice" interferes with normal sacrificial proceedings, the Isle's governor responds with the standard *contrapaso* for such an eruption: an arrow through the tongue. One arrow leads to another and civil war breaks out in the kingdom, "the son not respecting his father, nor the brother, his brother" (68). The result of all this patri- / fratricide is an island-wide conflagration in which all the barbarians are turned into "ashes" (70). The island self-destructs, one could say, because of a *non sequitur*. The power to sacrifice, it is suggested here, is posited on a confusion of language — on a paradigm of voice whose authority, although pernicious, is still precarious. It can be contested by other declensions of voice. In a sense, this contestatory work is what furnishes Cervantes's protagonists — as well as the mutes, polyglots, and ventriloquists who inform the population of the *Persiles* — their most interesting "labors." Dozens of characters across the text will be forced to contest authority as they quest for new, non-sacrificial, paradigms of voice.

The survivors of the Barbaric Isle holocaust, the protagonists and their companions, will be pushed out to sea from the smoldering island, out into an "economy of fluids" until, at the start of Book II, a number of them are identified as "the people who for the second time were born into the world out of the womb of this galley" (163).[22] The dynamics of this escape — from captivity in a barbaric sacrificial culture into elemental nature as the locus for a "second birth" — may be called the story-germ of the *Persiles*. These actions are very precisely paralleled by the plot of Feliciana's episode, a nativity story whose focus, as we shall see, is not an infant's birth but rather his mother's *re*birth into the symbolic order, her acquisition of narrative voice and authority. Although my understanding of Feliciana's episode contrasts sharply with that of Casalduero, we seem to be at one on the judgment that "the protagonist of this episode is neither the newborn child nor any of the other characters; the protagonist is the voice of Feliciana." Casalduero seems content to pronounce that protagonist-voice as "the sentiment of the woman-mother," glossing over the explicit *absence* of that sentiment that is such a psychologically tantalizing feature of this episode.[23] In my darker reading, that protagonist-voice is the voice of feminine desire, a voice muted on Cervantes's Barbaric Isle and in most of the canonical critical stances towards the *Persiles*. It is the voice of a woman allowed to describe her own nature. It is the only reality left to Auristela (Sigismunda) when, towards the end of the *Persiles*, a near-fatal poisoning so destroys her appearances that she can no longer be recognized "except through the organ of the voice" (456). And it is that same voice, "born" into a place of narrative authority, that contests the sacrificial paradigms of voice represented on the Barbaric Isle.

Feliciana's voice finds its chorus within the *Persiles* itself, wherever the fetishizing of women as property, a conspicuous hallmark of patriarchal history, is attempted. While still in the opening book we hear the story — interpolated in a double-voiced father-daughter narration — of the *ius primae noctis*, that "barbarous custom" (112) of an insular Irish culture which legally obliges all new brides to sexually satisfy their male in-laws. In the last book of the *Persiles*, a world that glitters with signs of sophisticated barbarism, we read about Alejandro Castrucho's foiled attempts to force his niece Isabela into a cross-cousin marriage in order to keep the wealth in the family.[24] There seems to be little difference, in short, between the male traffic in women practiced on the Barbaric Isle, the legislated rape in Ireland, and the forced nuptials in Italy. Each of these interpolated tales all subvert patrilineal descent systems in which female desire is conveniently scapegoated, in which women lose their "credit" when they determine their own sexuality. With its literalized male traffic in women, the Barbaric Isle narrative anticipates, in its homosocial structures of bonding, the European class narrative of triangular desire.[25] The chapters following the holocaust of the Barbaric Isle may be read — perhaps can only be read — as a critique of the limitation of these structures of desire. The bulk of the *Persiles*, in other words, is a quest for a re-creative narrative tradition. Both the main plot and its dozen interpolated stories seem to be working towards a regeneration of genres that look to survive the destruction of patriarchal fictions. How might language and literature refocus an erotic tradition that fetishizes women, cannibalizes men, and pulverizes hearts? The new discourse might begin, as does the *Persiles*, with a profound concern for the mechanisms of generativity — *of* children, *in* adults, and *for* texts.

The nativity narratives that constitute the tale of Feliciana, as I have earlier mentioned, open out the range of literary childbirth in order to reconceptualize the maternal position. The felicity of this position, as her story implies, depends upon the nature of one's kinsmen's ties to the patriarchal order. In Feliciana's situation, the rigor of these ties is exacerbated by an absent mother, a situation openly lamented by the daughter: "to my greater misfortune, I have no mother" (293). It may be argued that Feliciana involves herself in the pilgrimage to the Black Madonna of Guadalupe as a mother-quest, since Black Madonnas — those hermetic wonder-workers who preside over sex, pregnancy, and childbirth in Catholic countries — are especially venerated as the maternal aspect of Mary.[26] The intertextuality of Feliciana's tale, the ostensible presence within it of both biblical and Ovidian elements, moves us to inquire into their structural function within such a mother-quest. What kind of model-mothers subtend the surface text of Feliciana's narrative?

Mary is a pervasive subtext of Feliciana's story, not only as the subject of the above-mentioned hymn but also as an object of the text's deliberate allusiveness to the Nativity and Resurrection stories. Forcione's catalogue of the Cervantes text's Christian allusions underwrites his claim that "Cervantes had Christ in mind at this point in the composition of the work":

> the infant menaced by the knife of the enraged father (Herod), the flight of the parents toward Portugal, the shelter given them by shepherds, the concealment of the child by the shepherds, the triumphant reappearance of the missing child "on the third day," the allusion to baptism, and the approach of Easter.[27]

Cervantes must also have had Mary in mind, as a woman who, like Feliciana, was forced to deliver her son under traumatic circumstances. What is missing from the above catalogue of allusions — the mother's story — is supplied, as a personal agency narrative, in Cervantes's text of Feliciana. Indeed, I would argue that the recovery of this suppressed story is part of Cervantes's imitative strategy in this episode. The interplay between Feliciana and the Virgin Mary in Cervantes's text is not posited on a fallen woman's need for an elevating paradigm of asceticism, but rather on her need for a salvific mother-figure. What Freud could argue about his "hysterical" patient Dora — that "the notion of the Madonna is a favourite counter-idea in the mind of girls who feel themselves oppressed by imputations of sexual guilt"[28] — cannot in any form be applied to Feliciana, whose distinction is that she appears remarkably free of guilt over her "amorous escapades" (293). Her oppression, in any case, comes less from "imputations" than from very real threats of death from the two men "who claimed to be her brother and her father" (307).

Far more than the ascetic paradigm is turned on end in Cervantes's depiction of his flesh-and-blood heroine. Indeed, his portrait of Feliciana inverts with curious precision the traditional female virtues projected onto the image of the Virgin by Counter-Reformation Mariolatry: humility, obedience, and silence.[29] Feliciana is neither humble ("I have the best voice in the world") nor obedient ("I yielded myself to him in concealment from my father"); nor silent ("she let loose her voice to the winds") (299, 293, 306). To put it summarily, it is not the image of Mary as a patristic projection of an ascetic and speechless ideal that the text of Feliciana exploits, but rather the story of Mary's anguished concealment of her pregnancy, her flight from the patriarch Herod's knife, and her delivery within the cold pastoral world of Christ's Nativity. The text, in short, may be seen trying to recover Mary's *story* as opposed to her *image*.

The other side of Mary's story, as we suggested earlier, is the Ovidian myth of Myrrha. Numerous indications in Feliciana's episode show us that Cervantes also had Ovid in mind during its composition. The first ostensible allusion to Ovid is that which opens the chapter containing Feliciana's own narration (III.3). Here Cervantes anxiously proffers his reader one of the most deliberately allusive tropes in his opus: " 'Pregnant was the oak tree'—let's say it that way" (291). If the hortatory construction which here enlists the reader into approbation of this odd uterine metaphor seems a bit defensive, it may be in defense of Ovid, regarded in many Renaissance quarters as a perverse literary influence.[30] A "pregnant" tree, even one growing in the green world of Christian pastoral, gestures toward metamorphosis, here very ceremonially towards Ovidian metamorphosis. "Media gravidus tumet arbore venter" [the pregnant tree swells in mid-trunk], Ovid writes in one of the most moving depictions of childbirth in Western literature—a "vegetable" parturition with powerful metaphors for the human event, assisted throughout a "pitying Lucina" (*Met.*, X503–18). Cervantes's "pregnant" tree functions as an organic, if profoundly unsettling, allusion to this Ovidian childbirth. Myrrha, as we recall, becomes pregnant as the result of an incestuous affair with her unsuspecting father Cinyras, who drunkenly enjoys a bed-partner while his wife is away at the annual festival of Ceres. After many meetings, Cinyras becomes curious about the identity of his sexual partner. Speechless with horror at his discovery of Myrrha, Cinyras snatches his sword to kill her. Myrrha flees into the night and begins a fugitive existence across the broad lands of Arabia and beyond. Her exhausted wanderings are mercifully terminated when the gods, at her request, encase her laden womb with bark. Lucina helps the pregnant "tree" to deliver, through a fissure in its bark, the beautiful infant Adonis. The price of Myrrha's transgression is silence: "neque habent sua verba dolores, / nec Lucina potest parientis voce vocari" [the birth-pangs cannot voice themselves, nor can Lucina be called upon in the words of one in travail] (*Met.*, X.506–07). Ovid's myth of incestuous female desire reveals its subterranean outlines at strategic points in Feliciana's episode.[31] The interplay of this Ovidian subtext with Cervantes's surface text urges readers to confront what can only be called a perversion of pastoral.

How do we unperplex these three profoundly interrelated maternities? I have suggested that the text of Feliciana strategically sets up a network of differences between itself and its constitutive subtexts: a Christian and a pagan nativity story. Each of the three nativities sheds light on the others. At the level of the subtexts, a dialogue takes place between the infancy Gospels of the New Testaments (with all their historical repercussions) and the Ovidian myth of the birth of Adonis. The underlying Christian configuration of Feliciana's story includes, too, the Lucan Magnificat, for Mary's triumphant hymn of praise bears scrutiny as a literary precursor of Feliciana's hymn to the Virgin of Guadalupe.[32] No two conception accounts would appear more dichotomous: whereas the Virgin Mary did not "know . . . a man" (Luke I:34), Myrrha knew only the one man forbidden her by "pietas" [natural love] (*Met.*, X.333); whereas Mary was "impregnated by voice (through the ear, according to literalist interpreters of Origen)[33] and was thereby hailed as "plena gratiis" [full of grace], Myrrha was impregnated by her father's seed and is depicted by Ovid as "plena patris" [full of her father] (*Met.*, X469). That Mary felt no physical pleasure during her conception was famously argued by Francisco Suárez, a Marian theologian who died the same year the *Persiles* was published (1617): "the Blessed Virgin in conceiving a son neither lost her virginity nor experienced any venereal pleasure. . . . It did not befit the Holy Spirit without any cause of utility to produce such an effect, or to excite any unbecoming movement of passion."[34] The Ovidian Myrrha legend focuses intensely upon such "unbecoming" movements of passion.

It would seem that the virginal Mary and the venereal Myrrha function within Cervantes's text of Feliciana as a repetition, in an entirely sober key, of the comic opposition established in the *Quixote* between a "soberana señora," [sovereign lady] and a "sobajada señora" [pawed-over lady], with both ladies understood by the reader to be projections of Dulcinea by men who refuse to confront her.[35] The moment of reversal between female oppositions of this kind takes place in the Cave of Montesinos, where it is revealed to the "dreaming" hero that even "sovereign" ladies like Belerma can lose their teeth, have bags under their eyes, or suffer monthly periods (DQ, II.23). The question of the instability between oppositions of any kind is explicitly raised not only *by* the *Persiles* but also *in* the *Persiles* when the primary narrator, in one of his more discursive moments, suddenly chooses to dismantle the good / evil opposition for his readers: "It seems as if good and evil are such a small distance away from each other that they are like two coincident lines which, although originating from separate and different principles, end up in one place" (464). From the perspective of Cervantes's own text, then, and generated by a narrator who announces his doubts about the separability of the most cherished of hierarchic distinctions, could it be that Mary and Myrrha, in turn, are "such a small distance away from each other" that they, too, "end up in one place"?

Since it is now possible, at least without tumbling into heresy, to bring up some provocative connections between Mary and Myrrha, Cervantes's imitative subtexts, let me begin with perhaps the gloomiest one: the linkage between Myrrha's tears — "stillataque robore murra" [the myrrh which drips from her tree-trunk] (*Met.*, X.501), with which her son Adonis is anointed at his birth — and the myrrh carried by the Wise Men to Bethlehem (Matthew 2:1–12), its perfume foreshadowing Mary's own later sorrows as a *mater dolorosa*. A more surprising correspondence that works to undo the Mary / Myrrha opposition is etymological: according to some Church doctors, the name of *Mary* (also *Mariam* and *Maria*) is derived from the Hebrew word for *myrrh*. Also debated for centuries by church-men was Mary's "intact" post-partum condition, a feature that, in its unnatural perfection, separates Mary from the rest of her sex as much as Myrrha's bark does.[36] (It is suggestive, along these lines, that one of Cervantes's shepherds holds up Eve, rather than Mary, as a model post-partum patient: "I am certain . . . that when Eve bore her first son she didn't take to her bed, nor protect herself from the outdoors, nor affect any of the niceties nowadays used in deliveries" [299]). Another line of coincidence between Mary and Myrrha is their shared silence concerning the experience of childbirth: neither woman, unlike Feliciana, is allowed to tell her story. Mary rarely speaks across Matthew and Luke, the two infancy narratives that provide the quarry for Marian knowledge. And Myrrha's birth-pangs are explicitly depicted as not having "sua verba" [their own words] (*Met.*, X.506). But the opposition between Mary and Myrrha becomes perhaps most illusory when we arrive at the issue of the paternal relation, the main problematic of Feliciana's episode. Both Mary and Myrrha, in contrast to the surface text of Feliciana, are patriarchal women: each of them conceives — the one divinely, the other criminally — the father's child. Where Mary obeys and Myrrha seduces the patriarchal order, Feliciana, on the level of ironic repetition and interruption, moves beyond it. On the level of psychic structure, too, her maternity appears to eschew the daughter's seduction.[37] Indeed, her narrative systematically contests that logic by showing us that she cannot be firmly situated in either pole of the Mary / Myrrha projection. In this she is *like* the rest of her sex. Mediating between the virginal and desiring subtexts of her own story, Feliciana reforms various scholastic distortions concerning child-birth. Cervantes's notable departure from his maternal subtexts is in allowing his heroine a voice in fidelity to her own experience. By narrating her own delivery — in both senses of that word — Feliciana breaks through the limits of patriarchal discourse and into an economy of female creativity.

"Born again" after her embodiment within the "pregnant" oak, Feliciana acquires the voice of authority to render a story remarkable, in its reflective intelligence, for its radical questioning of authority. As she recounts the story of her "fall," she employs various conditional clauses to rethink the language naming her dishonor: "my infamy, *if* the conversation of betrothed lovers can be called infamy" (293); "the adulterer, *if* that's how one would put it" (294). The pure conventionality of each signifier here — *infamy, adulterer* — is observable under the control of a self-conscious narrator as she questions the ethical structures condemning her. Feliciana's ironic rewriting here, her regenerative creativity, adumbrates the character of Mari Cobeña, also given to figurative language in defense of her own premarital pregnancy. This peasant parody of Feliciana — depicted by her angry father as "nothing mute" — will cooly assure the civil authorities of Toledo that she is neither the first nor the last woman to have stumbled and fallen "into these ravines" (330).

Feliciana shows as well as tells how she has moved irrevocably beyond the literal order of those verbal "commonplaces" and doctrinal authorities who would define the maternal nature. When she first meets up with her infant, whom she has never really seen, she experiences a discontinuity, a marked (and textually remarked) absence of the sympathetic swellings conventionally expected of new mothers. Calling into question the sentiments of his acknowledged model Heliodorus — who pronounces the "maternal nature" as "a knowledge which cannot lie" — Cervantes chooses to depict Feliciana's maternal nature as problematized by her sufferings. She cannot "recognize," as yet, the creature which the text, in what might seem to be a superfluous coda, identifies as a boy-child: "They took it to her, she looked it over again and again, she removed its swaddling clothes; but by no sign could she recognize it as the child she had delivered; nor even — which is more significant — did any natural love move her feelings to recognize the child, which was a boy" (297). Heliodorus's argument for the maternal nature as biological and instinctual does not find its way into the Feliciana story because Cervantes is thinking in psychological terms, intuiting what many psychoanalysts today believe: that it is difficult to find evidence for any biological basis for parenting because physiological changes in mothers can be distorted by psychic upheaval. Cervantes conceptualizes the mother-infant bond in the Feliciana episode as temporarily undermined by her shocking post-natal circumstances. This implicit critique of a model for whom maternal love swells up "through a secret conformity and a convenience of nature" allows us to appreciate Cervantes's modernity and the force of his challenge to the classically-correct Greek romancer Heliodorus.[38]

When Feliciana finally gives her companions a sample of "the best voice in the world," she raises it in church, in the place where for centuries women had been debarred from teaching, preaching, or even speaking, on the grounds, as Peter Martyr Vermigli's collection of "commonplaces" authorized, that Eve's words had once beguiled Adam.[39] The conjunctions of voice with sexuality are ancient and, in Cervantes's final work, radically exposed. The voice that once beguiled Adam is here allowed to narrate the maternal implications of that once and future fall. The trajectory of that voice across Cervantes's opus is slow but steady. It begins perhaps with Marcela, whose economy of desire, stoutly defended by don Quixote, disdains a masculine object but then, in a moment of absolute reversal, appropriates the conventionally masculine ethic of autonomy. Unlike Feliciana's flight, Marcela's lends itself to depiction, in Poggioli's phrase, as a "pastoral of the self."[40] The burial at the denouement of Marcela's episode is exchanged, in Feliciana's, for a reunited family. And in the place of Marcela's defensive "Knight of the Mournful Countenance," we have Feliciana's industrious "Knight of the Infant." The most salient feature of Feliciana's story, however, is that it returns feminine desire to the reproductive site, exposing the duplicity apparent within — *as well as the duplicity necessary to maintain* — the opposition of the "virgin" mother and the "fallen woman."[41]

It would seem that across the *Quixote* Cervantes is working out the problem of woman's voice within a masculine position of desire, conceptualizing feminine desire as either absent, disruptive, or entirely split off from the maternal body. With the marginal *Persiles*, however, a missing text is restored. To extend the quixotic trajectory of masculine desire proleptically is to arrive at the Barbaric Isle, that paradigmatic locus of sacrifice whose custodians self-destruct. Plotted as a quest for new paradigms of voice, Cervantes's last romance moves its large, fluid, and fragmentary cast of characters away from the charred structures of the Barbaric Isle and towards a series of regenerative places — caves, hermitages, bowers — where these new paradigms might fit. Antonio's "uncouth cave," a generative retreat in which a Spanish soldier expiates the sin of anger and conceives his children, is one of these (71–83). Soldino's "dark cave," where an aged prophet retires to seek enlightenment before death, is another (392–98). The main protagonist's story-telling *self* is predicated as a place infinitely hospitable to new paradigms — a "place . . . where all things fit and nothing is out of place" (227). In this essay we have focused on Feliciana's creative enclosure — that place in mid-text at which life and language meet: the "pregnant" tree. And having earlier negotiated the Ovidian world invoked by its metaphor, it now seems appropriate to close with some response to its narrator's plea for rhetoric: " 'The oak tree was pregnant' — let *us* say it that way" (291).

If as readers we take up Cervantes's exhortation to co-create, we would move from the plot of Feliciana into the "plot" of her metaphor — into the figurative or "dialogical" space created by the metaphor, a space in which all plotting is suspended while a new meaning or "issue" is re-created. This conception of metaphor as creating a privileged space — traced within the English critical tradition by Patricia A. Parker[42] — may be usefully applied to the figurative "womb" into which Feliciana is returned before she can generate her story. Here at the spatial center of the *Persiles*, Cervantes's uterine trope emblematizes his long brooding on issues of female sexuality: pregnancy, childbirth, and the loss of "credit" suffered by women involved in "canonically irregular" liaisons.[43] One of the remarkable features of Cervantes's last romance is the dominance in it of the language of female embodiment and parturition. The work represents women, trees, a love-triangle, and even the text itself — as it "delivers" its hero out of a dungeon's "narrow mouth" (51) — giving birth. In this sense, the *Persiles* is a book (like Feliciana within her tree) enclosed by its own contents. The configurations used by Cervantes to organize his nativity narratives show that he was experimenting with wholly new structures of desire in the *Persiles*, that he was laboring to generate a non-linear, non-triangular, non-sacrificial paradigm of plot — a critique of the limitations of his prior works. For a fuller understanding of Cervantes's mind and art, it is essential to read his canonical and marginal texts side by side. The marginalized *Persiles* attempts to voice — after long silence and with all its gaps and interruptions — the mother's story. It is an underground story whose gaps are slowly being filled in by feminist pedagogy. Three days before his death, Cervantes closed the cycle of his creation by suggesting, in the famous prologue to the *Persiles*, that his own interrupted discourse would be resumed: "A time may come, perhaps, when tying up this broken thread, I shall say what is missing here, and what would have been fitting" (49).

Notes

1. *Los trabajos de Persiles y Sigismunda*, ed. Juan Bautista Avalle-Arce (Madrid: Clásicos Castalia, 1969), p. 299. All further references to the *Persiles* will cite this edition parenthetically by page number. Because of the many editions of the *Quixote* in use, I have chosen to refer to its passages by part and chapter number, preceded by the initials *DQ*. All translations of Spanish texts are my own, and all emphasis in quoted passages has been added. I am indebted to Barbara Johnson for insightful commentary on an earlier draft of this essay.

2. Joaquín Casalduero, for instance, explains why "in the *center* of the *Persiles*, Cervantes must intone his song. "He needs the immense space of his novel; he needs the time of life and of his life, all the time of man, so that his voice, filled with style and erudition, radiant with beauty, a voice in which the tradition of a noble culture has accumulated, elevates itself in full harmony to sing the great mystery of charity" (*Sentido y forma de "Los trabajos de Persiles y Sigismunda,"* [Madrid: Gredos, 1975], p. 184). Alban K. Forcione argues that Feliciana's hymn, "placed at the *center* of the Persiles," discloses the work's biblical shape (*Cervantes' Christian Romance: A Study of Persiles and Sigismunda* [Princeton: Princeton Univ. Press, 1971], pp. 86–89; see also pp. 19–21 and 123–28). Forcione reads this episode as a powerful expression of the traditional miracle narrative in *Cervantes and the Humanist Vision: A Study of Four Exemplary Novels* (Princeton: Princeton Univ. Press, 1982), pp. 328–35.

3. Now that it seems urgent to question the partialities and repressions that have gone into the making of our European literary canon, we might rethink *why* the politics of Cervantine canon formation have, since about 1630, conspired to delegitimate the text which Cervantes considered his masterpiece. Although occasional 18th and 19th century scholars regarded the *Persiles* favorably (see Rudolph Schevill, "Studies in Cervantes I. 'Persiles y Sigismunda': Introduction," *Modern Philology*, 4 [1906–7]:1–24, Continental criticism, in the main, has responded to the work with a long silencing tradition. As late as the 1930s, José Bergamín tried to challenge the mystique of a canon that could so serenely ignore its creator's

own judgments: "Cervantes, who knew himself very well, and also his qualities as a writer, believed, unfalteringly, that the *Persiles* was his *obra maestra*. Perhaps the time will come when criticism recognizes it as such" (*Laberinto de la novela y monstruo de la novelería*). That criticism has finally begun to recognize the *Persiles* as at least worthy of sustained scholarly attention is due to the efforts of such established critics as Rafael Osuna, whose prescriptive essay laments its "forgetting" ("El olvido del *'Persiles'*" in *Boletín de la real academia española*, XLVIII [1968]:55–75); Avalle-Arce, whose Spanish edition of the *Persiles* has superseded all others (although its "Introduction" underwrites the canonized critical approach by attesting to Cervantes's "hyper-valorization" of his late romance); Tilbert Diego Stegmann, whose German monograph includes a massive bibliography (*Cervantes' Musterroman "Persiles": Epentheorie und Romanpraxis um 1600* [Hamburg: Hartmut Ludke Verlag, 1971]); Alban K. Forcione, whose two studies serve as a quarry for much contemporary work on the *Persiles* (*Cervantes, Aristotle, and the 'Persiles'* [Princeton: Princeton Univ. Press, 1970], and *Cervantes' Christian Romance*; and Ruth El Saffar, who reads the *Persiles* as "the culmination of a life-time of writing" (*Beyond Fiction: The Recovery of the Feminine in the Novels of Cervantes* [Berkeley: Univ. of California Press, 1984]).

4. Francisco López Estrada, "La novela de Feliciana y Rosanio en el *Persiles* o los extremosos amores de la Extremadura," *Anales Cervantinos*, VI (1957):341.

5. For an enlightening discussion of the metaphysical logic of "unexplained and unjustified" dualities which dominate Renaissance notions of women, structures of thought inherited from Aristotle, see Ian Maclean's *The Renaissance Notion of Woman: A Study in the Fortunes of Scholasticism and Medical Science in European Intellectual Life* (Cambridge: Cambridge Univ. Press, 1980). From the repressive way in which the duality male / female functions so as to privilege or hierarchize the term *male* and to establish the term *female* as an opposite of privation ("species privata"), Maclean goes on to discuss the subtle dislocations which occur within that notion of woman. The Virgin / Fallen Woman pairing deployed by Cervantes's text — a sexual depiction of woman in "positive" and "privative" terms — would qualify as one of these dislocations. My use of the term "icons and fallen idols" consciously echoes the subtitle of Beth Miller's edition of *Women in Hispanic Literature* (Berkeley: Univ. of California Press, 1983), a text addressing the "consensus that misogyny [fallen idols] and idealization [icons] have been two aspects of a single tendency through centuries of literary production in Spanish" (p. 8).

6. Ovid IV, *Metamorphoses* II, with English trans. by Frank Justus Miller (London: Loeb Classical Library, 1916). All further references to the Myrrha legend cite this edition by book and line number.

7. Joaquín Casalduero, *Sentido y forma de "Los trabajos de Persiles y Sigismunda,"* p. 17.

8. Avalle-Arce uses the phrase "canonically irregular" about two other post-Tridentine marriages in the *Persiles* (391n.). See also Américo Castro's vast footnote on Cervantes and free love, which includes brief mention of the "natural and independent morality" of Feliciana de la Voz (*El pensamiento de Cervantes* [Madrid: Casa Editorial Hernando, 1925], pp. 349–52).

9. The practice of forced marriages is critiqued earlier in the *Persiles* by the sage Mauricio, himself a sager father than Feliciana's: "It seems to me just and even convenient that fathers marry their daughters with their consent and for their pleasure, as they are not giving them company for a day but for all the days of their lives, and from not proceeding in this manner there have followed, follow, and will follow thousands of difficulties, the majority of which tend to come to disastrous ends" (112).

10. In his reading of the Feliciana episode as a traditional miracle tale, Forcione explains that the emphasis in this literary form falls "on the intervention of a divine agency, which comes to the aid of heroes who are usually helpless, quite unheroic, and frequently even fallen" (*Humanist Vision*, p. 329).

11. This arrest ironizes the words of Auristela (Sigismunda), at the beginning of the chapter, in which she gives thanks for reaching Spain: "now we can continue our travels secure from shipwrecks, storms, and highwaymen because, according to Spain's fame throughout all regions of the world as a pacific and holy country, we can well promise ourselves a safe journey" (297).

12. López Estrada calls this "adventure" of don Diego de Parraces' assassination "an unexplained deed" and notes "the mute testimony" of a woman's picture and some verses (p. 336). Forcione, who uses this episode to illustrate Cervantes' technique of fragmentary exposition, regards the clarification of this brief episode as "barely satisfying; for it reveals merely that a relative of the young man committed the murder. Nothing is said of motive or circumstances" (*Christian Romance*, p. 21).

13. Auristela (Sigismunda) misreads Spain's freedom from brigands just before she is herself arrested for brigandage (297); one chapter later she is depicted as unable to read the verses of Feliciana's hymn: "they were more esteemed than understood by Auristela" (312). Auristela's defective understanding may be linked to her intense desire for the safety of a literal order. She wishes to go to Heaven, for example, "without any roundabout courses, without shocks, and without anxieties" (459). She is ever anxious to escape the sea, that locus of mutability and the unconscious, and even to avoid "the twisted roads and the doubtful paths" (461). The text never grants her these wishes.

14. See Forcione, *Christian Romance*, pp. 87–89; also El Saffar, *Beyond Fiction*, pp. 153–54.

15. In a critique of the patriarchal / canonical authority which the poem *Paradise Lost* deepens and extends, Christine Froula shows how Milton's nativity scenes reveal the degree of repression which shapes his epic story ("When Eve Reads Milton: Undoing the Canonical Economy," *Critical Inquiry* 10 [December 1983]:337). Within Froula's scheme, Cervantes would be found to have a "gnostic" stance towards authority (unlike Milton's "canonical" one).

16. Northrop Frye's label for romance in a study based on the thesis that "the structure of the Bible provided the outline of the mythological or imaginative universe for European literature" (*The Secular Scripture: A Study of the Structure of Romance* [Cambridge: Harvard Univ. Press, 1976], p. vii). My text intentionally echoes the title of René Girard's *Violence and the Sacred*, trans. Patrick Gregory (Baltimore: Johns Hopkins Univ. Press, 1977).

17. "VOCES daba el bárbaro. . . ." begins Cervantes's text, with the direct object "voices" wrenched into primacy through Latin word order. It is instructive to examine the ritual sacrifices of Cervantes's barbarians in the light of Walter J. Ong's "Latin Language Study as a Renaissance Puberty Rite," an essay which considers Renaissance Latin teaching within the psychological framework of violent puberty rites. These involved forcible removal from the maternal world of the vernacular, segregation within a closed male environment, and corporal punishment in order to instill "corage," i.e., strength of heart or "heartiness" — a most suggestive exegetical frame for Cervantes's heart-swallowing barbarians (*Rhetoric, Romance, and Technology* [Ithaca: Cornell Univ. Press, 1971]). I go into this in more detail in my essay "Cervantes' *Labors of Persiles*: 'Working (in) the In-between,' " in *Literary Theory and Renaissance Texts*, eds. David Quint and Patricia A. Parker (Baltimore: Johns Hopkins Univ. Press, forthcoming).

18. The idea of woman as incubator, man as imparter of life derives from Aristotelian accounts of sex determination *in utero*, principally from *De generatione animalium*. Although these notions were being heavily refuted by Galenists and others during the late 16th century (the fictional time of the *Persiles*), scholastic acceptance and expansion of Aristotelian biology was to have far-reaching consequences on attitudes towards human generation. See Maclean, pp. 37–39.

19. It was the invisibility of the paternal relation that led Freud into promoting

paternity under the banner of an "advance in civilization, since maternity is proved by the evidence of the senses while paternity is a hypothesis, based on an inference and a premiss" and, therefore, "more important than maternity" (*Moses and Monotheism: Three Essays*, in *Standard Edition of the Complete Psychological Works*, vol. 23 [London: Hogarth Press, 1964], p. 114). In a passage which sheds light on Cervantes's Barbaric Isle, Dorothy Dinnerstein notes that this uncertainty of the paternal relation drives men to engage in "various initiation rites through which they symbolically and passionately affirm that it is they who have themselves created human beings, as compared with the mere flesh spawned by woman" (*The Mermaid and the Minotaur: Sexual Arrangements and the Human Malaise* [New York: Harper & Row, 1976], p. 80).

20. Marxist anthropologists' analyses of women as objects of exchange within kinship systems have moved Luce Irigaray, among others, to analyze women as the "goods" through which patriarchal power passes ("Des Marchandises entre elles" [When the Goods Get Together], trans. Claudia Reeder in *New French Feminisms: An Anthology*, ed. Elaine Marks and Isabelle de Courtivron (Amherst: Univ. of Massachusetts Press, 1980), pp. 107–110.

21. This paradigm of male priority supporting the barbaric "Institution" appears in González's summary of an argument concerning the "bastardized, post-tragic" generic status of the *Persiles*. In various footnotes González nudges this same problem tangentially. At one point he fleetingly wonders about the women who are imported into Cervantes's fictional isle and there "barbarized." At another point he recalls, in order to eliminate, "the possibility of a perpetual life of isolated males" in the style of Pliny's *Natural History*, a text which describes an all-male community living alone, "sine ulla femina" (" Del *Persiles* y la Isla Bárbara: Fábulas y reconocimientos," *MLN* 94 [1979]: pp. 233, 255n., and 253n.). Actually, this last is a promising conjecture in that Cervantes certainly knew his Pliny and cites Book VIII of the *Natural History* within the *Persiles* itself (134). The *parodic* possibilities of such an isolated all-male community may very well have inspired the opening chapters of the *Persiles*.

22. For some pertinent differences between economies of solids and fluids — e.g., between the Barbaric Isle economy of unminted gold and the oceanic economy of water — see Irigaray's observations in "La 'Mechanique' des fluides," *L'Arc*, 58 (1974).

23. Casalduero, p. 183.

24. The custom of *ius primae noctis* was described in Francisco Thámara's *El libro de las costumbres de todas las gentes* (1556), whose source was probably Johann Boehme's *Repertorium . . . de Omnium Gentium Ritibus* (1520). I focus on Isabela Castrucha's subversion of her uncle's marriage plans in my essay on "Cervantes' Last Romance: Deflating the Myth of Female Sacrifice," *Cervantes*, 3 (Fall 1983): 103–20.

25. Those structures of desire, as René Girard's well-known study argues, look back to *Don Quixote*, the work he sees as seminal to "all the ideas of the Western novel" (*Deceit, Desire, and the Novel: Self and Other in Literary Structure*, trans. Yvonne Freccero [Baltimore: Johns Hopkins Univ. Press, 1965], pp. 1–52.

26. For a discussion of the maternal and midwifely aspect of Black Madonnas, see Marina Warner, *Alone of All Her Sex: The Myth and the Cult of the Virgin Mary* (New York: Vintage, 1983), pp. 273–75.

27. Forcione, *Christian Romance*, p. 128.

28. Sigmund Freud, *Dora: An Analysis of a Case of Hysteria* (New York: Collier, 1963), p. 125n.

29. Maclean argues that the figure of the Virgin Mary, despite her redemptive role in Medieval and Counter-Reformation literature, presents a "questionable advantage to woman-kind." As a perfect model of womanhood, her influence on the status of woman is remote: "Far from being the glory of her sex, she is *not of her sex* in its malediction, tribulation and imperfection" (*Renaissance Notions*, pp. 23–24). Along these same lines, Marina Warner's historical research into the cult of the Virgin Mary grew out of an intimation "that in the very

celebration of the perfect human woman, both humanity and women were subtly denigrated" (*Alone of All Her Sex*, p. xxi).

30. Rudolph Schevill, *Ovid and the Renascence in Spain* (Berkeley: Univ. of California Press, 1913), p. 134. See especially the sections on Ovid and Cervantes, pp. 132–98. See also *Quixote*, II.22, in which the guide to the Cave of Montesinos talks about "imitating Ovid in the burlesque style."

31. Cf. the passage in Cervantes which begins, "The gleaming of the sword . . ." (294) with Ovid's passage beginning, "He snatched his gleaming sword . . ." (l. 475, p. 98). That Cinyras is the grandson of Pygmalion, who falls in love "with his own work" (l. 249, p. 83) in the Ovidian story which precedes Myrrha's, points to a suggestive lineage of silenced females. I thank Rachel Jacoff for pointing out to me the spatial significance of the Pygmalion story, for stimulating discussions about Myrrha, and for helpful criticism of my readings of Cervantes reading Ovid.

32. Mary's *Magnificat*, her longest speech by far in the Bible, has a bellicose character not found in Feliciana's hymn, however. Although both are hymns of praise, Mary's *Magnificat* (in which she praises God and extolls herself) "is not a psychological poem on the mystery of the conception of Christ, or even on the miracle of the virgin birth — which she does not mention at all — but a rousing cry that the Jewish Messiah promised by God has arrived to vanquish his enemies" (Warner, p. 13).

33. The Greek exegete Origen (d. 254), by failing to distinguish between spontaneous generation and divine impregnation, suggested that Mary had conceived Jesus the *Logos* upon hearing the angel's voice. Origen's Alexandrine argument was taken literally in certain quarters, so that a hymn attributed to Fortunatus (d. 609?), marveling that "aure virgo concepit" [the virgin conceived through her ear], would be echoed by English medieval lyrics declaring to Mary how "through thine ear thou were with child" (see Warner's chapter on "Virgin Birth," pp. 34–49).

34. Francisco Suárez, "The Dignity and the Virginity of the Mother of God," Disputation I, V, VI, from *The Mysteries of the Life of Chirst*, trans. Richard O'Brien, S.J. (Indiana, 1954), p. 41.

35. Trying to re-create from memory the letter to Dulcinea which don Quixote forgot to give him, Sancho claims that if there's anything he remembers it's "that bit about the *sobajada* [pawed over, soiled from handling], I mean, the *soberana* [sovereign] lady" [*DQ*,I.30].

36. The meaning of the name Mary is elusive and etymologists have derived it from words for *lightbearer, ocean, stubborn,* and even *corpulent.* See Joseph Pohle, *Mariology, A Dogmatic Treatise on the Blessed Virgin, Mother of God,* ed. Arthur Preuss (London, 1953), pp. 34–35. For a precis of the debate about Mary's virginity both *in partu* and *post partum,* see Warner, pp. 43–49). I am indebted to Alan. S. Trueblood for his suggestive remarks on the linkages between Mary and myrrh.

37. At the psychoanalytic level, see Jane Gallop's *The Daughter's Seduction: Feminism and Psychoanalysis* (Ithaca: Cornell Univ. Press, 1982), a text which enlightens the familial roles of father and daughter by staging various encounters between psychoanalysis and feminism.

38. "I offer you the *Labors of Persiles,*" Cervantes declared in a 1613 pre-publication advertisement, "a book which dares to compete with Heliodorus, if for all its daring it doesn't emerge with hands on its head" ("Prólogo al lector," *Novelas ejemplares,* in *Obras completas,* ed. A Valbuena Prat, 10th ed. (Madrid: Aguilar, 1956), p. 770. The *Persiles'* avowed competition was with a text lavishly praised by the humanists, Heliodorus' *Historia etiópica de los amores de Teágenes y Cariclea,* trans. F. de Mena, ed. F. López Estrada (Madrid: Aldus, 1954), pp. 367–68. For current research into the "maternal instinct," see Nancy Chodorow's *The Reproduction of Mothering: Psychoanalysis and the Sociology of Gender* (Berkeley: Univ. of California Press, 1978), pp. 17–19, 21–23.

39. *Loci communes*, IV.I., pp. 588–89. Cited by Maclean, who notes that the biblical *locus* is I Tim. 2:14 (p. 18).

40. Renato Poggioli, *The Oaten Flute: Essays on Pastoral Poetry and the Pastoral Ideal* (Cambridge: Harvard Univ. Press, 1975), pp. 173 ff.

41. In *Des Chinoises*, Julia Kristeva examines the binary opposition mother-wife / "other woman"-mistress as a useful ideological assumption of the bourgeois family, since such an opposition locates disruptive female desire in the mistress or prostitute, i.e., at the margins of the family scene, while splitting it off from the mother, who cannot be imagined as having participated in an act of coitus or "primitive scene" of the kind inscribed exclusively for fallen women (*About Chinese Women*, trans. Anita Barrows [New York: Urizen Books, 1977], p. 26).

42. Patricia A. Parker, "The Metaphorical Plot," in *Metaphor: Problems and Perspectives*, ed. David S. Miall (Sussex, 1982), pp. 148–55.

43. In his recent biography, William Byron discusses the loss of "credit" of most of Cervantes's female relatives: "of the six children Doña Leonor de Cortinas raised to adulthood, Miguel was the only one known to have married. Every one of the women of her progeniture — Andrea and her daughter Constanza, Magdalena, Miguel's daughter Isabel — would turn out to be what pre-liberation morality would unhesitatingly have described as a whore" (*Cervantes: A Biography* [New York: Doubleday, 1978], p. 52).

SECONDARY BIBLIOGRAPHY

La Galatea

Avalle-Arce, J.-B. *La novela pastoril española*. Madrid: Ediciones Istmo, 1974. The most thorough study to date of the development of the pastoral novel in Spain, with a full chapter devoted to *La Galatea* and the radical ways in which it deviates from the tradition established by by Montemayer.

Casalduero, Joaquín. "La Galatea," In *Suma Cervantina*, edited by J.B. Avalle-Arce and E.C. Riley, 27–46. London: Tamesis, 1973. In addition to offering a fine reading of *La Galatea* as a whole, provides an excellent background in the pastoral tradition from the Greek Classical period through the Renaissance. A masterful article.

López-Estrada, Francisco. *La "Galatea" de Cervantes*. La Laguna de Tenerife: Universidad de la Laguna, 1948. A straightforward presentation of the organization and characters that make up Cervantes's pastoral novel.

Don Quixote

Allen, John J. *Don Quixote: Hero or Fool?: A study of Narrative Technique*. Gainesville: University of Florida Press, 1969. An interpretation of Don Quixote's character analyzed through a consideration of the pattern of his successes and failures as knight errant. The study includes a very useful discussion of narrative voice in *Don Quixote* and its role in structuring the novel.

Bandera, Cesáreo. *Mímesis conflictiva*. Madrid: Gredos, 1975. An application of René Girard's theory of mimetic desire to *Don Quixote*, especially Part 1. Through provocative readings of certain frequently discussed passages of the novel, proposes a vision of a world caught in desire, illusion, and conflict from which Cervantes, through engagement with it, was ultimately able to extricate himself.

Castro, Américo. *Cervantes y los casticismos españoles*. Madrid: Alfaguera, 1966. A study offering strong evidence of Cervantes's "New Christian" background and showing how that social marginality is reflected in *Don Quixote* as compared with Mateo Alemán's more cynical and embittered *Guzmán de Alfarache*.

– – –. *El pensamiento de Cervantes*. Madrid: Casa Editorial Hernando, 1925. An early study in which Castro links Cervantes ideologically with Erasmian humanism. Although Castro later repudiated the excessively ideological cast of his study, it has formed the basis for many major recent critical analyses of Cervantes, and was reproduced by Castro in amplified form in 1972.

Close, Anthony. *The Romantic Approach to "Don Quixote": A Critical History of the Romantic Traditions in "Quixote" Criticism.* Cambridge: Cambridge University Press, 1978. A book that challenges what has been the prevailing critical approach to *Don Quixote* over the past century by offering a critical perspective that places romanticism in its historical context. A good presentation of the history of Cervantes criticism.

Combet, Louis. *Cervantès ou les incertitudes du désir.* Lyons: Presses Universitaires de Lyon, 1981. A psycho-structural study which seeks to demonstrate, through an analysis of the role in all of Cervantes's work of the main character with respect both to his loved one and to his rival, a masochistic orientation in Cervantes's psyche that governs the structure of his *opus*.

Dudley, Edward C. "Don Quixore as Magus: The Rhetoric of Interpolation." *Bulletin of Hispanic Studies* 49 (1972):23–40. A fine study of the complex nexus of fiction and history that comes to a climax in Juan Palomeque's inn in *Don Quixote* Part 1.

Durán, Manuel. *La ambigüedad en el "Quixote."* Xalapa, Mexico: Universidad Veracruzana, 1961. An excellent example of a "perspectivist" reading of *Don Quixote*, one which highlights the difficulties of interpretation the text raises when one asks of it that it present a clear-cut set of attitudes toward the basic questions of history and fiction.

Efron, Arthur. *Don Quixote and the Dulcineated World.* Austin, Texas: University of Texas Press, 1971. A look at the prevailing schools of criticism in *Don Quixote* with the aim of revealing in every case their limitations. Proposes the idea that the idealizing habit of mind that makes Dulcinea possible pervades Cervantes's culture and Western Society as a whole.

El Saffar, Ruth. *Beyond Fiction: The Recovery of the Feminine in the Works of Cervantes.* Berkeley: University of California Press, 1984. A study of the changed roles of the female character in the two parts of *Don Quixote* and its effect on the structural and thematic issues that characterize the two works.

– – –. *Distance and Control in "Don Quixote:" A Study in Narrative Technique.* Chapel Hill: University of North Carolina Studies in Romance Language and Literature, 1975. A reading of the structural relations between author, character and readers as those relations are reflected in the interpolated tales of Part I and the invented deceptions which take their place in Part II of the novel.

Mancing, Howard. *The Chivalric World of "Don Quixote." Style, Structure and Narrative Technique.* Missouri: University of Missouri Press, 1982. A study that examines Don Quixote in the light of his chivalric enterprise: what chivalry means and how Don Quixote uses it to develop his self-concept.

Márquez Villanueva, Francísco. *Personajes y temas del "Quijote."* Madrid: Taurus, 1975. A rich mosaic of learned and original essays on some of the most often discussed and disputed episodes in *Don Quixote*.

Johnson, Carroll B. *Madness and Lust: A Psychoanalytical Approach to "Don Quixote."* Berkeley: University of California Press, 1983. An interesting

effort to analyze Don Quixote's adventures as symptoms of a psychosis
brought about by a midlife crisis in which unresolved early childhood crises
are reactivated.

Riley, E.C. *Cervantes's Theory of the Novel.* Oxford: Clarendon Press, 1962. A
basic study of Cervantes's contact with and expression of the prevailing
Renaissance and post-Renaissance schools of literary theory. Covers all of
Cervantes's major works, as it evaluates the issues of verisimilitude, the
marvelous, unity and diversity, and narrator reliability so important in neo-
Aristotelian poetics.

Spitzer, Leo. "Linguistic Perspectivism in the *Don Quixote,*" in *Linguistics and
Literary History.* Princeton: Princeton University Press, 1948. A beautiful
analysis of Cervantes's use of linguistic indefinition as a reflection of the
breakdown of the identity of word and thing, and, more generally, the
breakdown of a unitary concept of the world and the place of everything in
it.

The Novelas Ejemplares

Casalduero, Joaquín. *Sentido y forma de las "Novelas ejemplares."* Buenos Aires:
Revista de filología hispánica, 1943. A sensitive, nuanced reading of the
Novelas, in sequence, along with some profound considerations of the way
the collection forms as a whole. Special emphais on the issues of the Baroque
and the Counter-Reformation as they are expressed in Cervantes's work.

Dunn, Peter. "Las 'Novelas ejemplares." *Suma Cervantina.* Edited by J.B. Avalle-
Arce and E.C. Riley, London: Tamesis, 1973. A fine, close reading of *La
señora Cornelia* as part of an effort to demonstrate Cervantes's narrative
mastery in a *novela* frequently dismissed by critics. Supports the notion that
the whole collection reveals Cervantes's skill and consciousness as a crafter of
fiction.

El Saffar, Ruth. *Novel to Romance: A Study of Cervantes' "Novelas ejemplares."*
Baltimore and London: Johns Hopkins University Press, 1974. Proposes an
ordering of the dates of composition of the *novelas* that mirrors the
development of Cervantes's prose fiction in general and that leads from
works whose tendency is toward conflict or dissolution toward works
highlighting resolution, both structurally and thematically.

Forcine, Alban. *Cervantes and the Humanist Vision: A Study of Four "Novelas
ejemplares."* Princeton: Princeton University Press, 1983. A reading of the
Novelas ejemplares within the context of the influence of Erasmus on
Cervantes's consciousness. Extensive, informed, and sensitive readings.

Meregalli, Franco. "Le *Novelas ejemplares* nello svolgimento della personalità di
Cervantes." *Letterature Moderne* 10 (1960): 334–51. A study emphasizing
Cervantes's development as a novelist, and particularly proposing that the
critics not equate the so-called "Italianate style" of some of the *novelas* with
Cervantes's *juvenalia.*

The Persiles

Avalle-Arce, Juan Bautista. "Los trabajos de Persiles y Sigismunda, historia
setentronial." In *Suma Cervantina,* 199–212. London: Tamesis, 1973. A
presentation of the *Persiles* in the context of Cervantes's lifelong oscillation

between the poles of the "poetic" and the "historic" as outlined in the neo-Aristotelian literary theory. Sees the *Persiles* as an expression of the abstract, universalizing tendency in Cervantes's work. Proposes that the second two books were written well after the first two, and that the second half of the book reveals the more historically grounded fictional tendencies characteristic of the mature Cervantes.

Casalduero, Joaquín. *Sentido y forma de "Los trabajos de Persiles y Sigismunda."* Buenos Aires: Editorial Sudamericana, 1947. A reading of the *Persiles* that places it in the context of Baroque aesthetics and counter-Reformistic ideology. A close, sensitive exegesis which is sometimes burdened by too heavy an allegorical interpretation of its elements.

Forcione, Alban K. *Cervantes, Aristotle, and the "Persiles."* Princeton: Princeton University Press, 1970. A study of those places in Cervantes's *Don Quixote* and the *Persiles* where his resistance to the more literal and factual aspects of neo-Aristotelian poetics are most evident. An excellent presentation of the major neo-Aristotelian poetics and neo-Platonic Renaissance theorists, along with fine and original close reading of key passages in *Don Quixote* and the *Persiles*.

− − −. *Cervantes' Christian Romance.* Princeton: Princeton University Press, 1971. A study, influenced in large part by Northrop Frye, which presents the *Persiles* as a Christian allegory of transformation through tribulation. A solid framework of Renaissance literary and ideological currents supports the reading.

Schevill, Rudolph. "Studies in Cervantes: 1. 'Persiles y Sigismunda': The Question of Heliodorus." *Modern Philology* 4 (1907):677–704. An early recognition by a major Cervantes scholar of the merits of the *Persiles* and its relation to neo-Aristotelian poetics.

Theater

Canavaggio, Jean. *Cervantès dramaturge: Un théâtre a naître.* Paris: Presses Universitaires de France, 1977. Offers keen insight into the unsuspected complexities of Cervantes's theater, its implied debate with the complicities of Lope de Vega's *comedia nueva*, and its hidden social commentaries. Proposes a chronology for the composition of Cervantes's plays.

INDEX